GATEWAY

North Marsh and West Pond, Jamaica Bay

GATEWAY

Visions for an Urban National Park

ALEXANDER BRASH
JAMIE HAND
KATE ORFF
EDITORS

Princeton Architectural Press, New York

Endpaper photograph: Aerial view of Jacob Riis Park with the Marine Parkway
Bridge in the background, August 1937

Published by
Princeton Architectural Press
37 East Seventh Street
New York, New York 10003

For a free catalog of books, call 1-800-722-6657.
Visit our website at www.papress.com.

Editors: Laurie Manfra and Dan Simon
Designer: Elizabeth Azen, EA Projects, New York

Special thanks to: Bree Anne Apperley, Sara Bader, Janet Behning,
Nicola Bednarek Brower, Fannie Bushin, Megan Carey, Carina Cha, Tom Cho,
Penny (Yuen Pik) Chu, Russell Fernandez, Jan Haux, Linda Lee, John Myers,
Katharine Myers, Margaret Rogalski, Andrew Stepanian, Jennifer Lippert,
Paul Wagner, Joseph Weston, and Deb Wood of Princeton Architectural Press
—Kevin C. Lippert, publisher

The editors of this volume extend special thanks to Olympia Kazi, Fernanda Kellogg,
Tom Kiernan, Adi Shamir, and Mark Wigley.

Consulting Editor: Jeff Byles

Graphics: Sarah Williams and Minna Ninova, Spatial Information Design Lab (SIDL)

Research Assistance: Alexander Arroyo, Michelle Chang, Aimee Fix,
Aja Maria Hazelhoff, William Hood, Tawnee Rozier-Byrd, Darcy Shiber-Knowles,
Tse-Hui Teh, and Li-Chi Wang

This publication was generously supported by The Tiffany & Co. Foundation,
National Parks Conservation Association, and Furthermore: a program of
the J. M. Kaplan Fund.

Library of Congress Cataloging-in-Publication Data

Gateway: visions for an urban national park / Alexander Brash, Jamie Hand,
and Kate Orff, editors. — 1st ed.
p. cm.
ISBN 978-1-56898-955-6 (hardback)
1. Gateway National Recreation Area (N.J. and N.Y.)—Environmental conditions. 2. Gateway
National Recreation Area (N.J. and N.Y.)—Management. 3. National parks and reserves—
Public use—Gateway National Recreation Area (N.J. and N.Y.) 4. Natural areas—Public
use—Gateway National Recreation Area (N.J. and N.Y.) I. Brash, Alexander, 1958– II. Hand,
Jamie, 1978– III. Orff, Kate.
F128.65.G38G38 2011
974.9—dc22

2011006600

Thomas Vint, director of the landscape division at the National Park Service, presenting a master plan, 1934

Foreword Fernanda Kellogg

At first glance, perhaps no immediate logical connection may appear between a luxury jewelry brand like Tiffany & Co. and the future of Gateway National Recreation Area. But on second glance, if you consider the ideals of sustainability, the business values that Tiffany stands for, and the context and potential of Gateway, you may see the unique intrigue of the park itself and be excited by the innovative process that the Envisioning Gateway initiative has brought to the park and design communities. We hope you will not only take a second glance, but that you will be inspired, as we were, and join us in the conservation movement, what is arguably the preeminent global challenge of our time.

Since its inception in 1837 in New York, Tiffany & Co. has been guided by the belief that a successful company has a responsibility to the greater community. The Tiffany & Co. Foundation was established in 2000 to focus the company's philanthropic endeavors by providing grants to nonprofit organizations working in two main program areas: environmental conservation and design and the decorative arts.

The Tiffany & Co. Foundation was proud to partner with the National Parks Conservation Association on Gateway: Visions for an Urban National Park. The design research and competition that led to this publication exemplify the values of the Foundation and the company, highlighting the importance of environmental stewardship, sustainability, and good design. The Tiffany & Co. Foundation was established in large part to help preserve the environment and the beauty of the natural world that has inspired generations of Tiffany designs. One of the Foundation's early urban parks grants was for Gateway National Recreation Area, as the nation's largest urban park that spans New York Harbor and encompasses parts of Brooklyn, Queens, Staten Island, and New Jersey.

Green spaces and urban environments play an increasingly important role in the cities and communities in which we operate. As such, the Foundation has expanded our urban parks program to focus on the enhancement of visitor experiences and the beautification of these parks and gardens as a means of making an impact on the environment and the surrounding communities.

The fundamentals of sustainability are built on the fact that good design should last for generations, whether in jewelry or in park design. Both the Envisioning Gateway collaboration and Gateway: Visions for an Urban National Park contribute to the essential and ongoing dialogue that will help define the ways in which thriving cities and complex ecosystems can coexist and enrich each other.

The notion of sustainability—of the timelessness, the respect, and the love it represents—is absolutely central to our identity. The beauty of flora and fauna has long been a signature motif of Tiffany & Co. designs and it is our responsibility to protect the beauty that inspires us. Just as jewelry is passed down between generations, it is the responsibility of all of us to leave behind, for generations to come, a world every bit as beautiful and complete as the one we inherited. It is a trust that we dare not betray, and it propels us forward into restorative and visionary conservation work like Envisioning Gateway.

Preface Tom Kiernan, Mark Wigley, and Olympia Kazi

Since the creation of Gateway National Recreation Area more than three decades ago, the park has not received the support or attention it needs. Today it suffers from lack of identity, definition, and resources. New recreational facilities are needed to create an environment that is suitable for park visitors, and restored habitats are needed for the native wildlife and for plants to flourish. The National Parks Conservation Association aims to facilitate the transformation of this special place into a jewel of the U.S. National Park Service for millions of Americans. In 1903, Teddy Roosevelt famously said of the Grand Canyon, "Leave it as it is. You cannot improve on it. The ages have been at work on it, and man can only mar it." Yet the history of the National Park System illustrates that individuals and collective organizations have always helped protect and define them for the ages. Gateway's successful rebirth will ultimately involve an appreciation of what a national park is, the collective creation of such a vision for Gateway, and a collaborative effort led by local elected leaders, with the input and investment of city, state, and federal agencies, as well as the increased commitment of private philanthropic support. With the upcoming centennial of the National Park System in 2016, we have a historic opportunity to help redefine Gateway, and in so doing craft a new model for envisioning, building, and maintaining our parks.

Tom Kiernan
President, National Parks Conservation Association

Architects don't make buildings; they make new ways of seeing. If you listen to the ambitions of any architect, their goal is to generate new forms of the perception of the world. These ways of seeing the world represent a space that one could imagine inhabiting, so in a certain sense, the ambition of an architect is simply to rebuild the world, to reconstruct our image of nature. The role of Columbia University's Graduate School of Architecture, Planning and Preservation in the Envisioning Gateway project evolved into a kind of machine for a new collective imagination that has generated new ways of understanding and experiencing the park. This book provides a window into not only new ways of seeing the relationships between environmental systems and communities, but also new behaviors and conceptions of our actions.

A political ecology developed among the three partners, in which our separate missions joined together over time and evolved to form a new brand of informed activism. The partnership among the National Parks Conservation Association, the Graduate School of Architecture, Planning and Preservation, and Van Alen Institute represents a new kind of ecological model of thinking about and acting on the built environment that offers an alternative model to existing approaches to research, broadening and deepening the university's role in the remaking of New York City.

Mark Wigley
Dean, Graduate School of Architecture, Planning and Preservation, Columbia University

The name Gateway National Recreation Area doesn't quite render the full scope or true nature of a land that seems to escape definition, both physically and conceptually. Encompassing over 26,000 acres across the New York Harbor, Gateway is a unique environmental, infrastructural, and cultural resource. Calling it a recreation area or a park just won't do. Its sheer size, the motley of structures and activities that coexist there, the extreme variety of natural and built environments it embraces—in a word, its fundamental, mind-boggling complexity—pose seemingly intractable problems. How can one make sense of such vast land? How does one take care of an eco-system that is at once so beautiful, brutal, and fragile? How shall we treat such an exceptional urban ecology? Can design help us not just make its complexity intelligible but actually manage it? Can such an expanse of natural and human-made terrains be designed at all?

This volume traces the paths that Van Alen Institute, the National Parks Conservation Association (NPCA) and Columbia University's Graduate School of Architecture, Planning and Preservation (GSAPP) have charted over the past four years to address these questions. For us, envisioning the future of Gateway meant, above all, considering afresh the nature of the design and planning processes. Through the rich collaborative work with the NPCA and GSAPP, we devised a competition inspired by Gateway's exceptional character. Like Gateway itself, the competition was generous and open ended; it demanded a great deal from the participants, yet it left them the freedom to explore new territories and vistas. We invite you to travel with us through these paths and join in what is already an extraordinary collective project to reimagine the contemporary urban park.

Olympia Kazi
Executive Director, Van Alen Institute

YOSEMITE

GATEWAY
NEW YORK METROPOLITAN AREA
POP. 18,747,320 / AREA 6,720 SQ. MI

NATIONAL PARKS
URBAN AREAS

Map: SIDL

United States National
Parks and Urbanized Areas

Gateway region

Introduction An Urban National Park

Established in 1972 as one of two national parks in distinctly urban settings, Gateway National Recreation Area is an ecologically and culturally diverse park encompassing 26,607 acres across the New York–New Jersey harbor and coast. It supports 22 million residents in the tri-state region, and accommodates more than 8 million visitors annually. Serving as a vital sanctuary on the Atlantic flyway, it is home to diverse estuarine wildlife and habitats, as well as public beaches, historic military forts, navigational facilities, and New York City's first municipal airport—an astoundingly rich assemblage of nationally significant resources.

Gateway also serves another purpose; it acts as a crutch for the aging infrastructure of Greater New York, with combined sewer outfalls, treated wastewater effluent, abandoned buildings, degraded habitats, drowned marshes, former landfills, and vast asphalt runways. Over time these elements have burdened the park, compromising its ability to realize the National Park Service's (NPS) aspirations for historic preservation, environmental conservation, and active recreation, and to serve the needs of the surrounding urban population.

In 2006, the National Parks Conservation Association, Columbia University, and Van Alen Institute established a partnership to advance the dialogue about Gateway's future. The initiative sparked a collaborative process of research, outreach, and stakeholder engagement, ultimately leading to the Envisioning Gateway design competition in 2007.

The Envisioning Gateway initiative not only involved reconceiving this sublime stretch of land and water in the heart of the New York Harbor, but also required consideration of the increasingly vital role of urban parks in the twenty-first century. With more than half the world's population living in cities, human impact on the environment is a pressing concern. Parks and open spaces offer much-needed physical and psychological counterpoints to the density and pace of urban life. Not only do they improve public health, clean our air and water, and provide recreational opportunities, they are living libraries of biodiversity, serving as classrooms for environmental education and stewardship.

As a federally designated park adjacent to one of the world's largest metropolitan regions, Gateway is socially and physically entwined with the politics, culture, and infrastructure of Greater New York. The challenges that Gateway's managers face—preserving the park's resources, maintaining its infrastructure, and educating its visitors—must therefore be evaluated in relation to both the NPS mission and local urban conditions. Both are integral to reimagining Gateway's identity.

Gateway was designated a national recreation area on October 27, 1972, by an act of Congress—one century after Yellowstone was established as the country's first national park. The U.S. Department of the Interior assumed initial responsibility for Yellowstone and several other iconic Western landscapes set aside as public land during the latter decades of the nineteenth century, but it wasn't until Congress passed the National Park Service Organic Act in 1916 that the NPS was formally established. Its mission remains largely unchanged to this day:

> To promote and regulate the use of the…national parks, monuments, and reservations…which purpose is to conserve the scenery and the natural and historic objects and the wild life therein and to provide for the enjoyment of the same in such manner and by such means as will leave them unimpaired for the enjoyment of future generations.[1]

Since its founding, the National Park System has grown to encompass 391 parks totaling more than 84.6 million acres of land and 21 distinct unit types, ranging from dramatic landscapes like Grand Canyon National Park in Arizona to sites of historical significance, such as the Martin Luther King Jr. National Historic Site in Atlanta, Georgia. This diverse network of parks and monuments serves to honor the nation's collective heritage and preserve its most cherished resources in perpetuity. It is an institution and idea that continues to inspire other countries around the world.[2]

Among the greatest challenges that the NPS faces are the myriad interpretations of its founding legislation, directing it to serve what is effectively a dual purpose: NPS rangers are to preserve the parks "unimpaired for the enjoyment of future generations" while also providing for their daily use by visitors. In addition to the tension inherent in this mandate, NPS as a government organization must evolve in response to shifts in the nation's social, political, and environmental agendas. The formation of Gateway, as well as Golden Gate National Recreation Area in San Francisco, came at a time when park planners were adapting to shifting demographics and increasing urbanization throughout the country. They were the first two units of their type within the system, aspiring to preserve and protect "an area possessing outstanding natural and recreational features" explicitly for urban users.[3] It was within this context that Gateway was conceived as both a physical and symbolic entryway to the national park experience for the region's growing urban population. Today the park remains a global model for how diverse natural ecosystems can thrive alongside even the world's densest and fastest-growing cities.

The establishment of Gateway as a national recreation area was a major achievement in itself, requiring an array of city and state parkland to be turned over to the federal government for inclusion within the park's boundaries. Today Gateway complements one of the most extensive and successful municipal park systems in the world, New York City's Department of Parks & Recreation, but from the moment it was designated Gateway's mandate was distinct from that of other municipal and state parks in the region.

According to its enabling legislation, Gateway differs according to the unique characteristics of the park's three entities: the Staten Island, Sandy Hook, and Jamaica Bay units. The Staten Island and Sandy Hook units were designated as "having present and potential historical, cultural, or architectural significance" and their management was to include "appropriate programs for the preservation, restoration, interpretation, and utilization" of these sites.[4] The primary directive for the Jamaica Bay unit was "conserving the natural resources, fish, and wildlife located therein." Within the latter unit, the area known as Floyd Bennett Field was specifically designated to host the William Fitz Ryan Visitor Center, described as "the principal visitor center within the recreation area," and to be converted to relatively high-density recreational uses.[5]

These often-competing goals are at the heart of Gateway's mission and are prompting debate about how park managers can best provide recreational opportunities for the city's population while also conserving its natural and cultural assets. Building on the material generated during the Envisioning Gateway initiative, *Gateway: Visions for an Urban National Park* endeavors to more fully understand the park's historic conditions, the constraints it currently faces, and its potential to thrive in the future. We have invited designers, writers, historians, ecologists, and NPS managers to contribute to the dialogue about Gateway, and it is within this context of creativity, openness, and collaboration that we present new visions for the park.

ENDNOTES
1 National Park Service Organic Act, 64th cong., 1st sess., (August 25, 1916), 535, codified at U.S. Code 16 (1916), §1.
2 See Ken Burns's documentary *The National Parks: America's Best Idea* (2009).
3 U.S. Code 16 (1916), §460cc–2.
4 Ibid.
5 Ibid.

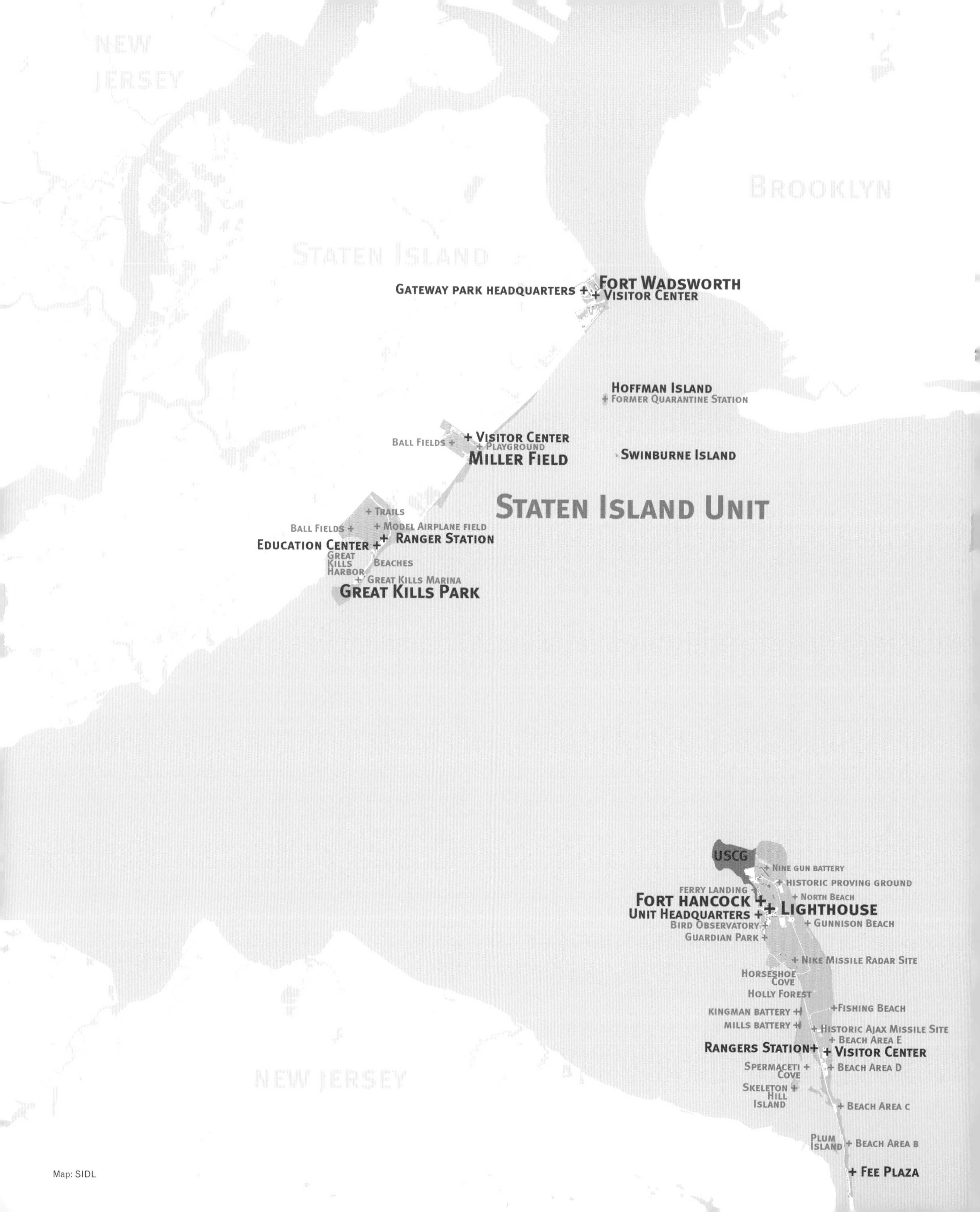

NEW
JERSEY

BROOKLYN

STATEN ISLAND

GATEWAY PARK HEADQUARTERS + + **FORT WADSWORTH**
+ **VISITOR CENTER**

HOFFMAN ISLAND
+ FORMER QUARANTINE STATION

BALL FIELDS + + **VISITOR CENTER**
+ PLAYGROUND
MILLER FIELD   **SWINBURNE ISLAND**

STATEN ISLAND UNIT

+ TRAILS
BALL FIELDS + + MODEL AIRPLANE FIELD
EDUCATION CENTER + + **RANGER STATION**
GREAT
KILLS   BEACHES
HARBOR
+ GREAT KILLS MARINA
GREAT KILLS PARK

USCG + NINE GUN BATTERY
+ HISTORIC PROVING GROUND
FERRY LANDING +
FORT HANCOCK + + + NORTH BEACH
UNIT HEADQUARTERS + + **LIGHTHOUSE**
BIRD OBSERVATORY +
GUARDIAN PARK + + GUNNISON BEACH

+ NIKE MISSILE RADAR SITE
HORSESHOE
COVE
HOLLY FOREST
KINGMAN BATTERY +| +FISHING BEACH
MILLS BATTERY +| + HISTORIC AJAX MISSILE SITE
+ BEACH AREA E
RANGERS STATION+ + **VISITOR CENTER**
SPERMACETI + + BEACH AREA D
COVE
SKELETON +
HILL
ISLAND   + BEACH AREA C

PLUM + BEACH AREA B
ISLAND

+ **FEE PLAZA**

NEW JERSEY

Map: SIDL

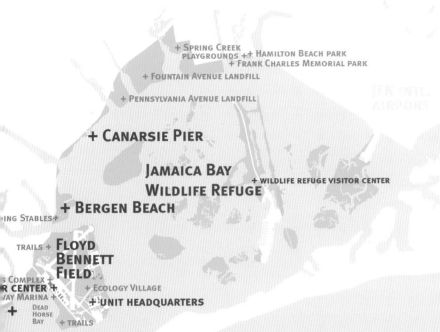

+ Spring Creek
PLAYGROUNDS ++ Hamilton Beach Park
+ Frank Charles Memorial park

+ Fountain Avenue landfill

+ Pennsylvania Avenue landfill

+ Canarsie Pier

Jamaica Bay
Wildlife Refuge   + Wildlife Refuge Visitor Center

+ Bergen Beach

ING Stables +

TRAILS +   Floyd
           Bennett
           Field

S Complex +
R CENTER +   + Ecology Village
AY Marina +
              +UNIT HEADQUARTERS
+
   Dead
   Horse
   Bay   + TRAILS

                     + Jacob Riis park   Jamaica Bay Unit
PLAYGROUNDS +
                  BEACH
           + Visitor Center
Fort Tilden

zy Point

                                                                    Gateway units

y Hook Unit

0   1.25   2.5   5   Miles   N

MILL BASIN INLET

FLATBUSH AVENUE

BELT PARKWAY

NORTH FORTY
NATURAL AREA

GRASSLAND
MANAGEMENT AREA

GATEWAY +
DRIVING RANGE
HISTORIC HANGARS +

+ AVIATOR SPORTS
COMPLEX

+ RYAN VISITOR
CENTER

GATEWAY MARINA +

HISTORIC HANGARS + COMMUNITY
GARDENS

FLATBUSH AVENUE

DEAD HORSE BAY

0   0.125   0.25   0.5 MILES

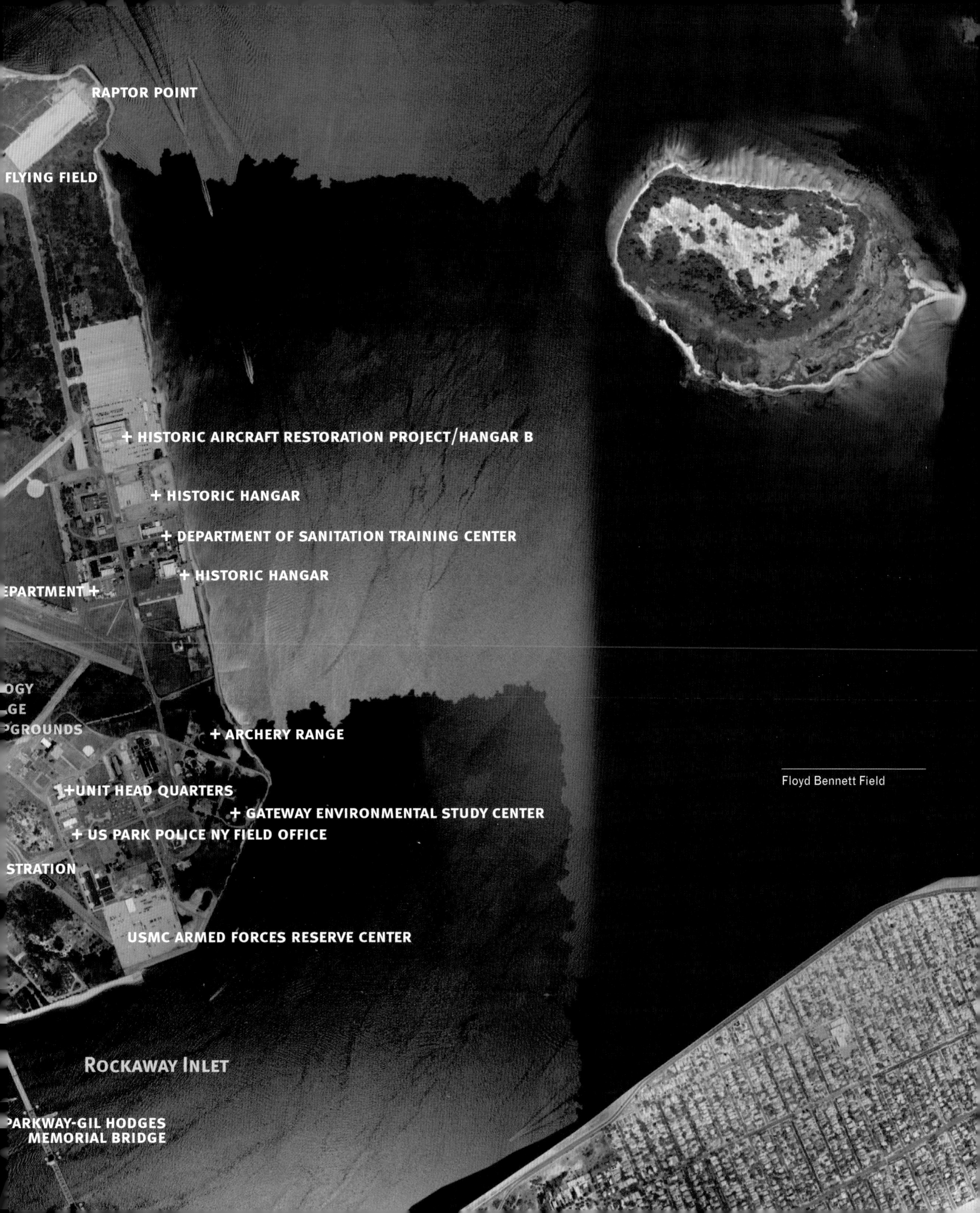

RAPTOR POINT

FLYING FIELD

+ HISTORIC AIRCRAFT RESTORATION PROJECT/HANGAR B

+ HISTORIC HANGAR

+ DEPARTMENT OF SANITATION TRAINING CENTER

+ HISTORIC HANGAR

EPARTMENT +

OGY
GE
GROUNDS

+ ARCHERY RANGE

+UNIT HEAD QUARTERS

+ GATEWAY ENVIRONMENTAL STUDY CENTER

+ US PARK POLICE NY FIELD OFFICE

STRATION

USMC ARMED FORCES RESERVE CENTER

Floyd Bennett Field

ROCKAWAY INLET

PARKWAY-GIL HODGES
MEMORIAL BRIDGE

THE PLACE

Gateway—Between the City and the Sea
Photographs by Laura McPhee

Capturing the haunting neglect and immense potential of Gateway's landscape of fields, marshes, structures, beaches, activities, and historic relics, Laura McPhee's photographs—taken over the course of one year with a large-format view camera of nineteenth-century design—portray eras past while simultaneously transporting viewers to a future not yet defined.

It is difficult to comprehend that all of the following images were taken in one park, but Gateway is composed of an agglomeration of municipal parcels and State lands that have collectively encountered nearly every imaginable impact a growing city and its inhabitants can muster. At various times in history, its sites have been exploited, celebrated as revelatory or precious, and adapted to meet military or security operations. Almost always unexpectedly beautiful, Gateway is a park in transition precisely because it is situated within a landscape and megaregion that are undergoing constant change themselves.

While a picture of the lush and rolling Sheep Meadow with skyscrapers in the background might convey the unique character of Central Park, and a shot of Half Dome at sunset illustrates the sublime wilderness of Yosemite National Park, what has become evident is that no one view of Gateway captures its full essence as a park. Its diverse range of landscapes is both an asset and a challenge for visitors to comprehend, and the park's future will depend largely upon an acknowledgment and celebration of this complexity. Caught as it is between the city and the sea, conservation of Gateway will be vital not only to the formation of a new ecological future for Jamaica Bay and its surrounding communities, but also to the City of New York, the Greater New York region, and the nation.

—The Editors

Invasive oriental bittersweet (*Celastrus orbiculatus*), Jamaica Bay Wildlife Refuge, Queens, New York, 2009

Concession stand from the 1930s, Plumb Beach, Brooklyn, New York, 2009

Plowed sand by the Rockaway Inlet, Fort Tilden Historic District, Queens, New York, 2009

Painting on plywood, Pennsylvania Avenue Remote Control Society, Floyd Bennett Field, Brooklyn, New York, 2009

Underground passage to the runway at New York City's first municipal airport, Floyd Bennett Field, Brooklyn, New York, 2009

The tidal marsh near JFK International Airport, Jamaica Bay Wildlife Refuge, Queens, New York, 2009

Incoming tide, Jamaica Bay Wildlife Refuge, Queens, New York, 2009

Birches (*Betula*) on East Pond Trail, Jamaica Bay Wildlife Refuge, Queens, New York, 2009

Indigenous and invasive plants displayed in found bottles, Jamaica Bay Wildlife Refuge, Queens, New York, 2009

Looking west from Building T-9, Army Machine Shop, Fort Tilden Historic District, Queens, New York, 2009

Soccer pitch, Floyd Bennett Field, Brooklyn, New York, 2009

Quarters A, U.S. Navy Commanding Officer's House, Floyd Bennett Field, Brooklyn, New York, 2009

Enlisted Men's Beach Club, Fort Tilden Historic District, Queens, New York, 2009

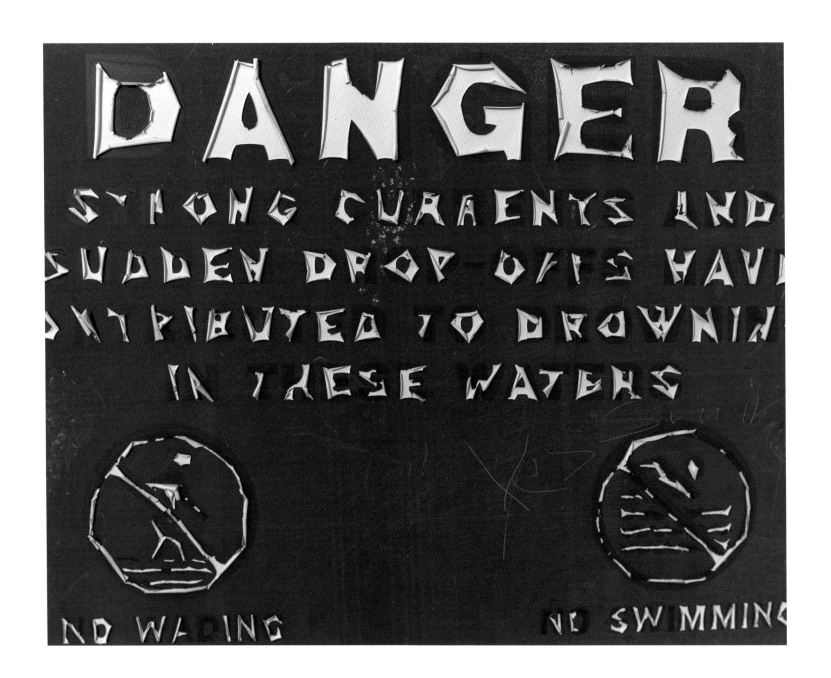

Danger sign, North Channel Bridge parking lot, Jamaica Bay Wildlife Refuge, Queens, New York, 2009

Eroding bank in a nesting area for diamondback terrapins (*Malaclemys terrapin*), Jamaica Bay Wildlife Refuge, Queens, New York, 2009

Building 89, U.S. Army laundry, Floyd Bennett Field, Brooklyn, New York, 2009

Fishing for Atlantic striped bass (*Morone saxatilis*) near the Marine Parkway-Gil Hodges Memorial Bridge, Floyd Bennett Field, Brooklyn, New York, 2009

Runway at Floyd Bennett Field, Brooklyn, New York, 2009

Tower expanded by Robert Moses to resemble the smokestack of a steamship, the bathhouse at Jacob Riis Park, Queens, New York, 2009

Doppler radar tower, NYPD Police Academy's driver training course, Floyd Bennett Field, Brooklyn, New York, 2009

Officers Row, Fort Hancock, Sandy Hook, New Jersey, 2009

Reconstruction of a 1940s boy's room, History House, Officers Row, Fort Hancock, Sandy Hook, New Jersey, 2009

Disembarkation point for soldiers returning from World War II, Fort Hancock, Sandy Hook, New Jersey, 2009

COSMOPOLITAN ECOLOGIES
KATE ORFF

"A town is saved not more by the righteous men in
it than by the woods and swamps that surround it."
—Henry David Thoreau

"It takes more than a good idea to make a great public improvement."
—Robert Moses

An Urban National Park

If the Cathedral Rocks at Yosemite represent the National Park Service's (NPS) most treasured landscape, and an icon of the nation's frontier, Jamaica Bay at Gateway National Recreation Area is its physical, conceptual, and spiritual opposite. With four sewage treatment plants, thirty combined sewer outfalls, vast expanses of airport tarmacs, acres of so-called "black mayonnaise," and a maze of bridges and highways, this collection of off-loaded land parcels has become a catalyst to set aside modern notions of "park" and rethink the role of the NPS altogether. Just as the scenic monumental landscapes of the American West shaped the nation's frontier mythology and nationalist ideology— symbolizing a land of promise and destiny—the muddy ecologies at Gateway have the potential to inspire a new ideology of global sustainable development and collaborative stewardship for the twenty-first century.

In contrast to America's relatively undeveloped countryside of 1916, when the NPS was founded, today we have dispersed settlement patterns characterized by unintended health consequences and wilderness in which nearly one quarter of the world's mammals, one third of amphibians, and more than one tenth of bird species are threatened with extinction.[1] Climate change alone is expected to force a further 15 to 37 percent of species to the brink of extinction within the next fifty years. This context represents a new opportunity to reinterpret the NPS's stated purpose to:

"conserve the scenery and the natural and historic objects and the wild life therein and to provide for the enjoyment of the same in such manner and by such means as will leave them unimpaired for the enjoyment of future generations."[2]

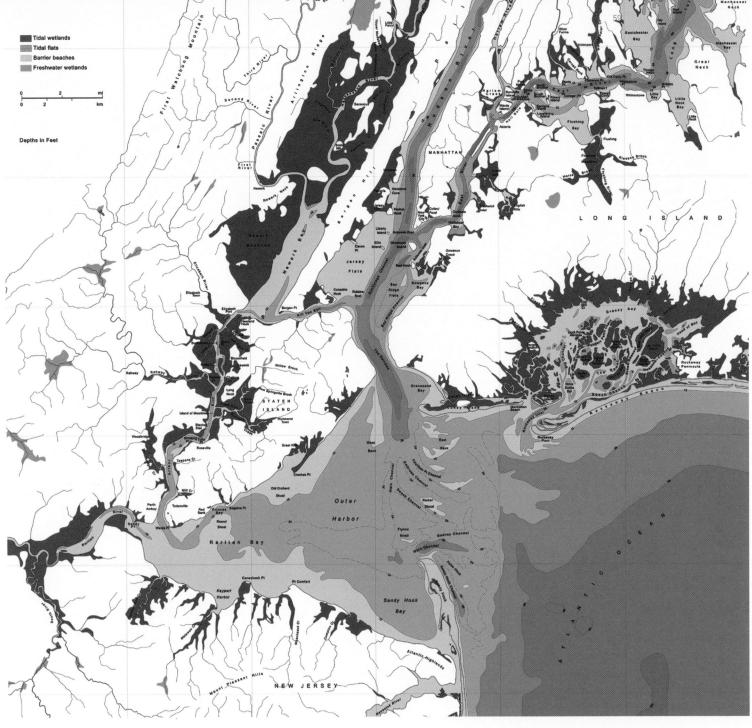

Plan of Greater New York showing extents of historic wetlands

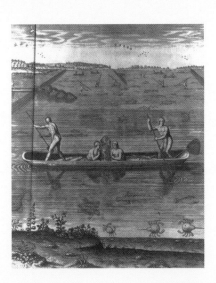

Lenape Indians fishing in the
bay, Theodor de Bry, 1590

What would it take to actually meet these goals in the context of Gateway? With the impending disappearance of Jamaica Bay's rich and biologically diverse matrix of salt marshes and grasslands in the next decade, as well as the inundation of large portions of the park due to sea level rise, the NPS would need to become a global deal-maker, municipal-interagency broker, and community organizer, while fostering the work of restoration ecologists, hydro-engineers, and visionary urban planners.[3]

Watershed to New York City

If Gateway is a harbinger of the new dialogues and methodologies needed at a national scale involving environment and development practices, then Jamaica Bay has the potential to trigger changes in the infrastructure and culture of New York City. This teeming ecosystem has, over the years, supported Lenape Indian settlements until the seventeenth century, small-scale farming during the colonial era, the once-prosperous fishing village of Canarsie, and the vibrant urban community of New Lots, Brooklyn, supplying much of the growing region with fish and shellfish. Today, the Jamaica Bay watershed, at 91,000 acres, is one of the largest and most densely developed urban water- and sewer-sheds in the country.[4] It receives waste and pollution from nearly 2 million people, who collectively produce 250 million gallons of treated wastewater (which contains 30 to 40 thousand tons of nitrogen) per day, all of which gets discharged, after varying degrees of treatment, into the tributaries or open waters of the bay. This marsh ecology is threatened by a confluence of conditions, including this enormous flush of treated wastewater, as well as polluted surface runoff, the bulkheading of its formerly soft shores, dredging, sea level rise, and bacterial contamination from combined sewer overflows that collectively exceed the ecosystem's capacity for regeneration.

Far from the perceived majesty of Cathedral Rocks or the novelty and wonder of Old Faithful, this hodgepodge of historically and ecologically significant recreational grounds—tied together by diverse wildlife habitats—eludes direct cultural and aesthetic interpretation. Henry Thoreau expressed a broad appreciation for the cultural and physical potential of what he called the "swamp on the edge of town."[5] Rather than the postcard-perfect iconic image of sublime rocky wilderness that affirms our country's past mythology, nature at the edges of towns and cities offers direct experience of natural processes and their reciprocal role in sustaining urban life. They are crucial to evolving our national ideology in response to environmental realities and in generating a joint approach to urban and natural systems. The muddy flats at Gateway offer a new, post-picturesque aesthetic to guide the remaking of America's increasingly urbanized landscape.

Jamaica Bay as Pilot Project

If Jamaica Bay were to become the site of a national pilot project on urban ecology, it could generate debate and fresh ideas about climate and infrastructure, and mobilize stakeholders, scientists, park rangers, and designers alike to form alliances to generate much-needed change. This vision is already being formulated from the ground up as a result of conversations among communities, school groups, fishermen, birders, and NYC Department of Environmental Protection employees who live and work in and around the bay area. The park's indefinable mud and dispersed footprint can provoke a new generation of ideas and a shift in the role of the NPS, from one of protector and conservator of the landscape to active shaper of the environment and policy coordinator on many levels. Based on its experiences with Gateway, the NPS could set a new agenda for integrating the formerly isolated urban-nature issues that America faces all across the country. This might foreground the role of natural landscapes in cities, and synthesize the nation's approach to land-use planning, biodiversity, energy, and food, all of which are collectively contributing to climate change. Such a program would guide the transformation of interstitial and derelict landscapes across the country toward more integrated policies and practices to better support our post-carbon settlement patterns and new cooperative ways of working and living.

A Brief History of Jamaica Bay

A gradient of land and water, local and federal jurisdictions, and contested ecological, social, military, and infrastructural contexts—both historic and contemporary—Jamaica Bay is a site of muddy ecologies and complex politics. A glance at a historic map of the region might lead one to believe that the lower third of Greater New York was once part of the bay's salt marsh system, known as the Flatlands. Its sinuous, meandering geometries are a result of the outwash from the Wisconsin Glacier's retreat nearly 10,000 years ago. Its outlines today remain in flux, changing with every storm and tidal movement through processes of erosion and deposition. Thirteen Lenape Indian sites have been identified within 3 miles of the bay, where remains of marine shellfish and bones indicate a former economy of fishing and hunting. The area still known as Canarsie was known for its vast planting fields and immense shell heaps. The Lenape fished with canoes up to 40 feet long, gathering clams, oysters, scallops, and whelk. They also hunted elk, bear, deer, beavers, raccoons, woodchucks, and various species of birds.

Dutch settlers had wrested ownership of the entire Jamaica Bay area by the mid-seventeenth century. The Dutch quite famously settled and fortified Lower Manhattan, but their cultural influence was equally strong in shaping New York's outlying territories. Their presence marked a shift in the mode of livelihood in "de Baye," from hunting and gathering to small-scale agriculture and dairy farming. The bay's salt meadows, for example, began to be periodically mowed as a source of fodder for livestock.[6] The following passage, dating from 1895, by the New Jersey State Geologist indicates the Dutch aversion to swampland and its perceived lack of productivity:

> The prejudicial effect of the proximity of these marshlands upon the healthfulness of the cities on their borders and on the salubrity of the adjacent country districts is the strong argument for their drainage and improvement. They are not only insalubrious, but also comparatively non-productive in an agricultural point of view. The possibilities of these meadows when drained and the sanitary advantages of their reclamation, aside from the aesthetic setting, make a strong impression upon all who have seen the rich and beautiful polders of Holland.[7]

The notion of the swamp as unproductive land having little or no economic potential contributed to its near decimation as the city rapidly industrialized in the nineteenth century. The significance of the marshlands continues to evolve in tandem with New York's economic and cultural context. Recently Manhattan has been called "the greenest community in the United States, and one of the greenest cities in the world," but the Jamaica Bay marshes, on the verge of disappearance, are only now being revalued.[8]

From Center to Periphery

By the turn of the nineteenth century the population of Jamaica Bay's surrounding communities had grown to nearly 1,000 inhabitants. It retained its agricultural base throughout the 1850s, just as horticulturalist and landscape designer Andrew Jackson Downing was penning a series of letters from Europe, urging "the necessity for a great [landscaped] Park." He was promoting a new way of inhabiting the landscape, not based on agriculture but on urban culture, that provided artful scenery, moral benefits, and healthful activity.[9] In that brief half-century, the population of New York City as a whole had grown to half a million. By 1850, nearly half of its residents were foreign-born, and they were dramatically reshaping the social, political, and physical form of the city, as well as its sanitary conditions. New York at this time was in the throes of the Industrial Revolution. The city was modernizing its housing stock, roads, and water and sewer systems in a complete technological transformation of its ecological fabric. The Croton Aqueduct, built to transport

G. Hayward. Lithograph.
D. T. Valentine's Manual of the City of New York for 1859.

Horse carts and rubble during the
construction of Central Park, ca. 1858

VIEW IN CENTRAL PARK.
Promenade. June 1858.

Dumping and filling at Jamaica Bay, *Brooklyn Daily Eagle*, 1930s

potable water to the city from upstate, was completed in 1842. Between 1850 and 1855, the city had built 70 miles of sewers. Jamaica Bay had shifted from being the center of a subsistence economy based on fishing, oystering, and agriculture, to the periphery of a rapidly industrializing one.

Cain and Abel

By the early twentieth century, just as Central Park was becoming a celebrated design achievement that "synthesized" city and nature, Jamaica Bay had degenerated into a backwater and dumping ground, receiving waste from its construction. There are many lessons, albeit paradoxical, to be gleaned from comparing the histories of these two parks. In 1858 the Board of Commissioners of Central Park chose the Greensward Plan submitted by Frederick Law Olmsted and Calvert Vaux for a new, centrally located public park in Manhattan. It became a model for integrating European picturesque aesthetics with modern scales of infrastructure. Its transverse roads hybridized roadway and park. Its new Reservoir, which connected to the upstate Croton water system, seamlessly embedded large-scale hydrological function in the form of a shapely naturalistic lake. Olmsted moved 2.5 million cubic yards of stone and earth by horse-drawn carts during its first five years of construction.[10]

The following year two horse-rendering facilities opened on Barren Island in Jamaica Bay. The first, built by Lefferts Cornell, processed dead horses shipped from Manhattan. The area, which had a number of other dump sites, became known as Dead Horse Bay. These horse rendering plants typically exported products such as oil for industrial uses and fertilizer back to Europe.[11] Hundreds of thousands of horses worked in New York City in the 1860s and 70s, and the average lifespan of a horse during this time was a meager two-and-a-half years. In 1879 the P. White & Sons establishment burned to the ground in a massive inferno that included six structures and 50 tons of horsemeat. The industrialization of nature in Jamaica Bay was at this time at its most gruesome and evident.

Central Park and Jamaica Bay have much in common. They are linked by reciprocal processes of construction and waste, growth, and decay. The creation of idyllic rural scenery and sculpted lakes at Manhattan's center happened in tandem with the creation of a vast wasteland and degenerate swamp on its periphery. What is now Gateway became a dump, harboring a self-contained colony of bone sorters, fish pickers, and metal scavengers; a place where it was said that nothing green could live and the smell would sicken at a distance of 2 miles.[12] As the last shovelful of earth was sculpted at Central Park and nearly 20,000 ice skaters flocked to its partially filled lake, fishing and farming had nearly ceased in the bay.

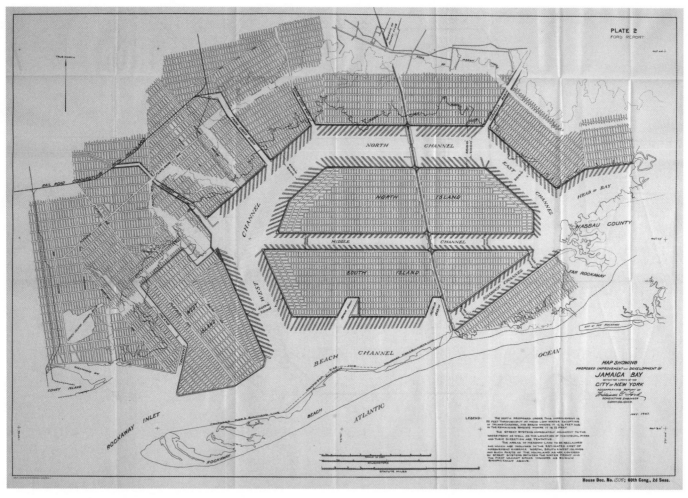

The world megaport proposal, William G. Ford, May 1907

Survey of Jamaica Bay showing marsh and settlement pattern, 1907

From Public to Cosmopolitan

In light of this shared history, the aspiration to park-ify this workhorse landscape in the Olmstedian tradition is not the right approach. Instead of a central, land-based park representing a singular capital construction project, Gateway has water at its center and is defined by a matrix of decisions and actions that exist almost wholly outside of its physical boundaries. Gateway represents a challenge to choreograph urban and natural systems as part of a global ecocity vision for the next century. At this moment, when nations are struggling to develop economic and financial models that redirect the most destructive aspects of our carbon- and waste-heavy lifestyles, the vision of a brave new world remains unclear and without consensus. What is clear is that our past approach to problem solving, with one-dimensional super-infrastructural solutions, has failed. We have learned from Robert Moses that widening a highway doesn't solve congestion, building larger power plants doesn't reduce consumption, barricading the water's edge doesn't reduce the intensity of hurricanes or the destructive forces of flooding. These static, independent, monofunctional, and purely physical solutions do not enable our cities to incorporate habitats or adapt to the consequences of climate change, nor do they attempt to alter the human behaviors at the root of the problem. Devising a dynamic, hybridized, and flexible approach that makes our cities adaptive in the face of climate turmoil and one that generates behavior change presents the central, new challenge to us as designers.

The Envisioning Gateway competition asked participants to imagine how to move beyond old notions of the public park and related processes of democratization and recreation, toward a modern idea for a cosmopolitan landscape in light of globalization and participatory research centered on urban ecology and global environmental change. Gateway must be simultaneously global and urban, community-based and federally coordinated. This requires a new psychological, ethical, and political agenda that would serve to prepare and train us for a new century of climate-based decisions and actions. Beyond the ideology of a public park "protected for users," Gateway could inspire a shared vision with broad benefits and a work plan for getting many hands dirty (or in this case, wet) in its remaking.

Redefining Infrastructure

Jamaica Bay challenges received notions of public, serves as a parable of modernization, and challenges its associated ideology of infrastructure. For much of the twentieth century, the bay has served as a fringe experiment for the city's massive, centralized engineering and capital-intensive projects. Its future will highlight a shift to soft, decentralized, and integrated landscape and community-based approaches.

A World-Class Port

Symbolic of the peak of modern twentieth-century ideology, the construction of a megaport was planned for the area that now encompasses Gateway. At around the turn of the twentieth century—after major water, sewer, park, and roadway infrastructure were built— the city planned to transform Jamaica Bay into a futuristic world-class port. A local news- paper called it "the greatest enterprise that the City has ever undertaken." The proposal, prepared by the U.S. Secretary of War and the City of New York, called for a forty-square- mile megaport to be dredged to a depth of 18 to 30 feet. Designed to serve ocean steamers and major ships, the intention was to reclaim New York's predominance as an international seaport by constructing the principal port of entry into the United States from the Atlantic. The aim was to surpass Boston, Baltimore, and other harbors on the Eastern Seaboard.

The megaport proposal was based on a report by the engineer William G. Ford, secretary of the Jamaica Bay Improvement Commission at the time. Ford's visionary plan, backed by meticulous calculations, was submitted to Congress for appropriation in May 1907.[13] The plan was to transform Jamaica Bay into a deep-water harbor by bulkheading the entire basin and performing a vast cut-and-fill operation using hydraulic dredges provided by the U.S. Army. A projected 267,815,575 cubic yards were to be dredged from the bay and used to backfill the bulkhead walls. This Faustian bargain was the outcome of deals with the federal government, the U.S. Secretary of War's office, and local authorities.[14] Phase one involved the federal appropriation of $250,000 to dredge channels, and for New York State to surrender its riparian rights to underwater land. Phase two was for New York City to build the bulkheads and piers at an initial expenditure of $1 million, to create a port with more capacity than that of Liverpool, Rotterdam, and Hamburg's ports combined.[15]

The bay and surrounding landscape's perceived lack of productivity continued to pro- vide the ideological grounds for its transformation from marshland to a grand futuristic illusion. Beyond its infrastructural benefits, the megaport plan fed New York's hunger for real estate, through fill operations at its edges. After the industrialization of agriculture and food distribution, Jamaica Bay and its surrounding environs, once valued as a produc- tive food source, had little value for a city that imported food from America's heartland. Its only perceived value was as real estate or potential conduit of manufacturing and services. In fact, the city's announcement of the megaport plan coincided with the total collapse of local fishing and oystering industries due to sewage and industrial pollution. By 1904 the bay was contaminated; shellfish were sufficiently infected to cause serious illnesses in those eating Canarsie's oysters and clams. The *New York Times* editorialized, "Except for

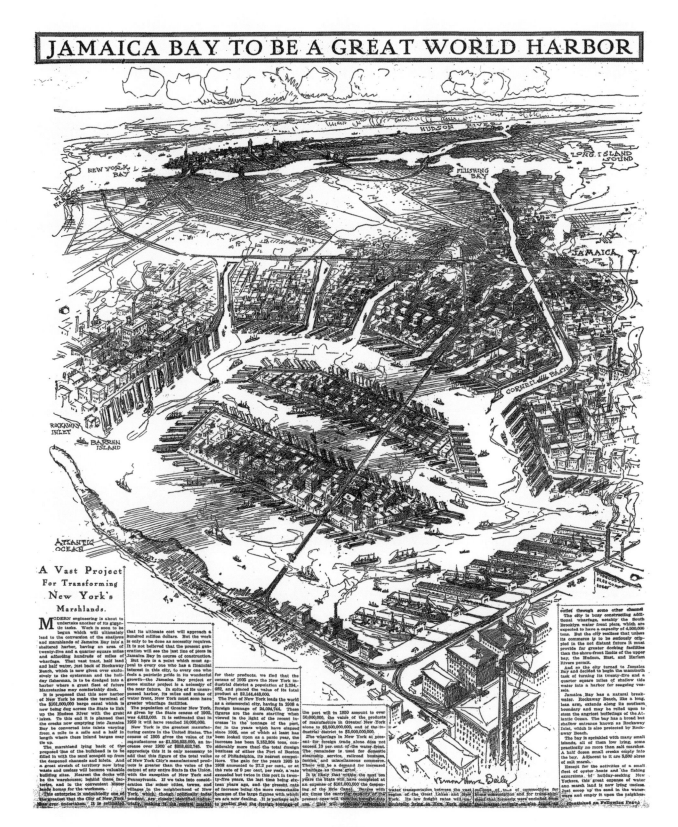

"Jamaica Bay To Be a Great World Harbor," *New York Times*, March 13, 1910

the activities of a small fleet of oyster boats and the fishing excursions of holiday seeking New Yorkers, this great expanse of land and water is now lying useless."[16]

Jamaica Bay was depicted as a hazardous zone in need of quarantine. The specter of Typhoid Mary was raised by a city health official in a report to the Society of Municipal Engineers.[17] The official stated that fifty-seven cases of typhoid had been reported in the Jamaica Bay area, and in addition to nine active carriers on its shores, "every single oyster from Jamaica Bay is coli infected."[18] By order of the Board of Health, the selling of oysters from its waters was strictly prohibited. Within this pattern of marginalization, the bay was transformed into a giant wastewater processing system and sewage treatment area overwhelmed by the city's burgeoning population.

From Megaport to Airport

The dredging of the bay was underway by 1912, but initial reporting by the *New York Times* portends the eventual abandonment of the plan:

> Harbor Work Begun in Jamaica Bay—Government Dredges Start on the Ship
> Channel that is to let in Ocean Carriers—Headway is Slow Now—Channels
> So Shallow that Great Dredges Can Only Work at High Tide.[19]

The mud won this particular battle. The projected twenty-year initiative, despite its failure to construct the port's physical infrastructure, had the legacy of centralizing authority over Jamaica Bay. On April 30, 1921, the Port of New York Authority (later renamed the Port Authority of New York and New Jersey) was established to administer and balance the shared infrastructural interests of the harbor. By this time, dreams of Jamaica Bay becoming a "Great World Harbor" had waned, in favor of building "America's Greatest Airport" at what later became Floyd Bennett Field—a consolidated landmass formed from the dredging and fill processes—which opened in 1931 to host several historic flights.[20] Four years later, the U.S. Postal Service decided to maintain Newark as the central airmail terminal for Greater New York, and Floyd Bennett Field became just an auxiliary runway.[21] It was turned over to the U.S. Navy in 1941. Not long after, Idlewild Airport (now JFK International Airport) opened on the bay's easternmost shore, occupying nearly 5,000 acres of new landfill. The first ambitious airport project in Jamaica Bay, Floyd Bennett Field was obsolete almost immediately upon completion.

More Dumps

The marsh that had served as a vital and productive resource for the region's former hunter-gatherer and agrarian economies was now deemed a dump—a primitive condition—

by the standards of an industrialized economy. A newspaper article appearing in the *Brooklyn Eagle* in 1912 described three refuse-disposal plants on Barren Island among the largest of their kind in the world. As the city expanded, waste dumps were dispersed along the bay's edges, littering the shores with decomposing materials. The landfill in Edgemere, Queens, and the Fountain Avenue and Pennsylvania Avenue landfills in Brooklyn accepted a range of sludge, construction debris, and millions of gallons of illegal toxic waste, mostly petrochemicals such as paint thinners and lacquers in the 1970s, according to the *Daily News*. The surfaces of these landfills are now undergoing rehabilitation; they will be capped and planted with shrubs as part of a city restoration project.

Waste Water

The natural biological and tidal processes of Jamaica Bay, which had handled the city's sewage for years (serving as an informal primary treatment system) collapsed around the year 1900. Fifty million gallons of raw sewage were being discharged daily into the bay by 1917, from the surrounding communities of Rockaway, Jamaica, the Twenty-sixth Ward, and Paerdegat Basin. By 1939, four large sewage treatment plants were built on the bay's edges, signifying a great improvement; however, treated freshwater is deemed a pollutant to salt marsh habitat, because marine and brackish water organisms have a limited tolerance for freshwater inundation. Eventually flounder fish, which are bottom feeders that settle on the bay's "black mayonnaise," tasted strongly of petroleum by the 1970s, due to the dumping of jet fuel and oil from JFK Airport.[22] Today's fish populations face a different set of problems. Trace amounts of petro-chemically derived hormone disrupters (commonly found in shampoos, lotions, and other grooming products) in treated wastewater may be linked to the feminization of fish caught in certain parts of the bay. One study showed a female to male ratio of ten to one.[23] New species are evolving out of these seemingly invisible cultural processes, particularly at the interface between Jamaica Bay and the communities that surround it.

Highways

Robert Moses was appointed Commissioner of the New York City Parks Department in 1934, bringing a new set of infrastructural visions and top-down methodologies into play in the region. Motor vehicle registrations in the United States had risen to more than 26 million by 1930.[24] Plans for the bay therefore shifted from accommodating international deepwater shipping and air travel to becoming a showcase for regional highways and bridges for cars.[25] All of a sudden Jamaica Bay was "in the way" of the contiguous suburban expansion of the

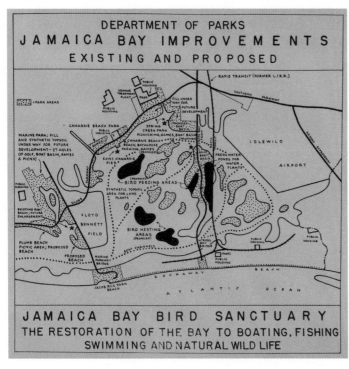

Gateway (Marine Park) picnic area, *Brooklyn Daily Eagle*, 1940s

Moses's master plan included recreation, public housing, development, and bird-feeding areas, *Brooklyn Daily Eagle*, 1950s

View from Jamaica Bay to North Shore, 2006

greater metropolitan region, toward the sandy beaches of Eastern Long Island and South to the Rockaways. The unveiling of a new master plan for the bay, at a party, gives a glimpse into the new planning methodology:

> On February 25, 1930, before five hundred civic leaders gathered in the Grand Ballroom of the Hotel Commodore for the Park Association's annual dinner, Robert Moses, dressed in a tuxedo and black tie, rose to his feet and tugged a cord which dramatically pulled the drapery from a huge map of New York City hanging behind the dais. Running across the map were heavy red lines. One, which started in Brooklyn at the Brooklyn Bridge, ran along the borough's western and southern shores, skirting Jamaica Bay, and then, in Queens, headed north along the city's eastern boundary. The shore-front portion, Moses said, was a "Marginal Boulevard"—he had not yet named it the Belt Parkway—which would provide a quick circumferential passage around Brooklyn.[26]

The collaring of the bay—with what was initially called "the Marginal," later "the Circumferential," and finally the Belt Parkway—established the trajectory on which it remains today. The bay's muddy and dispersed ownership meant there was no organized resistance, leading to relatively easy acquisition. The "greatest municipal highway venture ever attempted" was to follow Lenape Indian trails. Moses stated, "We have gone back to the aboriginal Indian trails for the Belt Parkway. A glance will indicate that the red men were smarter than their white successors in laying down lines of communication and travel."[27] The transition from intricate levels of land, water, and cordgrass to a uniform section of water, bulkhead, and highway for the Belt Parkway effectively cut off the surrounding community's access to the shoreline while concentrating pollutants along its edges. As natural systems and life forms were flattened, the region's vehicular infrastructure became thick and diversified in the form of forty-seven different bridges, one of which Moses proudly called the "club sandwich"—a triple intersection at the start of the parkway.

Just as the megaport project led to the consolidation of power in the Port of New York Authority, Moses used funding for the construction of the Belt Parkway as leverage to gain control of the Tunnel Authority. This effectively consolidated his monopoly over all new intracity water crossings. Historian Robert Caro later recalled the series of events, explaining that if then-mayor Fiorello Henry La Guardia "wanted New York to have the great Belt system, he would have to hand over to Moses, already far too powerful, more power still." In a formal "Memorandum of Understanding" between La Guardia and Moses, the deal was struck.[28] Traffic on the Belt became instantly notorious. "Four lanes of Belt Parkway had been jammed before the war. Now six lanes were jammed," according to Caro. Moses's definitive shaping of the bay's edges served to consolidate his power and eventually led to Gateway's current status as a recreational area and wildlife refuge.

Recreation "Area"

In 1938 Moses urged the complete abandonment of the megaport plan, citing the bay's "unlimited possibilities for recreational and residential development."[29] He demanded that dumping by the Department of Sanitation be prohibited. Soon after, jurisdiction for all of Jamaica Bay, including its islands and waters, was transferred from the Department of Docks to the New York City Parks Department. He designated bird feeding and nesting areas, as well as large tracts of public housing, as part of an overall plan to restore the bay to boating, fishing, swimming, and natural life. This modern notion of landscape being a place of recreation with scenic functions was consolidated and implemented in New York by Moses on a vast scale. Jamaica Bay, which had resisted definition for years, was recast as an area for boating, picnicking, and public bathing at modern beaches, as well as for the preservation of wildlife. This conceptualization of landscape, as either having passive-Olmstedian or active-Moses style recreational uses, continues to define and limit the regional landscape's physical and political potential.

In the 1970s New York City was in the midst of a fiscal crisis when the NPS assumed management of Jamaica Bay, along with a collection of decommissioned military properties, beaches, municipal tracts, and islands that today comprise Gateway. Moses, 82 at the time, publicly disapproved of the transfer to federal control. "No long-range thought has been given to the idea… I spent 20 years piecing together that land in and around Jamaica Bay under the Parks Department. The idea that this is something new being saved by the fellows in Washington is utter nonsense," he was quoted as saying in a *New York Times* article.[30]

A closer examination of the NPS's classification of Gateway as a "Recreation Area" prefigures current issues with the park's conceptualization and management. The word recreation carries an ideology of public use and enjoyment—structuring a relationship between park users and a landscape to be used. The recreation typology presents a different set of challenges and maintenance requirements than the traditional NPS mission of preserving awe-inspiring nationally symbolic landscapes to be interpreted and passed down from one generation to the next. The term area denotes a zone devoid of spatial content, as opposed to a specific place, phenomenon, or geological feature such as rocks, geysers, monuments, and historic houses. Despite the deep commitment of countless NPS staff members since the park's founding in 1972, there remains a discrepancy between the NPS mission, as defined by its charter legislation, and the actual ecological and infrastructural realities of Gateway.

Revitalization cannot be initiated by NPS alone. It demands a visionary federal agenda combined with a multilevel hybrid approach—a national reassessment of land use and infrastructure policy that cuts across federal, state, and local decision-making boundaries—and a ground-up effort to marshal park stakeholders and staff to become active researchers and stewards, effectively recasting the role of the typical national park visitor from enraptured wanderer to citizen scientist. This new reality demands an aesthetic that goes beyond the picturesque and sublime (a framework appropriate for a world existing outside of us) to one that empowers people and mobilizes participation, akin to the shared labor of gardening.

A Watershed Moment

Looking at the bay not as preexisting nature to be protected or a refuge for wildlife, but as a complex metropolitan watershed that supports people, plants, and animals—and placing the communities that influence it at the center of the solution—has the potential to inspire a new type of ground-up revolution. Small projects, dispersed throughout the watershed and based on an integrated idea of regeneration, could be coordinated at national and local levels and implemented to significant effect. A great deal has been written about the NYC Planning Department's restoration of Fresh Kills and the High Line as models of contemporary landscape practice; however, both require a top-down solution and are essentially surface treatments of formerly abandoned industrial infrastructure, offering leisure-based activities typical of the industrial era. Working to reset the dynamics of Jamaica Bay could potentially generate large-scale transformation within the city. As opposed to the iconic, capital-intensive mega-project, such an approach would combine a shared vision and strategy with the cumulative effects of small-scale interventions, transforming our understanding of the postindustrial landscape and expanding the concept of "public space" to include all aspects of the city, including marginal and residual zones, utilities, water, biodiversity, energy, and waste. This contemporary interpretation of public space encompasses a new ecological culture, reciprocal to the concept of "city."

Jamaica Bay—with its scattered surroundings of brownfields, solitary housing towers, leaching landfills, a hemmed-in global airport, decaying highways, and steel bridges—survives today as a living museum of the detritus of modern infrastructure. At this moment, it has the potential to become a tool for exploring new infrastructural paradigms: dispersed, community-based, decentralized, and regionally integrated.

Beach with sewer pipe, 1939

Aerial view of Jamaica Bay, 1940s

Park Commissioner Robert Moses shows progress
of work on the Belt Parkway at Marine Parkway and
Floyd Bennett Field to Federal Works Administrator
John Carmody. Left to right are Queens Borough
President George U. Harvey, Brooklyn Borough
President Raymond V. Ingersoll, John Carmody, and
Robert Moses, *Brooklyn Daily Eagle*, 1939

Marine Parkway, *Brooklyn Daily Eagle*, 1953

Out of the Quagmire and Into the Mud

Water defies regulatory and physical boundaries. Constantly in motion, interacting, changing, and connecting, it presents unique challenges when considered in relation to infrastructure. Gateway is a place where, one might argue, "The very idea of nature is getting in the way of properly ecological forms of culture, philosophy, politics and art."[31] Describing the bay as a dual condition of natural watershed and urban sewershed reframes it as a complex and shifting landscape with boundaries and publics that extend beyond any well-defined political or physical limits. Engaging and designing Jamaica Bay's water and sewersheds as a central element in the city's cultural history, for example, triggers the involvement of at least twenty-two regulatory agencies at federal, state, and local levels. Identifying actions that can be taken (and the corresponding scales of decision making) jumpstarts conversations that must take place if we are to address issues of water quality, biodiversity, and climate change. This expanded boundary of stewardship not only involves recreation seekers and park visitors, but also requires a larger shared vision of urban ecology and the value of "the swamp at the edge of town" that can bring about real change. Establishing a research station at Floyd Bennett Field and pilot projects for reintegrating Jamaica Bay into the urban and hydrological ecosystem may help identify the nation's long-term challenges and serve as a test case for addressing future crises of waste and water, climate change, and local governmental reform.

A dwindling window of opportunity is exerting pressure to think and act differently in both the short- and long-term. The Jamaica Bay Watershed Protection Plan Advisory Committee, established by local law in 2005, concluded after comparing satellite imagery over time that the marsh may be gone by 2012, presenting a three-year window to effectively bring about change. Beyond the loss of biodiversity and nesting habitats for migratory birds—significant in that it is one of the few large-scale sites on the northeastern seaboard—New York stands to lose the landscape's major infrastructural capacities: its role as a tertiary water treatment system and carbon sink. The marshlands sequester carbon as peat, keeping climate-warming greenhouse gases out of the atmosphere. Their disappearance may create a tipping point and provide a window into the dynamics of our ecosystem's future collapse.

Big Ideas, Little Projects

Cultural and ecological sustainability, as a key part of President Barack Obama's energy and environmental agenda and Mayor Michael Bloomberg's PLANYC 2030 sustainable development vision, could be jump-started with a renewed Jamaica Bay as its centerpiece.

If the city were to immediately implement homeowner-based tool kits, with incentives, for example, to reduce the amount of paving on surrounding property lots, install rain barrels, plant medians, switch to low-flow toilets, and build a network of rain gardens and oyster and eelgrass restoration patches, it may be possible to eliminate sewage overflow events. This is easily achievable within three year's time. This approach, in addition to a long-term transition from centralized bureaucratic infrastructures to decentralized democratic ones, is one possible way forward. It would empower individuals to participate within a loosened regulatory framework and through civic and financial incentives.

Envisioning and implementing a community-based watershed project to embed infrastructural capacities throughout the bay's drainage system could serve as a catalyst for rethinking New York City's relationship to its waterfront and trigger broad perception and behavioral changes. By addressing Jamaica Bay, the urban governance of New York City could be remade as a more environmentally focused city, where citizens are not passive consumers of pastoral park scenery but active participants in shaping a shared quality of life. Redesigning the city's residual public spaces and privately owned grounds and surfaces, such as roofs, driveways, and watery crevices, could lead to New York's emergence as an ecologically progressive cosmopolitan city. A pilot project already in the works in Jamaica Bay is reintroducing oysters, absent since the 1930s. A single adult oyster can filter up to 50 gallons of water daily, clearing away algae and contaminants. "We know we can get them to survive," says John McLaughlin, director of ecological services at the NYC Department of Environmental Protection. "The next step is, can we get them to reproduce?"

It comes down to a new kind of civic-scale gardening effort. In this way, Jamaica Bay has the potential to move the city from outdated notions of the iconic public park to a charged landscape of multiple operators and makers.

Cosmopolitan Nature

If Central Park is a landscape about democracy, Gateway is about cosmopolitanism. In an era when atmospheric carbon levels continue to rise, global cities are both the culprit and the answer. The globalized city has the potential to "become a vehicle for facilitating… different kinds of people—of strangers who share only the fact that they live in the same geographic area—to learn to live with, even to collaborate with, each other."[32] Viewing civilization and nature as one system—one that exists at local, global, and more significantly now at metropolitan scales of thinking—we have come full circle to a fully cosmopolitan ecology. Crucial within this paradigm is the understanding that all citizens share in the production of urbanity, in its making and remaking.

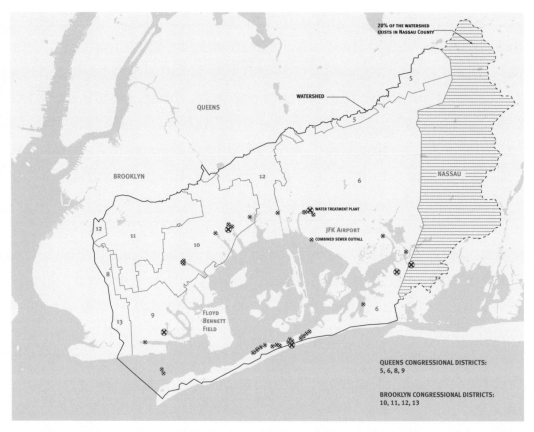

Diagram of joint watershed, sewershed, and congressional district map

Jamaica Bay, Foul With Sewage, Closed To Oyster Beds; 300,000 Bushels Gone

Jamaica Bay, which sends 300,000 bushels of oysters to the New York City market each year, will no longer be a source of supply. The waters have become so polluted as to constitute a menace to health, and the Health Department announced yesterday an order that will put a ban on the oyster beds. The oyster growers have until March 31 to "clean up" the beds and adjust their affairs.

The action of the Department of Health has the approval, it was said, of the State Department of Health, the United States Health Service and the Bureau of Chemistry of the Department of Agriculture. As the city has jurisdiction only within its limits, this cooperation was necessary to prevent Jamaica Bay oysters being shipped into this and other States.

Years ago Jamaica Bay was an ideal place for the culture of oysters. Now it has become the emptying place for forty trunk sewers, and the growing population along its shores has become an added source of pollution. The bay has narrow outlets and inlets through which the tides cannot circulate freely enough to freshen the waters.

Dr. Copeland said that an additional menace to the waters of the bay was the fact that there are several known typhoid carriers near the confines of the bay. As illustrating this danger he pointed to the case of "Typhoid" Mary, who is said to have been responsible for sixty cases of the disease and twenty deaths.

"Jamaica Bay produces between one-fourth and one-third of the entire supply of shell fish brought into the New York City market," said Dr. Copeland. "The stoppage of this supply may not only affect the price, but it may mean that a supply must be imported either from Canada or France to make up the deficiency. I have communicated with the health authorities of France for a report concerning the cultivation of oysters in France."

"Jamaica Bay, Foul With Sewage, Closed to Oyster Beds; 300,000 Bushels Gone," *New York Times*, January 30, 1921

Volunteers planting seed oysters at locations throughout coastal New York and New Jersey

Central Park engendered democratic debate and became part of a broader educative process that strengthened America's democratic culture. Today, just as Central Park's construction sharpened our concept of "the public realm" for an industrializing New York City, re-envisioning Jamaica Bay as a thriving cosmopolitan ecology would further evolve the concept of public space based on stewardship and cultivated wilderness for postindustrial contexts. It would reframe our understanding of infrastructure and the critical role of landscapes within cities, as well as highlight the city's responsibility toward global climate impacts for the next century. Emerging from this cooperative effort of scientific-, design-, community-, and water-based approaches is a potentially transformative set of ideas that will allow us to live together—alongside endangered species, mollusks, and migrating birds. In Jamaica Bay, the muck, now cultivated, becomes an amphibious garden: an array of spartina biofilters, racks of farmed oysters, a colony of female flounder.

ENDNOTES

First epigraph Henry David Thoreau, "Walking," *Atlantic Monthly* 9 no. 56 (June 1862): 657–74.
Second epigraph Robert Moses, quoted in "Belt Road to Open to Traffic Today," *New York Times*, June 29, 1940.
1 Ian Sample, "Earth Facing Catastrophic Loss of Species," *The Guardian*, July 20, 2006.
2 National Park Service Organic Act, 64th cong., 1st sess., (August 25, 1916), 535, codified at U.S. Code 16 (1916), §1.
3 U.S. Department of the Interior and the Jamaica Bay Watershed Protection Plan Advisory Committee, "An Update on the Disappearing Salt Marshes of Jamaica Bay, New York," (Aug 2, 2007). The report states that the rate of salt marsh loss, which was approximately 33 acres per year from 1989 to 2003, accelerated during the period from 2003 to 2005. "If the 2003–2005 observed loss for the five representative marshes is extrapolated to the entire bay, the bay's marsh islands would be projected to all disappear by 2012, just five years from now. Because this projection is based on a short time period and marsh loss rates vary between individual marsh islands, some islands may persist for longer and some for shorter." (p.1)
4 NYC Department of Environmental Protection, "Jamaica Bay Watershed Interim Report," (Sept 1, 2006), 8.
5 Henry David Thoreau, quoted in Daniel B. Botkin, *No Man's Garden* (Washington, DC: Island Press, 2000), 251.
6 Jaspar Danckaerts and Peter Sluyter, *Journal of a Voyage to New York and a Tour in Several American Colonies in 1679–80*, ed. Henry C. Murphy (Ann Arbor, MI: University Microfilms, 1966), 129–131. "There is towards the sea, a large piece of low flat land which is overflown at every tide, like the schoor (marsh) with us, miry and muddy at the bottom, and which produces a species of hard salt grass or reed grass. Such a place they call valet and mow it for hay, which cattle would rather eat than fresh hay or grass."
7 Kimberly R. Sebold, "Chapter 8: Conclusion," *From Marsh to Farm: The Landscape Transformation of Coastal New Jersey* (Washington, DC: NPS, 1992), http://www.nps.gov/history/history/online_books/nj3/chap8.htm.
8 In 1849 and 1850 Downing wrote a series of letters from London urging "the necessity of a great Park" for New York City. See Roy Rosenzweig and Elizabeth Blackmar, *The Park and the People: A History of Central Park* (Ithaca, NY: Cornell University Press, 1992), 15.
9 John S. Berman, *Portraits of America: Central Park* (New York: Barnes and Noble, 2003), 23.
10 Roy Rosenzweig and Elizabeth Blackmar, *The Park and the People: A History of Central Park* (Ithaca, NY: Cornell University Press, 1998), 150.
11 Frederick R. Black, "Jamaica Bay: A History, Gateway National Recreation Area, New York, New Jersey, Cultural Resource Management Study No. 3," 15.
12 Kirk Johnson, "All the Dead Horses, Next Door; Bittersweet Memories of the City's Island of Garbage," *New York Times*, November 7, 2000.
13 Ford Report, Report of the Jamaica Bay Improvement Commission, document No. 1506, 60th Cong., 2nd sess. (Washington, DC: Government Printing Office, 1909).
14 F. H. La Guardia, letter to the editor, *New York Times*, May 25, 1921. La Guardia requested that Congress authorize the dredging of Jamaica Bay to the depth of 30 feet, and requested a Congressional delegation be sent to review progress and to release appropriations to complete the dredging so that Jamaica Bay could accept large vessels and steam ships.

15 "Brooklyn Jubilant Over Jamaica Bay—Many Join to Celebrate the City's Plan to Create a Great Harbor There—Government Is Criticized—Fear Tardiness May Wrest From New York Her Supremacy as Chief Atlantic Port," *New York Times*, March 1, 1910.
16 "A Vast Project for Transforming New York's Marshlands: Jamaica Bay To Become Great World Harbor," *New York Times*, March 13, 1910.
17 Typhoid Mary was New York City's most infamous typhoid carrier, a healthy person reportedly linked to sixty cases of the disease. She was eventually quarantined on North Brother Island.
18 Royal S. Copeland, "The Pollution and Sanitation of Jamaica Bay," *The Municipal Engineers Journal*, Vol. 7 (1921): 18–24.
19 "Harbor Work Begun in Jamaica Bay," *New York Times*, September 15, 1912.
20 "Floyd Bennett Field at Barren Island Converted From Rubbish Dump Into Modern Air Base at Cost of About $4,000,000," *New York Times*, May 17, 1931.
21 "Whalen in Protest on Air Mail Decision; Mayor's Committee to Reply to Order Barring Floyd Bennett Field, He Says," *New York Times*, August 27, 1935.
22 Michael Harwood, "The 'Black Mayonnaise' at the Bottom of Jamaica Bay," *New York Times Magazine*, February 7, 1971.
23 Barbara Branca, "Estrogenic Compounds in Urban Waterways: An Interview with Anne McElroy" *A Publication of Sea Grant New York* 35, no. 2 (Spring/Summer 2006), 14.
24 Peter G. Rowe, *Making A Middle Landscape* (Cambridge, MA: MIT Press, 1991), 1.
25 Robert A. Caro, *The Power Broker* (New York: Knopf, 1975), 341.
26 Ibid., 343.
27 "Belt Road to Open to Traffic Today," *New York Times*, June 29, 1940.
28 Caro, *The Power Broker*, 643. The lone voice of opposition to the financing—$12 million from the New Deal, Public Works Administration, in addition to $17.9 million in city funds—was City Comptroller Joseph McGoldrick. Although no one dared to openly question the consolidation of Moses's power within the city, McGoldrick opposed the cost of the Circumferential, stating that due to the expenditure "not a single school, not a single new hospital, not a new police station or firehouse, not even a baby health station would be provided [in the budget of 1939 or 1940]...these are essentials, and in my considered judgment, we cannot embark upon new ideas until we have met these basic needs."
29 Marshall Sprague, "Jamaica Bay Area Urged as Playground; 'Waste' Waterfront Region May Fit into New York's Vast Recreational Scheme Rounding Out the Pattern Fishing and Crabbing Rezoning Proposed," *New York Times*, July 24, 1938.
30 "Moses the Park Builder, Opposes Gateway Recreation Project," *New York Times*, May 23, 1971.
31 Timothy Morton, *Ecology Without Nature: Rethinking Environmental Aesthetics* (Cambridge, MA: Harvard University Press, 2007), 1.
32 Gerald Frug, *City Making: Building Communities without Building Walls* (Princeton, NJ: Princeton University Press, 1999), 135.

THE UNIQUE VALUES OF OUR NATIONAL PARKS
ALEXANDER BRASH

Introduction

While the concept of *parks* is an ancient notion, America's national parks have been heralded as a unique and modern idea. Stretching from the Gates of the Arctic National Park and Preserve in Alaska to Dry Tortugas National Park near Key West, Florida, just over 390 national parks contain our nation's greatest natural and historical treasures. Forged in a cauldron wrought by the country's melting pot and cast into shape by generations of elected leaders in Congress, America's chosen landscapes and historical sites reflect the great rhythms of our nation. Our national parks are a special collection of American icons, imbued with a particular mission. Whether contemplating the birth of our nation as the mist wraps around the North Bridge at Minute Man National Historical Park in Massachusetts, or awed by the finite nature of human existence while gazing at the night sky over Rocky Mountain National Park in Colorado, visitors inherently know when they're in a great national park. When one can lose oneself in the majesty of a site or in the history for which it was preserved, then that park has succeeded in realizing the hopes of its founders.

Evolution of Parks

Frederick Law Olmsted—traditionally thought of as America's preeminent park designer—described the public park more than one hundred years ago as, "A large tract of land set apart by the public for the enjoyment of a rural landscape, as distinguished from a public square, a public garden, or a promenade."[1] Since then, the term park has been colloquially broadened to include almost any public place used for active or passive recreation. Parks not only include expanses of wilderness covering millions of acres, but also urban playgrounds, pocket parks, and rejuvenated brownfields. They come in an infinite array of sizes, structures, and intended uses; from the vast Olympic National Park near Seattle to the elevated High Line in New York City.

While the concept of a park is quite old, the desire to reserve space for certain intrinsic human values is tens of thousands of years older. With such distant origins, it is not surprising that the evolution of the park has been neither clear nor linear. What are considered parks today are perhaps more accurately described as open public spaces whose origins, values, and intended uses derive from multiple interwoven threads of human need. Several theorists have shed light on the origins of parks, but it was Olmsted's son, Frederick Law Olmsted Jr., and Theodora Kimball Hubbard who first broadly outlined the evolution of public parks.[2]

The oldest practice that has contributed to our view of modern parks is that of setting aside space for sacred purposes. Seventy-five thousand years ago, Neanderthals had developed mortuary practices and a "cult of the dead."[3] Evidence of culturally imbued human burial practices can be found all across Europe dating back 27,000 years, and by 10,000 years ago the cemetery had evolved among different human cultures, such as those of the Ténéré desert, now in present day Nigeria.[4] Grander examples of sacred places include Stonehenge in England and the Pyramids of Giza in Egypt.[5] More modern monuments such as the Kerameikos in Athens, Les Invalides in Paris, and the Vietnam Veterans Memorial in Washington, DC, as well as innumerable cemeteries, war memorials, and other sacred places, are the result of this, the oldest and most universal trend in the creation and preservation of public space.

The second strand woven into the idea of a park is that which has given rise to nature preserves and parks like Yellowstone today. The apogee of this practice dates to the eleventh century in Western Europe during the reign of William the Conqueror.[6] Originally preserves were not public spaces, but large parcels of land reserved to provide for the long-term supply of game or timber. While often attributed to European origins, preserves were in fact a universal concept. Fifteen hundred years before William the Conqueror, Persian rulers and their adversaries, Philip of Macedonia and his son Alexander the Great, saved vast areas as game preserves, while around the same time, the pre–Han Dynasty rulers in ancient China put aside extensive forested tracts for timber.[7]

A third idea leading to today's parks is derived from active recreation. While sports are another ancient and universal human concept, the act of setting aside space for these activities is more recent, and in the past several thousand years nearly every human culture has created separate fields or courtyards for outdoor games. Egyptians "batted the ball" around 4,000 years ago, and Mesoamericans used rubber balls on highly specialized ball-courts some 2,000 years ago. The Romans played pila, and the Chinese developed a primitive golf game during the Song Dynasty over 1,000 years ago.[8] In North America, Native Americans played lacrosse in myriad forms all across the continent well before Europeans arrived.[9] In today's society a great number of different games are played on an infinitely wide variety of fields, ranging from soccer fields, cricket pitches, and handball courts, to Yankee Stadium. Dedicated spaces for sports are found in, or exist entirely as, parks all across the world.

The fourth notion that has been woven into the origins of America's parks is that of the town common and the legacy of public access. The original English use of the word "common" in the late Middle Ages was actually to denote lands that were privately held, but used by many.[10] While a cottager or serf could use the area for certain purposes, the lord maintained ownership of the land, along with rights to its water, timber, and wildlife. The serfs paid an annual tithe to the owner, in effect paying rent to live on and use the land. This relationship between the inhabitant and the land is a reversal of that of the first settlers in North America, who brought with them the nomenclature of the common.

Historian Herbert Adams observed that in early New England, the town common arose from when "the English and Indians had a field in common fenced-in together."[11] In America early colonists applied the term common to sites based on shared usage patterns reminiscent of their European heritage, but in fact the common was actually derived from the Native American concept of usufruct. This term reflects the Native Americans' belief that people could only own what they wrought with their hands, such as weapons or tools, and that no one owned the land; instead, each village or tribe held sovereignty over various uses of it.[12] These uses were then allocated separately so that families or tribes might use a site for planting, pasturage, or other needs. While the English common was derived from land with a singular owner, where certain rights were given to the public, the Native Americans' system reflected a truly public land whose separate rights were subsequently bundled over time.

At first, commonly held fields were spread all across colonial townships. However, within decades, Native Americans faded from the scene and land-use trends shifted. Though some commons became famous, like Lexington Green, most others simply disappeared. As their value in an increasingly industrialized landscape waned, many of these commons or village greens were encroached on or given over to civil uses; they became sites on which new schools, libraries, and town halls were built. Fortunately, a number of these old commons evolved into parks, with some achieving historic status, such as the Boston Common created in 1634.[13]

A secondary impact that the town common has had in the evolution of public parks originates with its frequent use as a market and general gathering place. The common became a focal point not just for public interaction, but free speech. Even before the American Revolution, the common was cherished as a public forum, but in the nineteenth century this escalated, as typified by the ringing public debates that occurred in the fairgrounds and parks of Illinois between presidential candidates Abraham Lincoln and Stephen Douglas in 1858.[14] This trend might be said to have culminated one hundred years later, when Dr. Martin Luther King Jr. delivered his famous "I Have a Dream" speech on the National Mall in Washington, DC. Today, the rights of self-expression and free speech are embedded in the legal frameworks surrounding all our public parks.

←
Carlisle Graham, the first man to go through Whirlpool Rapids in a barrel,
Niagara Falls, NY, 1886

↑
upper left Running in Gettysburg National Memorial Park, Gettysburg, PA
upper right Wesleyan Chapel, Women's Rights National Historic Park, Seneca Falls, NY
lower left Fort Stanwix National Monument, Rome, NY
lower right Park bench at Gateway

The Evolution of Our National Parks

In the United States, the three place-based values of sacred spaces, nature preserves, and recreational areas were the threads in the fabric from which our public parks were cut, but our national parks are distinguished from other public parks by three additional and unique facets reflective of their more recent evolution. The first can be observed in the public's access and rights of ownership to our national parks. While this comes from the American tradition of having commons, the democratic principles underlying the national parks represent a new manifestation of this development. The second facet highlights the inherent urge of all societies to endure, and America's national parks serve to intellectually bind all citizens to a collective history by preserving and protecting historical icons or unique landscapes characteristic of the nation. Finally, the third facet is a culmination of Frederick Law Olmsted's unique philosophical insights regarding the beneficial purposes of parks.

Americans' rights of access to and ownership of public parks sprouted in colonial times, but were then dramatically expanded one hundred and fifty years later as Enlightenment values were embedded in our nation by the Founding Fathers. This democratization, often simply viewed as the public's right to enter and enjoy a park, is instead much more. Olmsted, for example, appreciated that in a park, citizens may socialize with others "unembarrassed by the limitations with which they are surrounded at home."[15] In essence, parks allow for more uninhibited social interactions among citizens. There is also another dimension to this idealism, which is intellectually deeper than the ideas of public access and equality. This idea, descended from the Founding Fathers' notion of the social contract, was rhetorically captured by President Franklin D. Roosevelt in 1934:

> There is nothing so American as our national parks. The scenery and wildlife
> are native. The fundamental idea behind the parks is native. It is, in brief, that
> the country belongs to the people, that it is in the process of making for the
> enrichment of the lives of all of us. The parks stand as the outward symbol of
> this great human principle.[16]

Not only did Roosevelt extol the notion that our national parks preserve key American landscapes and cultural icons, but he also moved well beyond that, to a symbolic level. He articulated the belief that America's national parks represent a component in the pact between our government and its citizens. Our national parks represent one of the reciprocal elements of the covenant whereby the citizens grant the right for a governing body to rule them; in return the government declares its trust in the citizens. In America, it is not simply that the parks are open to all; the nation's greatest treasures are entrusted to the people by the government as a tangible symbol of its faith in its constituency.

The second aspect that clearly defines our national parks is their propensity to memorialize America. The earliest large parks were set aside in the nineteenth century simply to protect great landscapes: Niagara Falls, Hot Springs, and three decades later Yellowstone and Yosemite. Simultaneous with this early park movement, however, a greater controversy, the Civil War, was shaking the nation. One of its repercussions was the permanent injection of Americanism deep into the park system.

By the time President Lincoln visited Gettysburg in the fall of 1863, the battle that had taken place there had moved beyond being simply viewed as a turning point in the Civil War. Lincoln used his famous address not only to honor the dead, but also to reframe the cause behind the war: a desire to maintain a united nation. His speech dramatically broadened America's view of the battlefield and the dead. When he used the phrase "this [hallowed] ground," Lincoln was referring to its value as both a memorial to the individuals who perished there as well as a tribute to the American ideals at stake in the battle.[17] Subsequent to the Civil War, Gettysburg and other great battlefields all across the nation were considered more than just sacred places. They were valued for their symbolism in the nation's history.

Shortly after the Civil War, a number of sites were set aside, but more than sixty years passed before the administration of these sites, as well as some from other wars, was transferred from the War Department to the National Park Service (NPS). Once this shift took place, the scope of our National Park System was profoundly broadened. Ethan Carr, a noted park historian, observed that this shift embodied the "vision of republican nationhood."[18] With the addition of such sacred American places, the national park moved irrevocably beyond the preservation of iconic landscapes to an idea that included historical sites and monuments.

The third facet of our National Park System that makes them singularly distinct from other park types descends from the philosophy of Olmsted. Though best known as the landscape architect who designed Central Park, Boston's Emerald Necklace, and hundreds of other projects throughout the country, Olmsted was far more than a great designer and craftsman; he was also a convincing advocate. Decades before the public had heard of Yellowstone or Yosemite, Niagara Falls was in danger of being destroyed by commercial avarice. By the early 1800s the land around the site had been divided up among numerous commercial interests, and the picturesque woodlands had been cleared away and replaced

with "a succession of claptrap buildings, factories, and shops that made Niagara one of the earliest victims of American cityscape blight."[19] In the 1860s, Olmsted joined the effort to have the commercialism pushed back, and have the falls properly appreciated for their intrinsic values; he finally succeeded in 1883, when it became a state park. He also worked on behalf of Yosemite at this time, and noted:

> It is the main duty of government…to provide means of protection for all citizens in the pursuit of happiness against all the obstacles…which the selfishness of individuals or combinations of individuals is liable to interpose to that pursuit.[20]

Olmsted's writings reveal that what he sought to preserve in the great landscapes and the design of new parks were values he deemed critical to the public's well-being. The core of Olmsted's philosophy was his belief in the role of parks in preserving human health. While this term carries broad implications today, for Olmsted it implied something very specific:

> It is a scientific fact that the occasional contemplation of natural scenes of an impressive character, particularly if this contemplation occurs in connection with relief from ordinary cares, change of air and change of habits, is favorable to the health and vigor of men and especially to the health and vigor of their intellect beyond any other conditions which can be offered them.[21]

To Olmsted, "human health" meant mental health, and he believed that visitors' mental health was significantly improved when they became so enraptured by their experiences in a park that they put aside their daily concerns. Nearly a century later when writing about Olmsted, the writer Joseph Sax described the value of this revelatory moment:

> It is the function of culture to preserve a link to forces and experiences outside of the daily routine of life. Such experiences provide a perspective—in time and space—against which we can test the value, as well as the immediate efficacy, of what we are doing.[22]

Olmsted believed that the ideal park provided the time and place where inspirational scenery allowed the average citizen to put aside their daily worries or cogitations, and experience, in essence, an epiphany. In such an epiphany, a person would be mentally freed to regain a proper perspective on life.

This experiential epiphany has subsequently been referred to in various ways by a number of other park philosophers and supporters. Just a few decades after Olmsted, the naturalist John Muir also wrote of this moment, though specifically with respect to the wilderness he so preferred. In 1901, Muir noted that such moments "can arouse

←
Half Dome in Yosemite National Park, CA

View of Gettysburg National Park

man from the stupefying effects of the vice of industry and the deadly apathy of luxury."[23] During the Mather Mountain Party's crossing in 1915 of what later became Sequoia National Park, Emerson Hough of the *Saturday Evening Post* wrote, "A sort of delirium seizes one in surroundings such as these. The world seems very far away."[24] In the mid 1950s, author-turned-interpreter Freeman Tilden honed in on the idea as he became a leading voice for our national parks. After writing generally about the parks' accepted values, he noted what he called their "fifth essence," their ability to unexpectedly bestow a sense of "renewal and affirmation" on people.[25] A decade later, author Wallace Stegner referred to the idea as that which "is good for us…because of the incomparable sanity it can bring…into our insane lives."[26] Even Congress, amid the environmental fervor that led to the first celebration of Earth Day in 1970, insightfully called for a "national park system preserved and managed for the benefit and inspiration of all the people."[27] Perhaps most recently, former NPS Deputy Director, John Reynolds, characterized his view of the experiential epiphany as "a sense of place…places that [are] touchstones of [our] existence."[28]

In writing about large public parks in general, landscape architect James Corner observed that experiential moments are at the core of the park paradigm, noting, "Large parks…capture what for many people are the ultimate virtues of such places—their full experiential range and consolidation of a public's sense of collective identity and outdoor life."[29] It is clear in the evolution of our national parks that they are unique because their focus on visitor experiences is even tighter and has crystallized at a higher standard. In our national parks, the primary goal is to foster an experiential epiphany that results directly from, and aligns with, the history and natural attributes of that site. Unlike other great public parks, the national parks were individually chosen because they are capable of being the primary source of inspiration for such experiential moments.

Early in the National Park System's history, these sought-after experiential epiphanies were tied to iconic landscapes. This relationship has since expanded to include hundreds of historic and cultural sites, and the goal of the epiphany encompasses a wide range of experiences—that moment when a visitor contemplates the scale of humanity against the sublime beauty of Yosemite Valley, or the thoughts of sheer horror evoked as one imagines running across the fields at Gettysburg. One of the newest national parks, the African Burial Ground in Lower Manhattan, delicately elicits intense emotions regarding the toll of slavery and the tumult associated with human diaspora. Today a great national park is defined by its ability as a secular place to trigger a transcendent experience.

Gateway's Epiphany

While a clear vision regarding the experiences provided and mission of our most iconic national parks has been articulated in the past, the support required to ensure that all other national parks reach the same expectations have not always been at hand. This challenge is even more pronounced for national parks in urban settings.

To be successful, a national park in an urban area must be accessible, it must be integrated with the region's infrastructure, and it must fulfill the broad spectrum of uses historically demanded of our public parks. Most importantly, however, in addition to serving as a flagship park for the surrounding communities, it must be designed to preserve and herald what it was created to protect, and it must never waver from its core mission of eliciting inspirational experiences. Joseph Sax understood this when he wrote that urban national parks have a rightful place within the National Park System, but only if they are able to bring the symbolism of the entire system to their visitors.[30] The hard part, as national park expert Ronald A. Foresta noted, is that historically the National Park Service does not know how to accomplish this.[31]

In stark contrast to most national parks with their iconic landscapes or historic significance, many of the large urban national parks like Golden Gate, Chattahoochee River, or Indiana Dunes struggle. Their convoluted pasts are complicated by a great array of potential uses and values, and unfortunately, the dynamics associated with uniting these elements usually conspires to derail the creation of a clear and compelling design for their future. Lacking a singularly compelling story, and burdened with too many interested stakeholders, too many possibilities, and the indiscriminate demand for open space in any urban area, these forces inevitably conspire to confound the delineation of a clear vision for most such parks. For example, it took more than three decades for planners and supporters of Golden Gate National Recreation Area to conceive of Crissy Field as a response to that park's aviation roots and the desire to provide San Franciscans with more open space as well as increased connectivity with the waterfront.

Designing great public spaces, as Olmsted and others have done, is arguably "easier," though of course not easy, when one is working with a blank slate of open space. However, in working with a site in the National Park System, a great design must not only improve access, aesthetics, interpretation, and all of the other critical issues associated with a park, it must also illuminate and highlight the values, or attributes, for which the park was created by Congress. Thus, a truly great design will create the time and space around the key values so that a visitor can find and attain their own experiential epiphany.

As an agglomeration of sites, Gateway really has no clear thematic past, nor has an easily recognizable and unifying vision for its future been embraced. One might posit that it is impossible to design a landscape or construct a park in order to elicit what has not been defined, and indeed Gateway stands in mute testament to this conundrum. However, it is with hope and faith and the belief that once Gateway's opportunities for an experiential epiphany have been articulated and agreed upon, then its true mission can commence. Until this time, however, vast expanses of Gateway National Recreation Area will remain essentially abandoned, unappreciated, and underused by millions of potential visitors.

Yet Gateway was once a font of life, a crucial slice of one of the great estuaries of the East Coast. Native Americans thrived around its edges, harvesting a multitude of products from the sea. Walt Whitman sailed its waters, and during World War II it hosted the largest naval airbase in the United States. Gateway must somehow evoke these moments or others to find a way to bring the next generation of visitors to its gates. As one of the first urban national parks created by Congress, it must also utilize such experiences to inspire appreciation for all other national park sites. When children have the opportunity to explore its marshes, see a peregrine falcon fly overhead, hear tales of a battle fought long ago, or touch the wings of a plane from their grandparents' era, those experiences will also help to open the doors to countless adventures all across our continent. In such a light Gateway will truly become the gateway it was meant to be.

ENDNOTES

1 Frederick Law Olmsted Sr., *Forty Years of Landscape Architecture: Central Park*, ed. Frederick Law Olmsted Jr. and Theodora Kimball (1928; repr., Cambridge, MA: MIT Press, 1973), 3.

2 Ibid., 3–17.

3 Yuri Smirnov, "Intentional Human Burial: Middle Paleolithic Beginnings," *Journal of World Prehistory* 3, no. 2 (June 1989): 199–233; and James Shreeve, *The Neandertal Enigma: Solving the Mystery of Modern Human Origins* (New York: Avon Books, 1995).

4 Margerhita Mussi, *Earliest Italy: An Overview of the Italian Paleolithic and Mesolithic* (New York: Kluwer Academic/Plenum Press, 2001); Ben Harder, "Evolving in Their Graves: Early Burials Hold Clues to Human Origins," *Science News* 160, no. 24 (Dec. 15, 2001): 380; Will Knight, "Ice Age Twins Found in Ancient Burial Ground," *Newscientist.com*, September 27, 2005, www.newscientist.com/article/dn8063; and Randolph Schmid, "Remains of a Cemetery Found in the Desert," *Washington Times*, August 14, 2008.

5 Marc Kaufman, "An Ancient Settlement is Unearthed Near Stonehenge," *Washington Post*, January 31, 2007.

6 Winston Churchill, *A History of the English Speaking Peoples, Vol. 1: The Birth of Britain* (New York: Dodd, Mead & Co., 1956), 172.

7 Waldemar Heckel, Lawrence Tritle, and Pat Wheatley, *Alexander's Empire: Formulation to Decay* (Claremont, CA: Regina Books, 2007); and Thomas T. Allsen, *The Royal Hunt in Eurasian History* (Philadelphia: University of Pennsylvania Press, 2006).

8 Peter A. Piccione, "Batting the Ball" (lecture, University of Charleston, South Carolina, 2003), http://www.cofc.edu/-piccione/sekerhemat.html; and Anthony A. Shelton, "The Aztec Theatre State and the Dramatization of War," in *War and Games*, ed. T. Cornell and T. B. Allen (New York: Boydell Press, 2003), 107–130.

9 Thomas Vennum, *American Indian Lacrosse: Little Brother of War* (Washington, DC: Smithsonian Institution Press, 1994).

10 Christopher Brooke, *Europe in the Central Middle Ages 962–1154* (London: Longman Group Limited, 1964); Herbert Adams, "Common Fields in Salem," "Village Communities of Cape Anne and Salem," and "The Great Pastures of Salem," in *Local Institutions*, ed. Herbert Adams, John Hopkins University Studies in Historical and Political Science (Baltimore: John Hopkins University Press, 1883), 357–401.

11 Ibid.

12 William Cronon, *Changes in the Land* (New York: Hill & Wang/Farrar, Straus & Giroux, 1983).

13 Boston Common Management Plan (Boston: City of Boston, Parks and Recreation Department, 1990).

14 "Lincoln-Douglas Debates of 1858," Lincoln/Net, http://lincoln.lib.niu.edu/lincolndouglas/index.html.

15 Witold Rybczynski, *A Clearing in the Distance* (New York: Scribner, 1999), 271.

16 John T. Woolley and Gerhard Peters, "Franklin D. Roosevelt: Radio Address from Two Medicine Chalet, Glacier National Park," August 5, 1934, the American Presidency Project, http://www.presidency.ucsb.edu/ws/?pid=14733.

17 Abraham Lincoln, "Transcript of the 'Hay Draft' of the Gettysburg Address," 1863, Library of Congress, http://www.loc.gov/exhibits/gadd/gatr2.html.

18 Ethan Carr, *Wilderness by Design: Landscape Architecture & the National Park Service* (Lincoln, NE: University of Nebraska Press, 1998), 25.

19 Joseph Sax, "America's National Parks: Their Principles, Purposes, and Prospects," *Natural History* (October 1976): 65.

20 Frederick Law Olmsted, *Yosemite and the Mariposa Grove: A Preliminary Report* (1865; repr., Yosemite, CA: Yosemite Association, 1995), 5.

21 Ibid.

22 Sax, "America's National Parks," 81.

23 John Muir, *Our National Parks* (Boston: Houghton Mifflin, 1901).

24 Horace M. Albright and Marian Albright Schenck, *Creating the National Park Service: The Missing Years* (Norman, OK: University of Oklahoma Press, 1999), 18.

25 Freeman Tilden, *The Fifth Essence: An Invitation to Share in our Eternal Heritage* (Washington, DC: The National Park Trust Fund Board, 1968), 17.

26 Wallace Stegner, "The Best Idea We Ever Had," in *Marking the Sparrow's Fall: The Making of the American West*, ed. Page Stegner (New York: Henry Holt and Co., 1998), 137.

27 National Park Service General Authorities Act, codified at U.S. Code 16 (1970), §1a–1.

28 John J. Reynolds, foreword, in *A Sense of Place: Design Guidelines for Yosemite Valley* (Washington, DC: National Park Service, 2005), 8.

29 James Corner, foreword, *Large Parks*, ed. Julia Czerniak and George Hargreaves (New York: Princeton Architectural Press, 2007), 11.

30 Joseph Sax, "America's National Parks: Their Principles, Purposes, and Prospects," *Natural History* (October 1976): 65.

31 Ronald A. Foresta, *America's National Parks and Their Keepers* (Washington, DC: Resources for the Future Press, 1984), 197.

TWO GATEWAYS:
THE FIRST U.S. URBAN NATIONAL PARKS
ETHAN CARR

The 1972 legislation that established Gateway National Recreation Area in New York City and Golden Gate National Recreation Area in San Francisco created, for the first time in the U.S., an explicit mandate for urban national parks. The acts expressed the optimism of a generation of policy makers who felt the federal government should create new kinds of parks that would directly address the deteriorating social and economic condition of the nation's cities. President Nixon may not have been as enthusiastic as Congress was about this expanded federal involvement in urban affairs, but he signed both pieces of legislation on October 27, 1972.[1]

There were earlier urban national parks, including many of the public spaces of Washington, DC, under the care of the National Park Service since Franklin Delano Roosevelt transferred their jurisdiction in 1933. Others included Independence National Historical Park in Philadelphia and the Jefferson National Expansion Memorial in St. Louis. These two urban historic sites, though, had specific legislative mandates to memorialize the founding and the westward growth of the nation. Their downtown locations did factor in their creation—both served as pretexts for the demolition of "blighted" areas—but meeting local needs for recreational opportunities was not their primary purpose. There were other national recreation areas and national seashores established before 1972, such as those at Lake Mead and on Cape Cod. These certainly experienced very high levels of recreational use, but were hardly urban parks even if their visitors did mostly come from nearby cities.

Gateway and Golden Gate came about through very different political motivations and for other sets of purposes. With the slogan "parks for the people, where the people are," the urban national parks of the 1970s originated in the idealism of the "New Conservation" of Stewart Udall (Secretary of the Interior under Kennedy and Johnson), and especially from the influential recommendations of the Outdoor Recreation Resources Review Committee (ORRRC) published in 1962.[2] The urban national recreation areas created in 1972 augmented existing local park systems by establishing and investing in federal parks within or just outside municipal boundaries. Like many of the environmental laws of the era, national urban park legislation was intended to increase federal responsibility in a critical area of environmental concern, in this case quality of life in the nation's cities.[3]

The stories of these two experiments in urban national park making, however, quickly diverged. The contexts and configurations of the two gateways differed significantly. In San Francisco, the historic Golden Gate Park had been established in 1875, but the municipal park system had since remained relatively undeveloped, at least compared to New York. Golden Gate, however, corrected the situation to a considerable degree.

It encompassed spectacular parkland on the city's waterfront, many significant historic sites (later including the Presidio), and regional reservations in Marin County. Neighborhood activism and advocacy organizations, such as the People for a Golden Gate National Recreation Area and the Sierra Club, successfully fought for the creation of Golden Gate National Recreation Area, which from the beginning required complex and innovative partnerships of governments, organizations, and the private sector. This coalition included powerful private and public interests that were able to secure the cooperation and policy innovations needed from the federal government.[4]

In New York, the establishment of Gateway National Recreation Area responded to a different set of circumstances. The success of Central Park in 1858 led to the development of more parks, playgrounds, and connecting parkways, eventually resulting in one of the country's finest nineteenth-century municipal park systems. By the early twentieth century, many of the most successful and influential examples of park design and diversification had occurred in and around New York City, from Prospect Park and its connecting parkways in Brooklyn, to the Bronx River Parkway and the system of automotive corridors that followed it in Westchester County and on Long Island. More was to come. During the 1930s, Mayor Fiorello La Guardia and his parks commissioner, Robert Moses, achieved a massive expansion of the city's parks largely by exploiting New Deal programs and funding. By 1941 the city had more than doubled its acreage of parkland, created a regional automotive parkway system, and provided playgrounds and recreation facilities on a scale that no other city in the United States at the time could equal.[5]

Robert Moses's transformation and expansion of the public landscape of the city—its park, playground, and parkway system—remains an extraordinary event in urban history, comparable to Baron Haussmann's famous transformation of Paris in the nineteenth century. By the 1960s, as New York convulsed under many of the same dramatic demographic and economic trends affecting other U.S. cities, it became evident that maintaining the city's extensive park system without Moses—and more significantly without the federal largesse of the New Deal—might be impossible. Park concessioners and private, nonprofit partner organizations began to take on a greater role in running city parks. Whereas in San Francisco the creation of Golden Gate was a product of local advocacy, the creation of Gateway in New York, at a time when the municipality was approaching insolvency, was part of a "load-shedding" strategy. The federal government, it was hoped, would subsidize New York's parks through the creation of a national park made up largely of former city parkland. In 1974, Mayor John V. Lindsay signed an agreement transferring approximately 14,000 acres of New York's parks to the NPS. Much of the rest of the 26,000-acre park was made up of decommissioned military properties, including Floyd Bennett Field in Brooklyn, Fort Tilden in Queens, Fort Wadsworth on Staten Island, and Fort Hancock on Sandy Hook, New Jersey. While on the West Coast a network of advocacy groups and private partners worked closely with a congressional delegation that had learned how vital the park was to its constituents, in New York officials hoped to subsidize the maintenance of thousands of acres of deteriorating parks they felt they could no longer afford.

Park Plans

Planning for Gateway was ambitious but from the start the enthusiasm around the creation of the first urban national park in the East was not matched by a commitment of federal funding. Neither was there a tradition or model to which NPS planners and landscape architects could refer. National historical parks, such as Independence in Philadelphia, had been treated as historic sites that happened to be in cities, not as specifically urban recreational centers. Other, more typical national recreation areas surrounded large reservoirs that provided for boating and swimming. The NPS had decades of experience designing such recreational and camping areas in both federal and state park systems; no other group of designers and engineers could claim the same level of expertise in this regard. But Gateway presented social and environmental issues and priorities that many national park planners had not yet encountered.

Much of the site was essentially unmaintained, marginal parkland along the shorelines of Brooklyn and Queens, for example. The illegal dumping of cars and other criminal activities were major concerns. While Jamaica Bay was an extremely significant migratory bird habitat, it also had serious water quality problems and JFK Airport jutted directly into it. New Deal–era recreational developments under Robert Moses, such as Jacob Riis Park, were beloved and heavily used, but they needed substantial and long-overdue maintenance and reinvestment. Historic designations for the Riis Bathhouse and the decommissioned military forts soon complicated matters even further. This array of urban planning issues did not fit easily into NPS culture or priorities (a situation Rolf Diamant describes elsewhere in this volume). In the end, just keeping up with maintenance proved challenging enough. Expensive proposals for the park would need to wait for a political climate that would bring the funding to match the promise of the initial legislation.

Money was not the only problem. Earlier traditions of national park design and landscape architecture, as successful as they were, would not easily provide solutions for how a truly urban national park should function, be planned, or even what it should look like. One of the greatest challenges facing Gateway planners, for example, was that of public accessibility. Only the Jamaica Bay Wildlife Refuge was accessible by subway in New York, and even that still required a three-quarter mile walk. Sandy Hook, across the harbor in New Jersey, was completely inaccessible except by private car. Only bus lines connected other areas to one another and to the majority of the city's population.

Public transportation to and between the units of Gateway was a major feature of park plans from the beginning. Funding for mass transit—a major political issue in New York in the 1970s—had been one motivation for the park proposal. In 1969, when federal officials first put forward their vision for Gateway, they also proposed an extensive ferry system crisscrossing New York Harbor and unifying the otherwise dispersed and marginal elements of the park.[6] In 1971, Mayor Lindsay told Congress that the entire Gateway proposal would fail unless it included funding for the extension of at least one subway line along with other transportation improvements. This was not a minor concern for the mayor, who stalled the park legislation in Congress that summer with his demands that funding for public transportation be considered integral to the park concept.[7] Improved transportation systems were at the heart of the Gateway idea; without them, the individual pieces of scattered properties would remain inaccessible to the public and to one another. Without the transportation component, there was no cohesive "gateway" park at the mouth of New York Harbor, only a collection of somewhat derelict sites used primarily by the local neighborhoods around them.

In the coming years, however, convincing Congress to fund Gateway at all proved difficult. Modest initial funding came after the land transfers were completed in 1974, but multi-million-dollar transportation schemes would prove impossible to implement. This perhaps was the most decisive difference between the two gateway parks. In San Francisco, many of the areas of Golden Gate were more accessible to the public and closer to the center of the city. In New York, the properties that made up Gateway were mostly marginal and relatively inaccessible, and they remained so. The money that Congress provided to initiate and maintain the park never amounted to what local advocates had hoped for: an extensive redevelopment of the individual units combined with a new connecting ferry system and a subway extension. When the NPS presented its park development alternatives in 1976, the proposals disappointed many. Advocates at the Regional Plan Association and elsewhere reacted angrily, claiming that Gateway's "potential as one of the great ocean and beach bay parks in the world, located in the heart of a densely populated region," had not been recognized.[8] Subsequent plans followed, as did some funding. But in 1980, a *New York Times* reporter still asked

New York City Mayor John Lindsay and National Park Service Director Ronald H. Walker sign the agreement under which 14,000 acres of NYC land became part of the new Gateway National Recreation Area, 1974

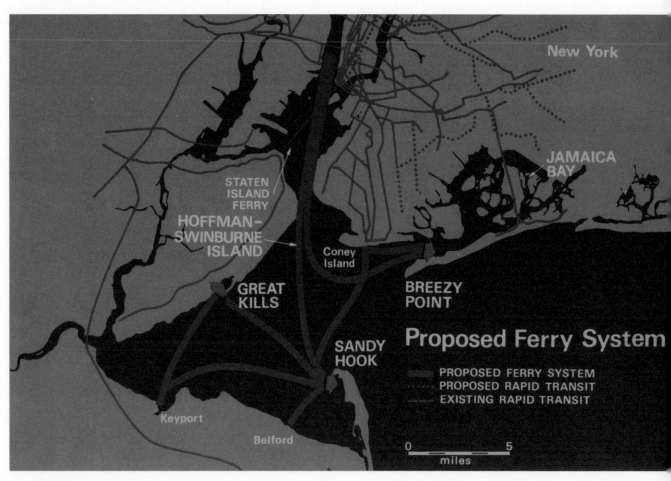

Proposed ferry plan, 1969

rhetorically how Gateway might yet become "a true national park and not just the guardian of scattered pieces of real estate that were in danger of being lost to public use."[9] Today many are asking that question again.

Persistent Issues

The differences between Golden Gate and Gateway national recreation areas are instructive because the former is cited as a successful example of an urban national park, while the latter continues to have its potential suppressed by persistent issues apparent from its inception. The ferry and mass-transit systems that planners have considered a basic requirement of the Gateway idea since 1969 would not only be expensive, but would also probably be controversial for local residents who may be ambivalent about the prospect of large numbers of other New Yorkers coming to their neighborhoods to enjoy beaches, bike paths, and the waterfront. Historian Ronald A. Foresta identified the problem of Gateway planning, in part, as the victory of a "localist view" over nonlocal interests, a victory enabled by the mandated public process and participatory planning techniques put in place by the NPS in the early 1970s.

As soon as local interests were allowed a place at the planning table, in other words, they helped hamstring any efforts to implement ambitious plans for Gateway. Combined with a national political climate that became increasingly less favorable to large-scale, federal park and transportation plans, it is not surprising that Gateway was not transformed into the showcase beach and harbor park its backers had envisioned. Increased concern for the preservation of natural and historic resources, and an emphasis on environmental education over active recreation, have also shifted priorities for park planning. At Gateway, Foresta concludes, "Emphasis on preservation and education allowed [the NPS] to shift planning away from mass access" to beaches and other recreational resources, a shift that was also an expedient response to the results of the local public planning process.[10]

But the social and legislative contexts for Gateway have changed dramatically in the last twenty years, a fact best indicated by the renewed interest, activities, and uses of the park. Above all, the economic resurgence of Brooklyn has changed how not only Gateway, but also Coney Island, the Atlantic train yards, the Brooklyn Heights waterfront, and other locations throughout the borough are regarded by both public officials and private interests. Brooklyn has always been vastly underserved in terms of park acreage. As the borough gentrifies, this reality is finally being addressed.

For designers who may be drawn into plans for the still underachieving Gateway, an understanding of what an urban national park was once intended to be should be a useful guide in moving to a fresh vision of what it could become. Gateway remains very different socially, politically, and geographically from its sister park on the West Coast. Much of its territory was born out of the New Deal. The standard city park construction details that once characterized the parks, playgrounds, and esplanades along the Belt Parkway, for example, have more bearing on Gateway's design history than NPS traditions. The unhappy postwar fate of much of that New Deal legacy—the widening of the Belt Parkway and the expansion of JFK Airport into Jamaica Bay come to mind—have also been the fate of some of the land and waters that later became part of Gateway.

But neither is Gateway the assorted collection of municipal parkland and obsolete shore fortifications it once was. More than thirty-five years as a federal entity has added a new layer of complexity to the site's history, creating another persistent question: how does Gateway fit within the rest of the National Park System and its design traditions? In the past the answer might have been, not at all. In the future, however, it may serve as a prototype for what national park making can still become in urban areas. As the Envisioning Gateway design competition has already indicated, future design solutions will create dramatically new responses to the difficult environmental, social, and logistical puzzle that the urban national recreation area has proved to be. Gateway is a national park. This reality demands that a national interest be served, and that interest may conflict with some local priorities. Congress indicated in 1972 that the whole country had a stake in enhancing and investing in this portion of the public landscape of New York. Its cultural and natural resources also merit the enhanced stewardship that being part of the national park system should guarantee.

The unique history and context of Gateway will continue to push the NPS to work beyond the precedents of other parks in the federal system. This is an era in which many exciting municipal park design competitions and projects, particularly in New York, are providing great inspiration. Federal officials need to examine these recent developments. They are some of the most creative and successful in the world right now, as are the public policies and processes that have allowed them to occur. Projects such as the Hudson River Park, the High Line, and the Brooklyn Bridge Park represent the converging interests of real estate developers and park advocates, who have had to forge new kinds of partnerships to achieve significant results. Gateway must take its place, with these parks and others, in this contemporary transformation of New York's public landscape. The potential, still there, is to become a new kind of national park that will set a precedent for safeguarding and enhancing the environmental and public health of New York, and by example all of the nation's cities.

Park benches and railing along the Belt Parkway, December 1940

ENDNOTES
1 For the legislative history of Gateway National Recreation Area, see contemporary accounts in the *New York Times*. Also see Lary M. Dilsaver, ed., *America's National Park System: The Critical Documents* (New York: Rowman and Littlefield, 1994), 380–384.
2 Outdoor Recreation Resources Review Commission, *Outdoor Recreation for America: A Report to the President and to Congress by the Outdoor Recreation Resources Review Commission* (Washington, DC: Government Printing Office, 1962); and Ronald A. Foresta, *America's National Parks and Their Keepers* (Washington, DC: Resources for the Future, 1984), 178.
3 Foresta, *America's National Parks*, 169–222.
4 Hal K. Rothman, *The New Urban Park: Golden Gate National Recreation Area and Civic Environmentalism* (Lawrence, KS: University Press of Kansas, 2004).
5 See Hilary Ballon and Kenneth T. Jackson, eds., *Robert Moses and the Modern City: The Transformation of New York* (New York: W. W. Norton, 2007).
6 Richard L. Madden, "National Park Urged for Harbor," *New York Times*, December 12, 1969.
7 Ibid., "Mayor Says Gateway Proposal Will Fail Without Cheap Access," *New York Times*, July 17, 1971.
8 John C. Devlin, "Panel Criticizes 3 Gateway Plans," *New York Times*, March 28, 1976.
9 David Bird, "Gateway Park Is Confronting a New Challenge," *New York Times*, May 9, 1980.
10 Foresta, *America's National Parks*, 205–212.

Establishing a Design Framework for Gateway Jamie Hand

The real mission of this initiative is to find ways to move everybody—everybody—to see the situation differently. Without the capacity to see differently, no action is possible.
—Mark Wigley

Seeking to establish a new vision for Gateway and to build a foundation for the significant public, political, and financial support needed to ensure the park's restoration, the National Parks Conservation Association (NPCA) stepped outside its traditional sphere of operations and formed a partnership in 2006 with two design institutions: Columbia University's Graduate School of Architecture, Planning and Preservation (Columbia) and Van Alen Institute (VAI). Generously underwritten by The Tiffany & Co. Foundation, this somewhat unlikely collaboration came together with the broad goal of examining the potential of Gateway's social, ecological, and urban landscapes through extensive research and an international design competition.

By the NPCA's estimation, Columbia's expertise in cutting-edge design research and education, and VAI's century-long commitment to fostering design excellence in the public realm, would surely bring attention and innovation to the site. A design competition for Gateway would build upon the great and growing tradition of landscape design competitions in New York City—from Central Park in 1857 to the revitalized Fresh Kills, Governors Island, and High Line parks in the last decade—and generate public desire and political support for yet another beloved, world-class park. Better yet, our efforts would lead to a single, graceful design solution, as competitions had famously done at Jefferson National Expansion Memorial in St. Louis, Missouri, in 1947 and the Vietnam Veterans Memorial on the National Mall in Washington, DC in 1981.

It didn't take long, however, to realize that Gateway could be neither invented nor reinvented in the same manner as its iconic predecessors. As a park, Gateway was already highly used, highly public, and highly defined by the federal legislation that created it. As a natural landscape, Gateway was so intrinsically tied to the region's urban future and ecological health that there were few civic institutions that weren't already fiercely invested in its management and planning. Any efforts on our part would succeed decades of initiatives spearheaded not only by the National Park Service (NPS), but also by the U.S. Army Corps of Engineers, the New York State Department of Environmental Conservation, the Regional Plan Association, the Port Authority of New York and New Jersey, the New York City Mayor's Office of Long Term Planning and Sustainability, and countless other foundations and nonprofit groups.

With these challenges in mind, we returned to the fundamental question: How might architects, landscape architects, and urban designers and planners contribute to the dialogue about Gateway? How might an ideas competition, positioned as part academic exercise and part development strategy, impact Gateway's future in a meaningful way?

An ideas competition, generally speaking, provides an exceptional forum for designers to perform at their most rigorous and creative capacities—free from political and financial constraints but attuned to the very real challenges that these limitations create. The competition process has been an integral element of architecture's educational model and professional practice for centuries; that is to say, it is very familiar to designers as a platform for engagement. It can be equally understood, however, as a tool for shaping how the broader public thinks about a site, a place, or an issue. Even without the guarantee of a competition proposal's realization, the contributions of significant site research and unexpected alternatives can shift perceptions and catalyze new approaches to the design and planning of public infrastructure.

An ideas competition typically includes background information in what is commonly referred to as a "brief"—a collection of site plans, a narrative description, a series of photographs, or anything that paints a picture of the conditions designers are expected to consider and incorporate into their submissions. Recognizing that Gateway's complexity presented an unparalleled opportunity to engage design disciplines in dialogue with ecology, geology, engineering, social sciences, policy, and other fields that have shaped the park's many landscapes, we endeavored from the start of the collaboration to set a new and rigorous standard for our competition brief.

Nearly a year before the competition launch, a team of Columbia researchers led by Kate Orff, assistant professor and director of the Urban Landscape Lab, and Sarah Williams, director of the Spatial Information Design Lab, was organized to hold graduate-level design studios; prepare a report comprising essays, extensive mappings, external primary sources, and site photographs; and bring together leaders in the fields of urbanism, ecology, and park management for an academic conference entitled Nature Now: The Urban Park as Cultural Catalyst. VAI took the material generated by this team and built a website dedicated to the initiative: www.vanalen. org/gateway. The website was designed to be both an online portal for the competition process as well as a centralized forum for designers, planners, regional stakeholders, and the public at large to engage with comprehensive data about Gateway's past, present, and future. The website remains available as a public resource.

The depth of Columbia's research also played a major role in framing the design challenge, or "program." One might argue that landscape- and urban-scale competitions, as a whole, are less proscribed than their architectural counterparts. Indeed, Gateway as a competition site represented a substantial jump in scope and complexity for VAI despite decades of competition management under its institutional belt. The park is immense and multi-faceted, and from a design standpoint it poses first and foremost a question of scale. Should it be treated as one site or many? Would it be realistic to ask competitors to essentially redesign all 26,607 acres in detail, or to try to solve all of the park's conflicting issues? We saw the competition program not as an explicit assignment but as an organizing strategy that encouraged responses across multiple scales and allowed each design team to identify what they deemed the highest priorities. We hoped the competition would reveal those issues most worth bringing to the attention of the NPS in the future.

More specifically, we broadly outlined eight overarching conditions and challenges that surfaced during Columbia's research, and then charged competitors with the task of designing both a master plan and a smaller scale "park within a park."

> *Gateway Master Plan* Develop a new master plan and strategy for creating a unified experience when visiting Gateway National Recreation Area. Proposals should link the diverse recreational, ecological and historic opportunities located within the three exist-ing units of the park: Jamaica Bay, Sandy Hook, and Staten Island.
> *Park Within a Park* Within the larger approach developed above, design a new park sited at Floyd Bennett Field within the Jamaica Bay Unit of Gateway, which includes the Wildlife Refuge, Riis Beach and Fort Tilden. Floyd Bennett Field has the opportunity

not only to become a premier destination within Gateway, but to provide facilities and resources for the entire park. Floyd Bennett Field is a 1,358 acre piece of land that was New York City's first municipal airport; today it hosts myriad activities but suffers from a lack of identity and definition, representing a microcosm of the larger issues facing Gateway. Competitors may intervene on as much or as little of Floyd Bennett Field and its surrounding waters as they choose, and should define the programmatic elements of a "park" in terms of contemporary urban conditions and social/recreational needs and desires.[1]

The open-ended nature of the competition program reflected the contemporary realities at Gateway, and we extended this approach to the jury process as well: in May 2007, we convened twelve jurors in an abandoned airplane hangar at Floyd Bennett Field to review and debate the entries at length. Over 230 designers registered for the competition from twenty-three countries around the world, and the jury's ultimate task was to select six winning proposals from the ninety-seven submitted.

The Envisioning Gateway jury was composed of renowned designers in addition to historians, environmentalists, scientists, and political and philanthropic leaders from the region.[2] This diversity of perspectives was critical to the success of the deliberations—design integrity and innovation were high priorities, but balanced within the context of the NPS mission and tempered by ecological and political realities. As individual jurors gravitated toward certain approaches over others, the park's inherent conflicts—and six priorities for its revitalization—became clear.

The competition did not result in a single, tidy solution to Gateway's many challenges; instead it revealed the most pressing issues at hand and the multiple ways in which these issues might be addressed. The material that follows represents a selection of winning and notable competition entries, grouped according to these pressing issues, presented alongside graphics and texts adapted from the research originally generated by Columbia's team. This framework directly reflects the competition process, during which rigorous data about the site's past served to inform and inspire imaginative speculations about its future. In jury co-chair Mark Wigley's words, "The report itself was the launching pad for a range of concepts and strategies that emerged in the competition. Research and design both informed and gave depth to each other."

Taking the idea a step further, the Envisioning Gateway collaboration as a whole might be viewed as a new design methodology in itself—one where the competition entries, taken collectively, reveal a new set of principles for understanding the site. And one where a commitment to design thinking, throughout the process, enables a new way of seeing.

ENDNOTES

Epigraph Mark Wigley, introductory remarks to the competition jury, May 12, 2007.
1 Excerpt taken from Envisioning Gateway competition program, ©Van Alen Institute, 2007, http://www.vanalen.org/gateway/logistics_prog_req.php
2 See Partners & Participants on page 216 for a list of the Envisioning Gateway competition jurors by name and professional affiliation.

Jury deliberation co-chairs Mark Wigley, Dean of Columbia University's Graduate School of Architecture, Planning and Preservation, and Adi Shamir, then-Executive Director of Van Alen Institute

Competition jurors discuss a submission, clockwise from left: Peter Latz, Anuradha Mathur, Wendy Paulson, Lindy Roy, John Loring, Kate Orff, Andrew Darrell, Ethan Carr, Nanette Smith, Adi Shamir, and Marian Heiskell

Competition jurors selected winning entries through three rounds of debate and discussion. Clockwise from right: Walter Hood, Marian Heiskell, Anuradha Mathur, Randall Luthi, Ethan Carr, John Loring, Andrew Darrell, and Adi Shamir (standing)

COMPETITION THEMES

Who Goes There?

HONORABLE MENTION: Urban Barometer
/ PORT Architecture + Urbanism

So Near, Yet So Far

HONORABLE MENTION: [Un]natural Selection
/ W Architecture and Landscape Architecture

Shifting Ground

FIRST PRIZE: Mapping the Ecotone
/ Urban Found Architecture

Eco-Harbor

SECOND PRIZE: Reassembling Ecologies
/ North Design Office

Down in the Dumps

HONORABLE MENTION: H2grOw
/ EFGH

Past as Prologue

THIRD PRIZE: Landmarks, Seamarks, Ciphers
/ Virginia Polytechnic

Who Goes There?

It is no longer sufficient to look only within the boundaries
of a park when making management decisions. Parks are
part of broader communities; actions in parks affect their
communities just as actions in communities affect parks.
—Denis Galvin, former deputy director, U.S. National
   Park Service

One of Gateway National Recreation Area's greatest distinctions as an urban national park is the range of diverse ethnic communities that border its 41 square miles. Unlike the majority of NPS sites, all three of Gateway's units are surrounded by relatively dense residential and commercial development—from small fishing villages and summer beach communities on the New Jersey shore to New York City Housing Authority apartment towers and big-box retail stores. This broad cross-section of cultures, with an equally broad range of demands on Gateway's natural resources, gives the park tremendous potential as a vibrant public space, yet poses challenges for stewardship and outreach efforts as park stakeholders set a socially inclusive course for the future.

The park's multinational constituency is showcased in the areas around the Jamaica Bay unit, where predominantly white, middle-class neighborhoods adjoin some of New York's largest Haitian and Caribbean immigrant communities. More than 138 languages are spoken in Queens and Brooklyn, the two New York City boroughs that border the unit, and these ethnic groups have not always lived in harmony. While race and class tensions have tempered in recent years, they are very much a part of the area's past. The Staten Island unit is surrounded by a more suburban community, constituted principally of car-reliant residents who occupy single-family homes—a demographic largely representative of the borough as a whole. Sandy Hook, Gateway's only unit in New Jersey, is the least urban of all: while many individuals commute by car or ferry to Manhattan, communities retain the feel of small, coastal towns with many second- and third-generation residents reflecting the population's deep roots along the dune-lined shore.

Collectively, Gateway's neighboring communities are far more diverse than the constituency that the national parks have attracted over the past century. This proximity of permanent residents from widely varying social and economic backgrounds has shaped Gateway's physical landscape and, in many ways, its mission. A stark statistical difference between Gateway and many other national parks is its relatively high rate of visitation, likely due to its proximity to such a densely populated region. In 2005,

Gateway was the second most-visited national recreation area in the country, host to approximately 8.4 million visitors, and in 2006 it was the fifth most-visited park in the entire national park system. However, by the same token, many visitors to Gateway might not even recognize that they were on federally owned land. Gateway's location makes it more akin to a municipal park, drawing local constituents with the potential to become powerful advocates on behalf of Gateway's manifold natural and recreational resources.

This usage pattern was indicated in a 1990 study conducted by the University of Idaho's Park Studies Unit, which found that 36 percent of Gateway's visitors had been to the park more than ten times prior, and 98 percent of all visitors to Gateway were from the United States. Such data suggests that park visitors are more habitual, regional, and local in character, rather than one-time destination seekers. This aspect of Gateway stands in dramatic contrast to that of other national park sites; in 2005, for example, 18 percent of visitors to Yosemite National Park were visitors from outside the United States and visiting these destinations for their first time. With its present configuration and facilities, Gateway serves a regional population that is a markedly different subset from the National Park Service's typical visitor demographic, and its recreation and education programs have evolved as a result.

In addition to hiking, fishing, historic tours, and enjoyment of public beaches—fairly standard activities for a national park site—a number of active recreation opportunities have been created at Gateway, including soccer and baseball fields, cricket pitches, ice rinks, boating marinas, and archery and golf driving ranges. Some of these facilities have been developed with substantive investments from private partners, and others are a result of local enthusiasts reclaiming neglected open spaces for specific hobbies and pursuits.

Floyd Bennett Field, for instance, has become a meeting area for a diverse mix of informal programs; the vast former runways are frequently appropriated for parasailing, bike racing, model-airplane flying, and drag racing. A number of annual cultural events take place at Floyd Bennett Field, and several formal clubs have obtained special use permits to occupy public space in the park. These include the Floyd Bennett Garden Association, which operates the largest community garden in New York City; the Historic Aircraft Restoration Project, which restores antique airplanes inside one of the former hangars; and Friends of Gateway, which operates a greenhouse and education center for the cultivation of trees and plants to be replanted in the park.

In addition to Gateway's neighboring constituents, with their diverse activities and enthusiasms, the National Park Service must accommodate the wide variety of national, state, and local

Neighborhoods and districts

Diversity and foreign-born
population

Map: SIDL

20% OR LESS

20 - 40%

40 - 60%

60 - 80%

80% OR MORE

0 1 2   4 Miles

N

Map: SIDL

interests intersecting at Gateway and the surrounding metropolitan area. NPS works with more than twenty-two agencies representing these different scales, each with its own claims to jurisdiction over Gateway's land and water resources. The U.S. Army Corps of Engineers, the Department of Homeland Security, and the Port Authority of New York and New Jersey are three such institutions, responsible for major restoration and infrastructure projects in Jamaica Bay. Though the harbor has become less significant for national defense since battleships were strategically superseded by cruise missiles, Gateway continues to be used by several agencies responsible for public safety, including the New York City Police Department's Special Operations Division. Since the late 1970s, Floyd Bennett Field has also provided space for educational organizations including, among others, the New York City Department of Education and Outward Bound.

This exceptional range of uses and visitors at Gateway—reflective of the demands on a metropolitan area with rich cultural heritage—adds a unique layer of complexity to the park's identity and role in the National Park System. Combined with Gateway's prime location in what is arguably the most diverse city in the world, this complexity strengthens the park's potential to set a new standard for visitor outreach and programming. Gateway can become a model for urban parks that both reflect and sustain the communities around them.

The competition entry Urban Barometer, by Christopher Marcincowski and Andrew Moddrell of PORT Architecture + Urbanism, reframes the issue of public use by emphasizing Gateway's broader potential as a site for research, experimentation, and scientific learning. The proposal goes beyond the traditional relationship between a park and its users to propose a greater focus on the national need for scientific research institutions and creative public-private partnerships. The proposal accentuates Gateway's metropolian context and, through the idea of ongoing and interactive public research, highlights Gateway's potential to offer urban dwellers an experience markedly different from other national parks, which emphasize recreational uses and the interpretation of the site's cultural or natural history. The selected competition entries that follow similarly focused on an expansion of programming and activities at Gateway in conjunction with creatively recasting the relationship between the region's institutional resources and its communities.

Gateway Stakeholders

Governmental Organizations / Federal

Environmental Protection Agency
National Aeronautics and Space Administration
National Oceanic and Atmospheric Administration
National Park Service
New York Sea Grant
New Jersey Sea Grant
U.S. Army Corps of Engineers
U.S. Coast Guard
U.S. Department of Agriculture
U.S. Fish and Wildlife Service
U.S. Geological Survey

Governmental Organizations / Regional

Interstate Environmental Commission
New York/New Jersey Port Authority
New York-New Jersey Harbor Estuary Program
New Jersey Coastal Heritage Trail

Governmental Organizations / State

New Jersey State Department of Environmental Protection
New Jersey State Department of Transportation
New Jersey State Maritime Resources
New Jersey Fish and Wildlife
New Jersey Water Supply Authority
New York State Department of Environmental Conservation
New York State Department of Health
New York State Department of State
New York State Department of Transportation
New York State Office of Parks, Recreation, and Historic Preservation

Governmental Organizations / City

New York City Council
New York City Department of City Planning
New York City Department of Education
New York City Department of Environmental Protection
New York City Department of Health and Mental Hygiene
New York City Department of Parks and Recreation
New York City Department of Sanitation
New York City Department of Transportation
New York City Office of the Mayor
New York City Soil and Water Conservation District
New York City Police Department
Town of Hempstead, Long Island, New York

Governmental Organizations / Borough / County

New York City Borough of Queens
Queens Community Board #10
Queens Community Board #12
Queens Community Board #13
Queens Community Board #14
New York City Borough of Brooklyn
Brooklyn Community Board #5
Brooklyn Community Board #15
Brooklyn Community Board #18
New York City Borough of Staten Island
Staten Island Community Board #1
Staten Island Community Board #2
Staten Island Community Board #3
Monmouth County, NJ

Governmental Organizations / Municipal

Atlantic Highlands Borough, Monmouth County, NJ
Highlands Borough, Monmouth County, NJ
Middletown Township, Monmouth County, NJ
Rumson Borough, Monmouth County, NJ

Non-Governmental Organizations

American Littoral Society
CIESIN, Columbia University
Clean Ocean and Shore Trust
Fishermen's Conservation Association
Friends of Gateway
Gaia Institute
Gateway Greenhouse Education Center
Metropolitan Waterfront Alliance
Regional Plan Association
National Resources Defense Council
National Resources Protective Association
New York Academy of Sciences Harbor Consortium
New York/New Jersey Baykeeper
New York-New Jersey Trail Conference
Citizens for NYC
Coastal Conservation Association of New York
Linnaean Society of New York
Neighborhood Open Space Coalition
New York City Audubon Society
New York Botanical Garden
New York City Environmental Fund
New York State Ornithological Association
TreeBranch Network
Berlin Airlift Historical Foundation
Brooklyn Bird Club
Brooklyn Polytechnic University
Concerned Citizens of Bensonhurst
Deep Creek Yacht Club
Diamond Point Yacht Club
Eastern Queens Alliance
Floyd Bennett Field Garden Association
Gerritsen Beach Cares
Jamaica Bay Ecowatchers
Jamaica Bay Task Force
Manhattan Beach Community Group
Marine Park Civic Association
Marine Science Research Center, SUNY Stonybrook
New York Aquarium
Norton Basin Edgemere Stewardship Group
Pennsylvania Avenue Radio Control Society
Riverhead Foundation for Marine Research and Preservation
Rockaway Point Yacht Club
Salt Marsh Alliance
Sebago Canoe Club
Southern Queens Parks Association
Wildlife Trust
Alice Austen Museum
Great Kills Yacht Club
Natural Resources Protective Association
Richmond Model Flying Club
Rosedale Civic Association
Army Ground Forces Association
Bayshore Regional Watershed Council
Brookdale Community College Ocean Institute
Clean Ocean Action
Earth Share of New Jersey
Friends of Gunnison
Institute of Marine and Coast Sciences, Rutgers University
Marine Academy of Science and Technology
Monmouth County Audubon Society
Monmouth County Friends of Clearwater
Navesink Maritime Heritage Association
Navesink River Environmental League
Navesink River Rowing
New Jersey Audubon Society
New Jersey Conservation Foundation
New Jersey Environmental Federation
New Jersey Lighthouse Society
New Jersey Marine Science Consortium
New Jersey Water Resouces Research Institute
Raritan Basin Watershed Alliance
Sandy Hook Bay Catamaran Club
Sandy Hook Bird Observatory
Shrewsbury Sailing and Yacht Club
Shrewsbury River Yacht Club
The Fort at Sandy Hook
Twin Lights Historical Society
Save Sandy Hook

ENDNOTES
Epigraph Denis Galvin, "Directors Orders: Communicating the NPS Mission," http://www.nps.gov/refdesk/DOrders/DOrder52A.html. At the time of this statement in 2001, Galvin was the acting director of the U.S. National Park Service.

Current recreational activities at Floyd Bennett Field

Urban Barometer
Christopher Marcinkoski and Andrew Moddrell (PORT Architecture + Urbanism)

Our proposal introduces cutting-edge science and active research into Gateway's programming agenda. We do not believe that Gateway should be enhanced and transformed so that it functions as just another natural recreation area. We propose that Gateway, in particular Floyd Bennett Field, becomes the site of a new type of national park—one whose role is to provide a productive urban infrastructure and a public realm and ecological amenity. We call this a National Eco-Urban Research Zone—a territory that both promotes stewardship of existing natural and native resources, but also engages in the active exploration of the relationship between dynamic ecosystems and ongoing anthropologic urbanization.

The mandate of this new designation will be to encourage policy, design, and public awareness of the potentially fertile synthesis of urban and natural landscapes. This work could be undertaken through a unique public-private partnership between the U.S. National Park Service (NPS) and related city and state agencies, corporate entities, nongovernmental organizations, and local and regional academic institutions. Under this model, incubators, laboratories, and research facilities will become a fundamental part of the park's landscape, allowing for field exploration of the evolving interrelationship between the city and the natural systems in which it sits. Further, the introduction of this program will create a revenue stream necessary for the continued operation and maintenance of the park, thereby reducing the financial obligation of the NPS. Ultimately, we envision that the NPS could manage similar zones in each of the twenty-five largest U.S. metropolises as a way of promoting the continued engagement of intelligent urban growth that is both environmentally and economically sustainable.

In addition to newly proposed flagship open spaces like Fresh Kills, the High Line, Governors Island, Brooklyn Bridge Park, and the Greenpoint-Williamsburg waterfront, New York City already has more than seventeen hundred municipal parks, playgrounds, and recreation facilities across the five boroughs, totaling nearly 29 thousand acres. As NYC's current Parks Commissioner Adrian Benepe proudly notes, "Already, three-quarters of New Yorkers live within a 10-minute walk of a park."[1] The NPS alone currently operates four distinct types of national park within the New York metropolitan region. Our proposal will add a fifth, special research zone. It's enough to make one wonder: Is the continued development of parkland through conventional means alone enough to sustain and guide the transformation and changes that the megalopolis will undergo over the next century?

The concept of sharpening Gateway's particular role relative to research and science moving forward into the twenty-first century becomes significant. Rather than solely focusing on the preservation of varied ecological systems within an urbanized context, we propose a more progressive, science-based approach, exploring how seemingly oppositional structures can be integrated into a fertile, productive ground capable of sustaining both intelligent urbanization and vibrant, varied ecological systems.

1 John Koblin, "A Central Park Figure," *New York Observer*, http://www.observer.com/node/36958.

"ALREADY, THREE-QUARTERS OF NEW YORKERS LIVE WITHIN A 10-MINUTE WALK OF A PARK."
NYC Parks Commissioner Adrian Benepe http://www.observer.com/printpage.asp?iid=14384&ic=Sit+Down

URBAN BAROMETER

The National Park Service currently operates 20 types of National Park – four types of which can currently be found within the New York Megalopolis. New York City alone has more than 1,700 parks, playgrounds and recreation facilities across the five boroughs. City Parks' properties total more than 28,000 acres.

Add to this proposed new flagship open spaces like Fresh Kills, the Highline, Governor's Island, Brooklyn Bridge Park and the Greenpoint-Williamsburg waterfront redevelopment – as well as the 20 or so existing New York State parks within the metropolitan area – and the question of Gateway's role within the New York Megalopolis moving forward into the 21st century becomes considerable.

Capital investment in public open space at the scale currently seen within New York is both worthwhile and commendable. HOWEVER, IS THE CONTINUED DEVELOPMENT OF CONVENTIONAL PARKLAND ALONE ENOUGH TO SUSTAIN THE TRANSFORMATION AND CHANGES THAT THE MEGALOPOLIS WILL UNDERGO OVER THE NEXT CENTURY?

IN ADDITION TO STEWARDSHIP AND PRESERVATION, WE PROPOSE CUTTING-EDGE SCIENCE AND ACTIVE RESEARCH. WE PROPOSE GATEWAY TO BECOME A NEW TYPE OF NATIONAL PARK – A TRUE SCIENTIFIC, ECONOMIC, AND URBAN INFRASTRUCTURE AS MUCH AS A PUBLIC RECREATIONAL AMENITY.

GATEWAY SHOULD BE RE-DESIGNATED AS THE FIRST NATIONAL ECO-URBAN RESEARCH ZONE – A TERRITORY THAT BOTH PROMOTES STEWARDSHIP OF EXISTING NATURAL AND NATIVE RESOURCES, BUT ALSO ENGAGES IN THE ACTIVE EXPLORATION OF THE RELATIONSHIP BETWEEN DYNAMIC ECOSYSTEMS AND ONGOING ANTHROPOGENIC URBANIZATION.

This work will be undertaken through a unique public-private partnership between the National Park Service and related public agencies; corporate entities, as well as local and regional academic institutions. Ultimately, it is envisioned that the National Park Service could manage similar zones in each of the 25 largest metropolises in the United States as a way of promoting the continued engagement of intelligent urban growth that is both environmentally and economically sustainable.

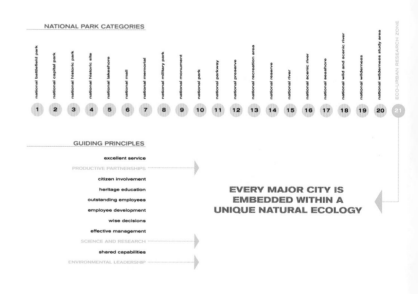

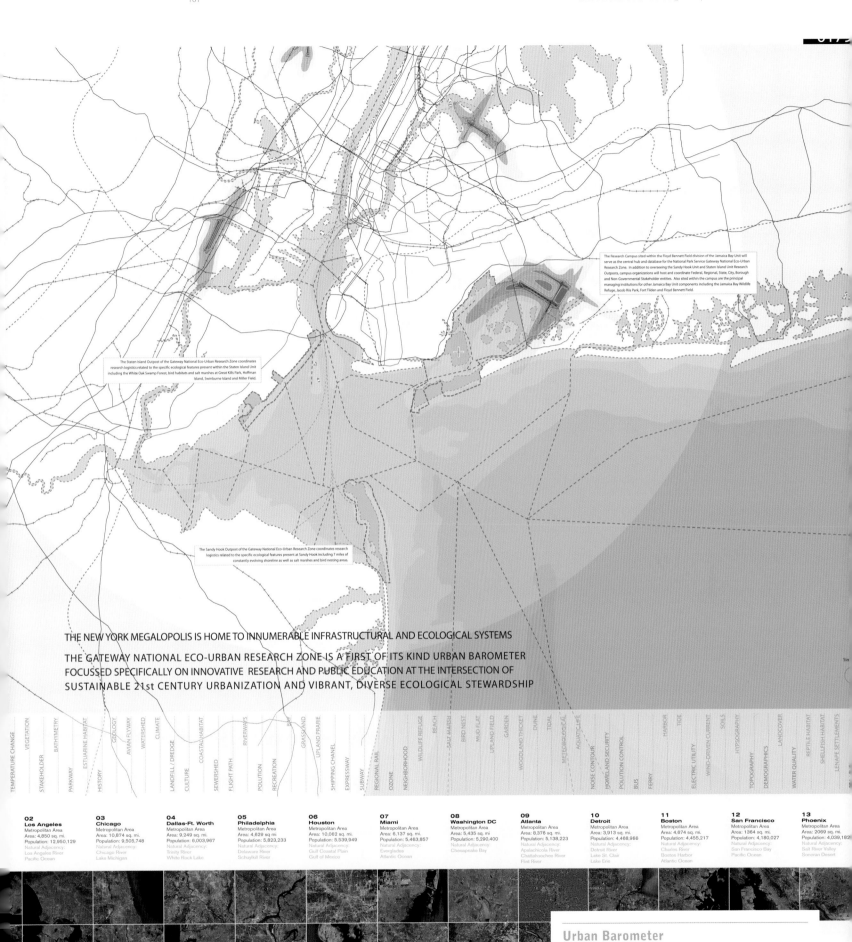

The Research Campus sited within the Floyd Bennett Field division of the Jamaica Bay Unit will serve as the central hub and database for the National Park Service Gateway National Eco-Urban Research Zone. In addition to overseeing the Sandy Hook Unit and Staten Island Unit Research Outposts, campus organizations will host and coordinate Federal, Regional, State, City, Borough and Non-Governmental Stakeholder entities. Also sited within the campus are the principal managing institutions for other Jamaica Bay Unit components including the Jamaica Bay Wildlife Refuge, Jacob Riis Park, Fort Tilden and Floyd Bennett Field.

The Staten Island Outpost of the Gateway National Eco-Urban Research Zone coordinates research logistics related to the specific ecological features present within the Staten Island Unit including the White Oak Swamp Forest, bird habitats and salt marshes at Great Kills Park, Hoffman Island, Swinburne Island and Miller Field.

The Sandy Hook Outpost of the Gateway National Eco-Urban Research Zone coordinates research logistics related to the specific ecological features present at Sandy Hook including 7 miles of constantly evolving shoreline as well as salt marshes and bird nesting areas.

THE NEW YORK MEGALOPOLIS IS HOME TO INNUMERABLE INFRASTRUCTURAL AND ECOLOGICAL SYSTEMS

THE GATEWAY NATIONAL ECO-URBAN RESEARCH ZONE IS A FIRST OF ITS KIND URBAN BAROMETER FOCUSSED SPECIFICALLY ON INNOVATIVE RESEARCH AND PUBLIC EDUCATION AT THE INTERSECTION OF SUSTAINABLE 21st CENTURY URBANIZATION AND VIBRANT, DIVERSE ECOLOGICAL STEWARDSHIP

TEMPERATURE CHANGE · VEGETATION · STAKEHOLDER · BATHYMETRY · PARKWAY · ESTUARINE HABITAT · HISTORY · GEOLOGY · AVIAN FLYWAY · WATERSHED · CLIMATE · LANDFILL / DREDGE · CHICAGO · CULTURE · COASTAL HABITAT · SEWERSHED · FLIGHT PATH · RIVERWAYS · POLLUTION · RECREATION · GRASSLAND · SHIPPING CHANEL · UPLAND PRARIE · EXPRESSWAY · SUBWAY · REGIONAL RAIL · OZONE · NEIGHBORHOOD · WILDLIFE REFUGE · BEACH · SALT MARSH · BIRD NEST · MUD FLAT · UPLAND FIELD · GARDEN · WOODLAND THICKET · DUNE · TIDAL · METEOROLOGICAL · AQUATIC LIFE · NOISE CONTOUR · HOMELAND SECURITY · POLLUTION CONTROL · BUS · FERRY · HARBOR · ELECTRIC UTILITY · WIND-DRIVEN CURRENT · SOILS · HYPSOGRAPHY · TOPOGRAPHY · DEMOGRAPHICS · LANDCOVER · WATER QUALITY · REPTILE HABITAT · SHELLFISH HABITAT · LENAPE SETTLEMENTS

02 Los Angeles	03 Chicago	04 Dallas-Ft. Worth	05 Philadelphia	06 Houston	07 Miami	08 Washington DC	09 Atlanta	10 Detroit	11 Boston	12 San Francisco	13 Phoenix
Metropolitan Area	Metropolitan Area	Metropolitan Area	Metropolitan Area	Metropolitan Area	Metropolitan Area	Metropolitan Area	Metropolitan Area	Metropolitan Area	Metropolitan Area	Metropolitan Area	Metropolitan Area
Area: 4,850 sq. mi.	Area: 10,874 sq. mi.	Area: 9,249 sq. mi.	Area: 4,629 sq mi	Area: 10,062 sq. mi.	Area: 6,137 sq. mi.	Area: 5,435 sq mi	Area: 8,376 sq. mi.	Area: 3,913 sq. mi.	Area: 4,674 sq. mi.	Area: 1364 sq. mi.	Area: 2069 sq. mi.
Population: 12,950,129	Population: 9,505,748	Population: 6,003,967	Population: 5,823,233	Population: 5,539,949	Population: 5,463,857	Population: 5,290,400	Population: 5,138,223	Population: 4,468,966	Population: 4,455,217	Population: 4,180,027	Population: 4,039,182
Natural Adjacency:	Natural Adjacency:	Natural Adjacency:	Natural Adjacency:	Natural Adjacency:	Natural Adjacency:	Natural Adjacency:	Natural Adjacency:	Natural Adjacency:	Natural Adjacency:	Natural Adjacency:	Natural Adjacency:
Los Angeles River	Chicago River	Trinity River	Delaware River	Gulf Coastal Plain	Everglades	Chesapeake Bay	Apalachicola River	Detroit River	Charles River	San Francisco Bay	Salt River Valley
Pacific Ocean	Lake Michigan	White Rock Lake	Schuylkill River	Gulf of Mexico	Atlantic Ocean		Chattahoochee River	Lake St. Clair	Boston Harbor	Pacific Ocean	Sonoran Desert
							Flint River	Lake Erie	Atlantic Ocean		

Urban Barometer
Christopher Marcinkoski and Andrew Moddrell, *Larchmont, NY*

15 Seattle	16 Minneapolis	17 San Diego	18 St. Louis	19 Tampa Bay	20 Baltimore	21 Denver	22 Pittsburgh	Portland	Cleveland	Cincinnati
Metropolitan Area	Metropolitan Area	Metropolitan Area	Metropolitan Area	Metropolitan Area	Metropolitan Area	Metropolitan Area	Metropolitan Area	Metropolitan Area	Metropolitan Area	Metropolitan Area
Area: 2459 sq. mi.	Area: 2316 sq. mi.	Area: 2026 sq. mi.	Area: 2147 sq. mi.	Area: 2077 sq. mi.	Area: 1292 sq. mi.	Area: 1768 sq. mi.	Area: 2207 sq. mi.	Area: 1227 sq. mi.	Area: 1675 sq. mi.	Area: 1739 sq. mi.
Population: 3,263,497	Population: 3,175,041	Population: 2,941,454	Population: 2,796,368	Population: 2,697,731	Population: 2,658,405	Population: 2,408,750	Population: 2,370,776	Population: 2,137,565	Population: 2,114,155	Population: 2,104,218
Natural Adjacency:	Natural Adjacency:	Natural Adjacency:	Natural Adjacency:	Natural Adjacency:	Natural Adjacency:	Natural Adjacency:	Natural Adjacency:	Natural Adjacency:	Natural Adjacency:	Natural Adjacency:
Lake Washington	Mississippi River	San Diego Bay	Missouri River	Tampa Bay	Chesapeake Bay	Great Plains	Allegheny River	Willamette River	Cuyahoga River	Ohio River

RESEARCH

STEWARDSHIP

RECREATION

EDUCATION

Urban Barometer
Christopher Marcinkoski and Andrew
Moddrell, *Larchmont, NY*

Site Research and Design Proposals: Who Goes There?

FUNDING MECHANISM

By utilizing tax and enterprise incentives at the various levels of government, land leasing less than 4% of the entire GATEWAY land mass for incubator and research facilities will generate significant supplemental operation capital as well as potential pioneer technologies that can improve the sustainability and eco-character of urbanized areas throughout the U.S. and the world.

If this investment were to be properly capitalized, the potential for Gateway's continued success would almost certainly be assured.

N STRIP

developable territory, set aside for public/private research r facilities. This zone provides the functional mechanism for –URBAN RESEARCH designation at GATEWAY. The STRIP is a public education campus engaged in the study enic urbanization and its relationship to the diverse the Megalopolis.

RECREATION BOW / RUNWAY PROMENADE

This zone encompasses the majority of Floyd Bennett Field structured recreation areas including playfields, campgrounds, pedestrian + bike circuits, as well as public gardens and agro-research plots. The center piece of the zone is the RUNWAY PROMENADE – stretching along the longest leg of the historic FBF runway – this element not only provides recreational facilities, but also helps manage stormwater on the FBF site.

ECO-BLADDERS / HABITAT NESTS

Utilizing the existing geometry and structure of the Floyd Bennett Field runway, a strategy for stormwater maintenance and habitat growth is deployed in the unpaved polygons within the asphalt lattice. These "soft" polygons have been engineered to collect and hold water while also providing fertile ground for the establishment and growth of various ecological habitats under research within the GATEWAY territory.

CONSTRUCTED WETLAND TERRACE

In order to structure research and public understanding of the relationship between ongoing urbanization and global tide levels, the southern section of Floyd Bennett Field has been engineered into a series of wetland terraces. This element of FBF will offer a unique context for researching the impact of tidal fluctuations on urbanized areas of the globe, while offering a direct form of public engagement on the issue.

SERVICE BAR

The service tenants of Floyd Bennett Field – including the Department of S tion, as well as the various Homeland Security constituents present – shou remain part of the GATEWAY territory. Their facilities at FBF are concentrat along the structured eastern edge of the plot, thereby providing shared res and infrastructure around which their services can be integrated into the research agenda of the GATEWAY ECO-URBAN RESEARCH ZONE.

These entries highlight how Gateway's diverse visitors and stakeholders can play a key role in remaking the park.

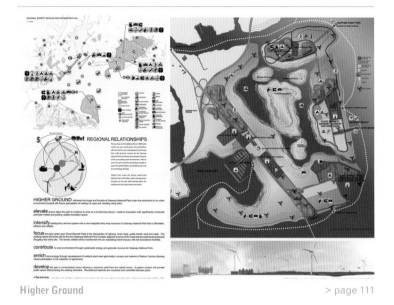

Higher Ground

> page 111

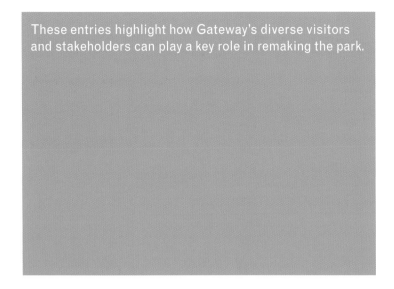

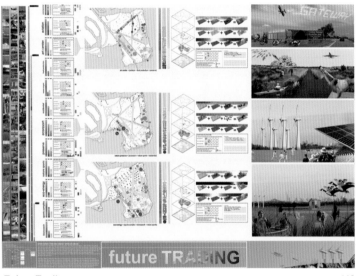

Future Trading

> page 112

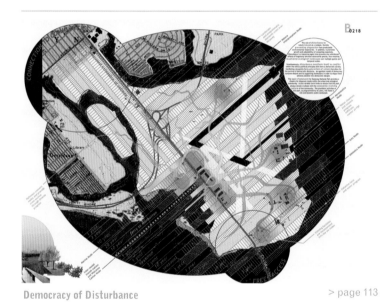

Democracy of Disturbance

> page 113

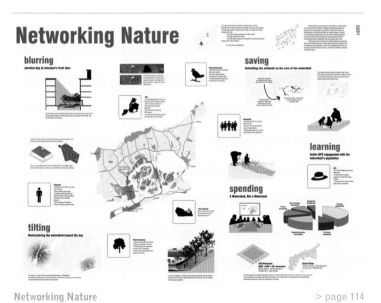

Networking Nature

> page 114

Gateway for Change

> page 115

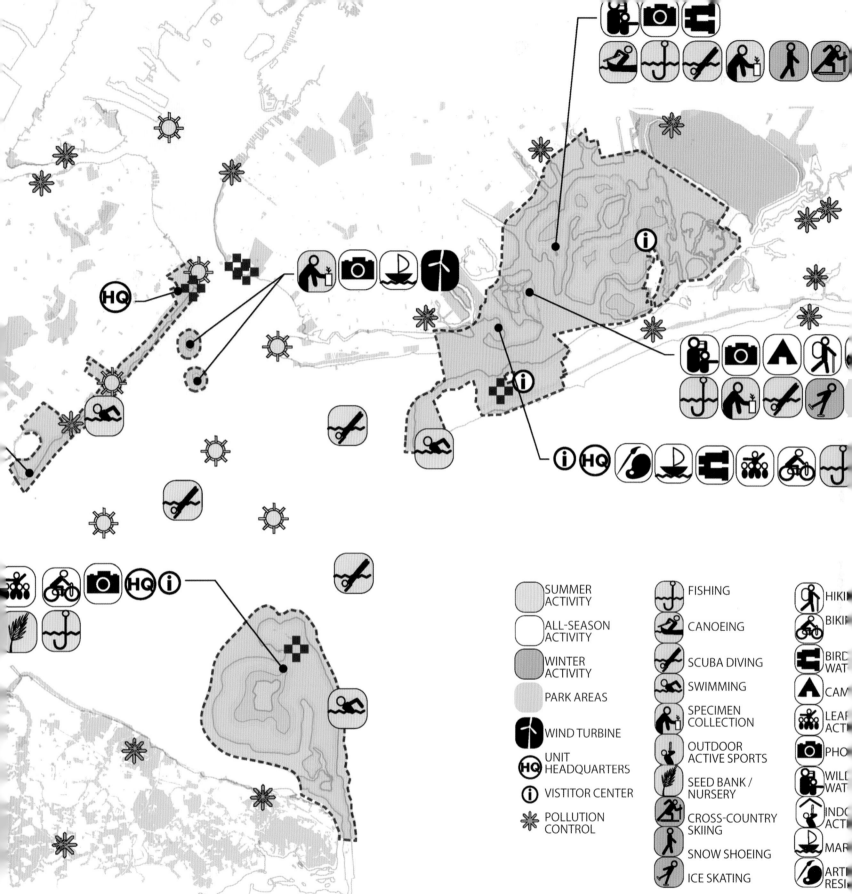

LEGEND

(light gray)	SUMMER ACTIVITY
(white)	ALL-SEASON ACTIVITY
(dark gray)	WINTER ACTIVITY
(medium gray)	PARK AREAS
(wind turbine icon)	WIND TURBINE
HQ	UNIT HEADQUARTERS
(i)	VISITOR CENTER
※	POLLUTION CONTROL

(icon)	FISHING
(icon)	CANOEING
(icon)	SCUBA DIVING
(icon)	SWIMMING
(icon)	SPECIMEN COLLECTION
(icon)	OUTDOOR ACTIVE SPORTS
(icon)	SEED BANK / NURSERY
(icon)	CROSS-COUNTRY SKIING
(icon)	SNOW SHOEING
(icon)	ICE SKATING

(icon)	HIKI...
(icon)	BIKI...
(icon)	BIRD WAT...
(icon)	CAM...
(icon)	LEAR... ACT...
(icon)	PHO...
(icon)	WILD WAT...
(icon)	INDO... ACT...
(icon)	MAR...
(icon)	ART... RESI...

Higher Ground
Michelle Lazar, Matthew Sweig: "Enrich local ecology through development of wetland plant seed germination nursery and network of Nature Centres allowing citizen partici-pation in the collection of specimens." *Toronto, ON, Canada*

IN DEPTH IDEA EVALUATION FORM

1. Please rate the following aspects of the idea (check the box that applies).

Visitor experience: [X] excellent / very good / good / poor / very poor

Environmental quality: excellent / [X] very good / good / poor / very poor

Marketing potential: [X] excellent / very good / good / poor / very poor

2. Please write "yes", "no", "maybe" or "NA" for each statement:

Public transportation allows easy and pleasant access. — yes
Wilderness areas and endangered species will flourish here. — yes
I could see people showing up to visit. — maybe
Overall, the value of the site is higher than before. — maybe probably
The various elements of the site are cohesive. — yes

3. Comments:
The eco-resort I prob. wouldn't visit, b/c I live in NYC. The gardens I like, but not so sure about compost waste.

IN DEPTH IDEA EVALUATION FORM

1. Please rate the following aspects of the idea (check the box that applies).

Visitor experience: excellent / [X] very good / good / poor / very poor

Environmental quality: excellent / [X] very good / good / poor / very poor

Marketing potential: [X] excellent / very good / good / poor / very poor

2. Please write "yes", "no", "maybe" or "NA" for each statement:

Public transportation allows easy and pleasant access. — yes
Wilderness areas and endangered species will flourish here. — maybe
I could see people showing up to visit. — yes - definitely
Overall, the value of the site is higher than before. — yes
The various elements of the site are cohesive. — maybe

3. Comments:
This city really needs more playing fields + facilities. Bio research sounds vague - is it good for the environment?

Future Trading

Emilie Hagen, Annie Suratt, Michael Szivos: "This project creates a microcosm of that process: functioning like a tournament playoff chart or survival of the fittest, the field is narrowed through a series of iterations and combinations, until in the final product the weak concepts have been eliminated, while the dominant/desirable strains have been combined into a mutant/hybrid made of all the best elements of the many possible plans." *New York, NY*

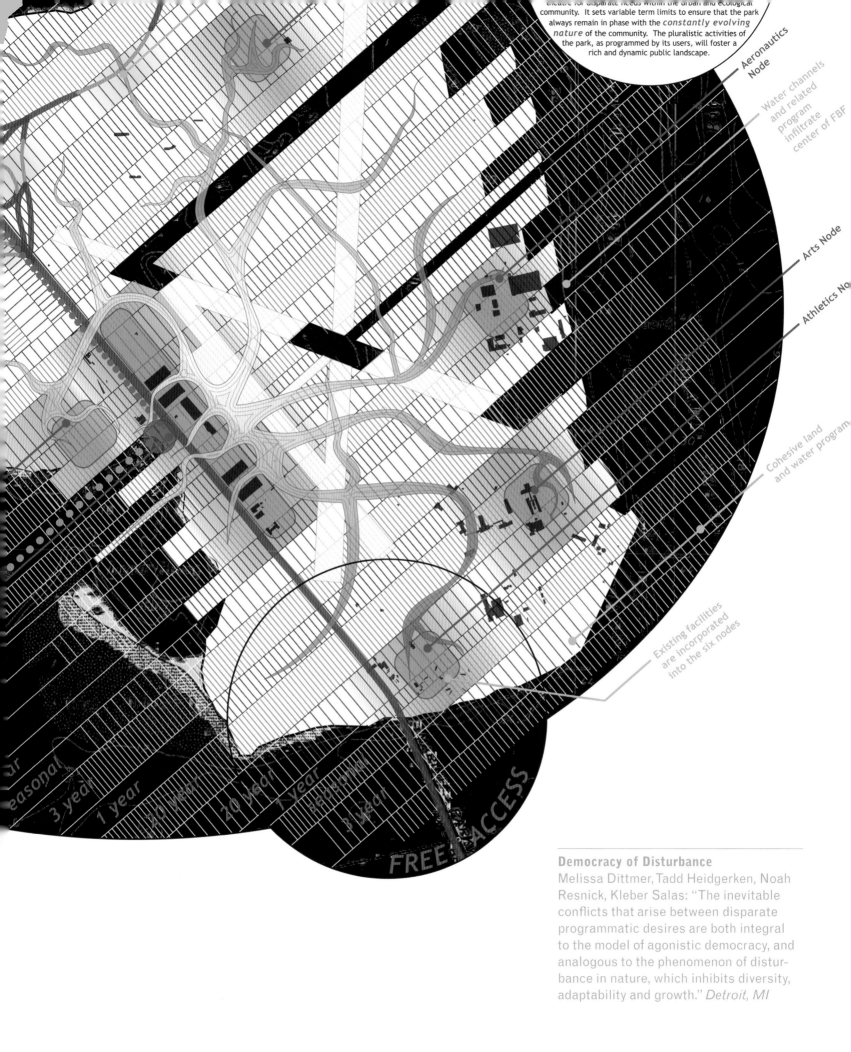

theatre for disparate needs within the urban and ecological community. It sets variable term limits to ensure that the park always remain in phase with the *constantly evolving nature* of the community. The pluralistic activities of the park, as programmed by its users, will foster a rich and dynamic public landscape.

Aeronautics Node

Water channels and related program infiltrate center of FBF

Arts Node

Athletics No

Cohesive land and water program

Existing facilities are incorporated into the six nodes

FREE ACCESS

Democracy of Disturbance
Melissa Dittmer, Tadd Heidgerken, Noah Resnick, Kleber Salas: "The inevitable conflicts that arise between disparate programmatic desires are both integral to the model of agonistic democracy, and analogous to the phenomenon of disturbance in nature, which inhibits diversity, adaptability and growth." *Detroit, MI*

saving
Rebuilding the wetla

3 million yd³ of clean fill
are dredged from NY Harbo
each year by the Port Autho

This fill should be
deposited at Jamaica Bay
instead of far out to sea
saving a great deal of mo

front door

incorporated easily into the wide (54' typ.) streets of the
ed. These 6-foot strips would absorb stormwater that
e bay.

converted to green roofs,
duced.

ark. Tax credits would
nal construction methods.

ual

eer for the NPS in the park
he city
aintain green strips
er replacing traditional
th green roofs and paved
rs with permeable

vantage of the Bay's
ecreational opportunities

shed toward the bay

If half the streets were converted,
this would produce 1,300 acres of
new open space in the watershed.
That is an area 1.5 times the size of
Central Park.

NYC
-Pay for proposed green strips out
of existing CSO mitigation budget
-Utilize remaining money for
improvements throughout
watershed
-Find new sites for existing
FBF tenants
-Co-administer education program
for watershed school children

Animal Community
-Pollinate the plant community
(birds and insects)
-Clean the water (oysters)
-Contribute to the food chain
-Provide beauty and enjoyment
for the human community

Community
-Volunteer for NPS in the park
and in the city
-Assist in the care and maintenance of green streets
-Actively participate in the creating the future of the watershed

spending
A Watershed, Not a Watertank

Port Authority
Work to make Jamaica Bay
primary regional site for
depositing clean fill

Plant Community
-Improve water quality in the bay
-Improve air quality in the city
-Provide beauty and enjoyment
for the human community
-Provide food and habitat for the
animal community

**CSO Waterta
(600' x 600'
Holding Capacity -
Estimated Cost - $

Networking Nature
Abby Feldman, Daniela Jimenez, Frank Ruchala Jr., Elizabeth Stoel: "Instead of only
being a passive observer of their environment, visitors will be offered the opportunity
to actively engage in its construction and understanding." *Brooklyn, NY*

027

Gateway for Change -- the Green~~~ of Barren Field

Floyd Bennett Field will combine existing & new recreational opportunities with a new center for the research, development & deployment of green technologies.

The United States is the world's largest single emitter of carbon dioxide, accounting for 23 percent of energy-related carbon emissions worldwide. (U.S. Department of Energy)

Producing Energy

Wind Turbines: Wind turbines could supply about 20% of the nation's electricity. Wind energy resources for generating electricity can be found in nearly every state. (Pacific Northwest Laboratory)

Biofuels: Relative to oil and natural gas systems, switchgrass pellets have the potential to reduce fuel heating costs and greenhouse gas emissions in eastern North America by approximately 30% and 90%, respectively. (Northeast Regional Biomass Program) The plants grown for biofuels also store carbon in soil, which acts to mitigate the effects of industrial greenhouse gas emissions. (USDA)

Water Turbines: In water moving between 4 and 5.5 miles per hour, a water turbine could generate as much energy as a wind turbine with a diameter four times larger. (Environmental and Energy Study Institute)

Solar Panels: When compared with electricity produced by fossil fuels, each kilowatt of solar-produced electricity offsets up to 830 pounds of nitrogen dioxide, 1,500 pounds of sulfur dioxide and 217,000 pounds of carbon dioxide each year (San Francisco Chronicle)

Reducing Energy

Hybrid buses: Hybrid buses reduce emissions up to 90% compared to conventional diesel buses currently on the road today. Hybrids also operate on ultra-low sulfur diesel fuel, which produce cleaner emissions than conventional diesel buses. (Capitol Area Transportation Authority)

Building Reuse: Reusing building materials can help avoid 10 negative environmental impacts: global warming acidification, eutrophication, fossil fuel depletion, water intake, criteria air pollutants, ecological toxicity, human health, ozone depletion and smog. (Wastematch.org)

Tree Planting: A single mature tree can absorb CO2 at a rate of 48 lbs/year and release enough oxygen back into the atmosphere to support two human beings. An acre of trees absorbs enough CO2 over one year to equal the amount produced by driving a car 26,000 miles (Brooklyn Times, USDA Forest Service General Technical Report)

Solar Powered Fixtures: All lighting throughout the park will be replaced with solar powered fixtures, greatly reducing operating costs and the carbon footprint for the park.

Research Campus: Many of the existing buildings can be reused as part of a research campus for green technologies. Within the campus there is space for additional buildings as needed as well as housing for visiting researchers.

Floyd Bennett Field Visitor Center

FLOYD BENNETT FIELD AQUATIC CENTER

TREES

REUSED STRUCTURES

CIRCULATION

Gateway for Change

VertNY: Martha Desbiens, Nicholas Desbiens, Tricia Rubenstein, Kristi Stromberg Wright: "At Floyd Bennett Field visitors will have the opportunity to observe firsthand about current Green Technologies including green roofs, wind turbines, photovoltaics, tidal turbines, and biofuels." *Brooklyn, NY*

So Near, Yet So Far

The most important urban parks are accessible—fifteen minutes from your house or your home. And if it's more than that, then getting there needs to be part of the recreation experience.
—Robert McIntosh, Associate Regional Director (retired), Planning, Resources Stewardship, and Science, U.S. National Park Service

Gateway National Recreation Area is one of few national parks situated in such close proximity to vast municipal and regional transportation networks. Indeed, Jamaica Bay is home to one of the busiest airports in North America, putting Gateway at the center of a sprawling system of subway, highway, bus, and regional rail routes that serve this global transportation node. The millions of passengers who fly in and out of John F. Kennedy International Airport every year are granted some of the most spectacular views of Gateway's marsh habitats and historical sites. And yet for those on the ground, getting there is not at all straightforward, and navigating the park's massive scale presents a significant challenge.

Gateway owes its enormous promise as a public resource to the fact that parts of the recreation area are merely a subway ride from Times Square. In the words of one Brooklyn resident, "Gateway is New York City's Serengeti. It is the only place in the world where 10 million people might someday access a 'WOW!' moment in nature via public transit."[1] But New York City's mass-transit systems are not oriented to effectively service Gateway as a major destination. None of the subway lines, for example, take visitors all of the way to a park entrance. Subway access requires a walk, bike ride, or municipal bus transfer from the nearest station, and the pedestrian route is often lengthy or poorly marked. The Jamaica Bay Wildlife Refuge, arguably the most accessible site within Gateway, requires a fifteen-minute walk through a residential neighborhood from the A train subway stop in Broad Channel—a manageable trek for many visitors, but daunting for school groups, the elderly, or those unfamiliar with the area.

Aside from subways, other modes of public transit fall far short of their potential to connect Gateway and its users. Paramount among these is ferry service, a natural way to reach this shoreside park. A regional transportation plan was proposed at the time of Gateway's founding—including a major expansion of regional ferry service both to the park and between the park's three distinct units—but was never realized due to political and financial hurdles. And although several proposals to develop ferry service in the region have been under consideration in the decades since the park was established, few focus on Gateway itself. In recent years, private ferry operators have provided seasonal commuter-ferry service from Manhattan to Sandy Hook and Riis Landing; however, such service offers no connection between Jamaica Bay, Staten Island, and Sandy Hook, and the rest of Gateway remains relatively inaccessible. "We need and must provide a better waterway system," notes Marian Heiskell, chair of the National Parks of New York Harbor Conservancy. "Not only would water transportation make the park more accessible, but it could also be an enjoyable part of the 'getting away from the city' experience of visiting Gateway."

For now, private transportation remains the easiest means of visiting Gateway. New York City's expanding network of bicycle lanes has made cycling to and through the park an increasingly viable option. Several stretches of the New York City Greenway, a right-of-way designated specifically for cyclists, pedestrians, and other nonmotorized forms of transportation, traverse Gateway's Jamaica Bay and Staten Island units, though do not yet connect to one another, to the larger Greenway network in Brooklyn and Queens, or to nearby subway stations and communities.

A private car is still the most efficient way to navigate the park, and is in fact the only way to visit all three units of Gateway in one day. Sandy Hook remains somewhat remote because only one road provides access on and off the peninsula, but in Staten Island local arterial roads connect Fort Wadsworth, Miller Field, and Great Kills Park, and in Jamaica Bay the six-lane Belt Parkway circumscribes the unit's northern boundary while other four- and six-lane roads connect to Jacob Riis Park, Fort Tilden, and Breezy Point on the Rockaway Peninsula.

The effect of the Belt Parkway on the local landscape typifies the tensions inherent in planning transportation infrastructure for an urban national park. Since its construction in the late 1930s, the Belt Parkway has ironically protected Jamaica Bay's wetlands and habitats by preventing dense development along the bay's perimeter. By the same measure, however, this high-speed roadway has made it difficult for communities on the other side of the parkway to access Gateway at all. The Jamaica Bay Watershed Protection Plan Interim Report, published in 2006 by a consortium led by the New York City Department of Environmental Protection, recommended better public access to Jamaica Bay as part of significant policy and infrastructural changes necessary to improve quality of life.

Given Gateway's ecological fragility and the demands of its urban population, the NPS mandate to both preserve its parklands and make them publicly accessible becomes particularly challenging. Likewise, the ability of the public to conceptually connect

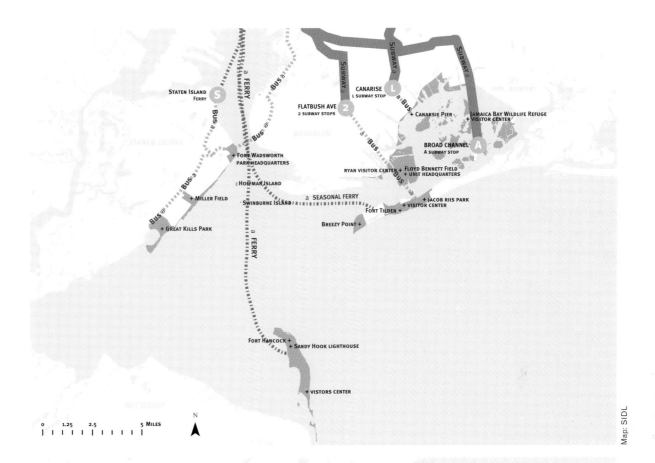

Public transportation in the region

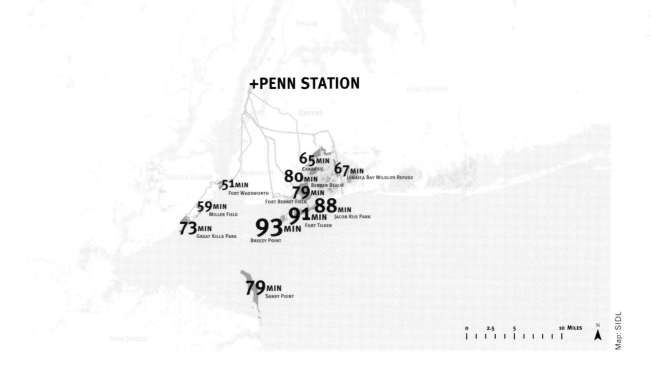

Travel time via public transit from Penn Station to Gateway sites

the diverse features of a park into a unified experience is arguably as important as a physical connection to the park itself. Unlike other iconic parks (Central Park or Prospect Park, for example) Gateway is geographically dispersed and decentralized; partly due to this fragmentation, millions of New York City residents simply do not know this national park exists in their backyard. Those that do often do not grasp its unique resources; few visitors to the popular boardwalk at Riis Beach realize that one of North America's premier bird sanctuaries, or the region's most endangered wetland marsh, is minutes away.

This disjointed quality of the park is not only a result of geographical fragmentation, but also of an inadequate wayfinding system that fails to give Gateway a coherent identity as a place. Though traditional National Park Service signage designates major landmarks within the park, no comprehensive system integrates the three units or guides visitors from one resource to the next. Such inconsistencies contribute to the broader challenge Gateway's stakeholders face as they work to connect the urban national park to its public and vice versa. Gateway thus remains unfulfilled in its potential to strengthen physical and recreational connections among its three distinct units, and to introduce an urban population, largely dependent on public transit, to the cultural, recreational, and ecological resources it has to offer.

The competition entry [Un]natural Selection proposed by W Architecture and Landscape Architecture offers a series of strategies that "reorient the experience of the visitor from the fragment to the whole." By linking disparate parts of the park to one another and unifying visitor experience through expanded public transportation, additional wayfinding elements, and new recreational opportunities, Gateway becomes legible as a figure and as a destination. The selected competition entries that follow similarly addressed Gateway's need for a well conceived and integrated transportation plan that would support and extend a much needed park-wide identity.

ENDNOTES
Epigraph Robert McIntosh, opening remarks, Nature Now: The Urban Park as Cultural Catalyst conference, Columbia University GSAPP, October 14, 2006.
1 Anonymous comment submitted online at www.npca.org, solicited by National Parks Conservation Association as part of public outreach efforts following the design competition (2007–8).

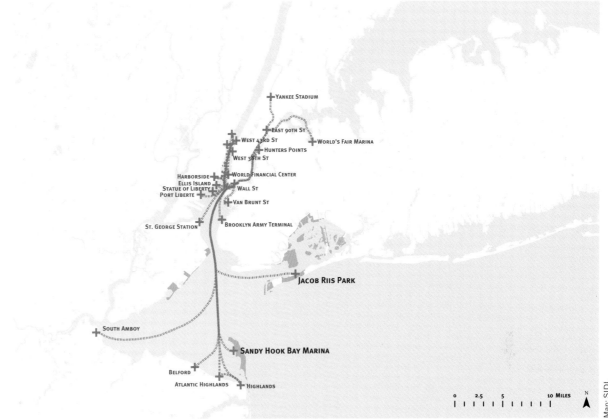

Map: SIDL

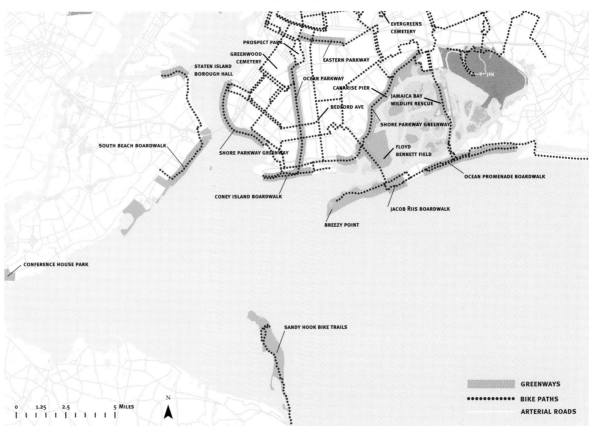

Map: SIDL

[Un]natural Selection
W Architecture and Landscape Architecture

National parks have historically been about preserving and protecting places of scenic beauty—removed from and, ideally, untouched by humanity. Gateway National Recreation Area is different. It is all about human contact with the environment and the resulting changes that take place over the centuries.

Our design celebrates the process of (un)natural selection. In the twenty-first century we are beginning to understand that human health and ecology exist within, and not separate from, the surrounding environment. Gateway, situated between the nation's greatest concentration of humanity and the ocean, presents a special opportunity to explore the connections and tensions inherent in this amalgam of ocean, land, air, and settlement. Our design strategy involves three overlapping steps that will celebrate the connection between humans and the rest of the natural world, while modeling innovative stewardship that protects flora and fauna, mitigates human waste, and honors cultural relics. We want to reorient the experience of the visitor from the fragment to the whole, restore elements we have lost or disturbed to create a new balance, and preserve those remaining elements that have cultural value.

At Gateway, the new identity of the park begins by uniting the disconnected sites with their surrounding communities including the water and the air above through a waterfront greenway and critical areas zone. Creating the greenway will require forming relationships between surrounding jurisdictions and communities, linking the parts to the whole both physically and programmatically. The creation of critical area zones will provide for the protection and conservation of endangered plant and animal species at this critical interface within the park. Best management practices for stormwater quality and quantity will be mandated for the site as well as other innovative strategies that will improve the relationship between people and the bay. Public transportation linkages will be improved, unifying the park and

connecting it to the city. This will be achieved through additional ferry and water taxi services, uniting the loop around the bay in addition to linking the park to other harbor attractions.

One of these sites, Floyd Bennett Field, symbolizes the synthesis of the built and natural environments and the layering of water, land, and air. Here we propose regenerating its original wetlands, while preserving the runways of the historic airport. Boats, ferries, bike paths, and light rail unify the park and provide various modes for visitor exploration as well as new connections to New York City. Visitors leave their cars behind at the Airfield Orientation Center, to explore and discover the overlapping web of man-made and wetland ecology. The runways become corridors for exploring the wetlands as well as the history of aviation. The additional wetland areas will help increase the available wildlife habitat, filter wastewater, and will provide for varied recreational opportunities.

The new Gateway combines relics of the past with contemporary problems unique to its urban context. Forts strategically located at the mouth of the harbor, New York's first airfield, and historic waste processing in Dead Horse Bay exist alongside disparate ecological and cultural issues. Sewage disposal, the ecological health of the tidal marsh and estuary in our living harbor, and recreational access for uses like bird watching and surfing all highlight our pivotal role in this complex network of contemporary events, programs, and ecological systems.

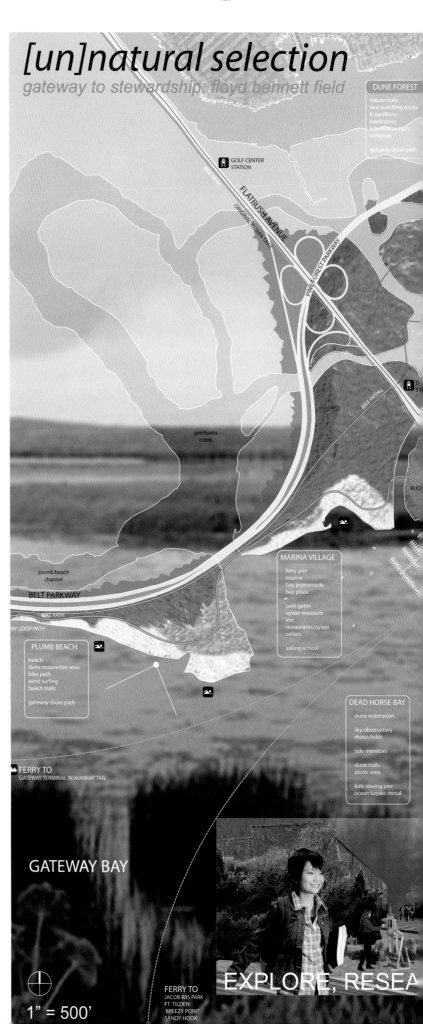

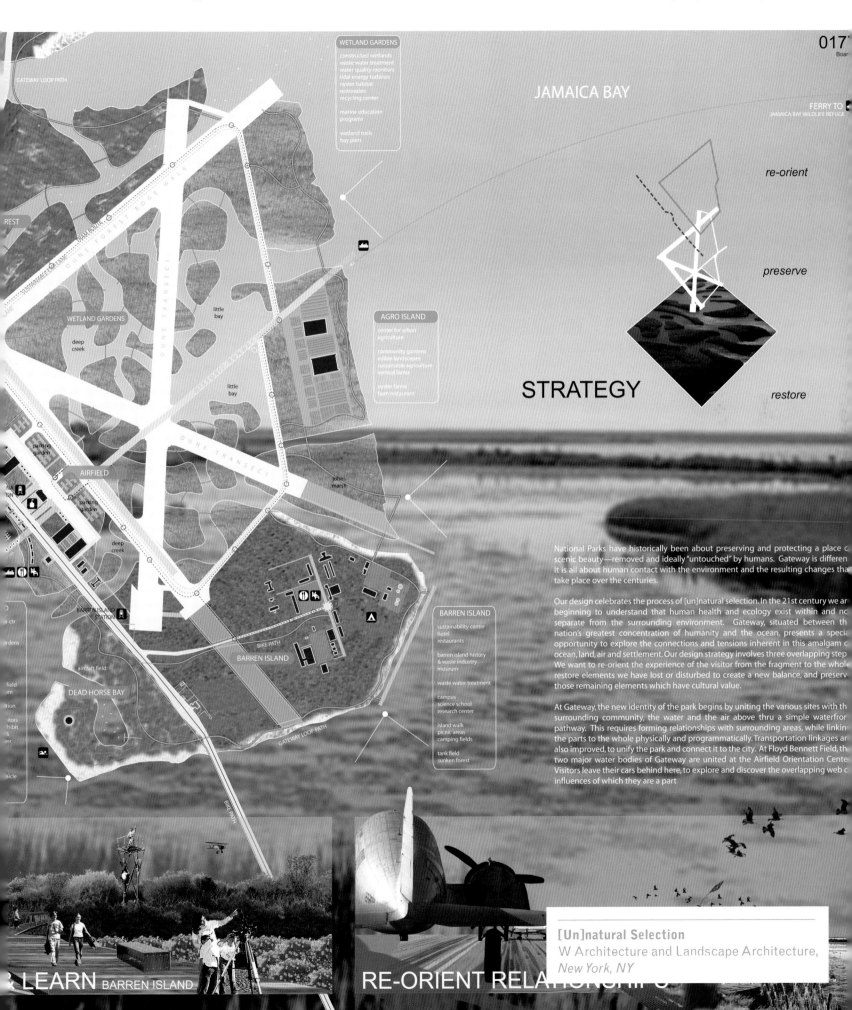

017
Boar

JAMAICA BAY

FERRY TO
JAMAICA BAY WILDLIFE REFUGE

GATEWAY LOOP PATH

REST

WETLAND GARDENS

constructed wetlands
waste water treatment
water quality monitors
tidal energy turbines
oyster habitat
restoration
recycling center

marine education
programs

wetland trails
bay piers

little
bay

WETLAND GARDENS

deep
creek

little
bay

AGRO ISLAND

center for urban
agriculture

community gardens
edible landscapes
sustainable agriculture
vertical farms

oyster farms
farm restaurant

re-orient

preserve

STRATEGY

restore

parking
garden

AIRFIELD

parking
garden

johns
marsh

deep
creek

BARREN ISLAND
STATION

BIKE PATH

BARREN ISLAND

aircraft field

DEAD HORSE BAY

field

BARREN ISLAND

sustainability center
hotel
restaurants

barren island history
& waste industry
museum

waste water treatment

campus
science school
research center

island walk
picnic areas
camping fields

tank field
sunken forest

GATEWAY LOOP PATH

BIKE PATH

National Parks have historically been about preserving and protecting a place c
scenic beauty—removed and ideally "untouched" by humans. Gateway is differen
It is all about human contact with the environment and the resulting changes tha
take place over the centuries.

Our design celebrates the process of [un]natural selection. In the 21st century we ar
beginning to understand that human health and ecology exist within and no
separate from the surrounding environment. Gateway, situated between th
nation's greatest concentration of humanity and the ocean, presents a specia
opportunity to explore the connections and tensions inherent in this amalgam c
ocean, land, air and settlement. Our design strategy involves three overlapping step
We want to re-orient the experience of the visitor from the fragment to the whole
restore elements we have lost or disturbed to create a new balance, and preserv
those remaining elements which have cultural value.

At Gateway, the new identity of the park begins by uniting the various sites with th
surrounding community, the water and the air above thru a simple waterfror
pathway. This requires forming relationships with surrounding areas, while linkin
the parts to the whole physically and programmatically. Transportation linkages ar
also improved, to unify the park and connect it to the city. At Floyd Bennett Field, th
two major water bodies of Gateway are united at the Airfield Orientation Cente
Visitors leave their cars behind here, to explore and discover the overlapping web c
influences of which they are a part

& LEARN BARREN ISLAND

RE-ORIENT RELATIONSHIPS

[Un]natural Selection
W Architecture and Landscape Architecture,
New York, NY

[un]natural selection
gateway to stewardship

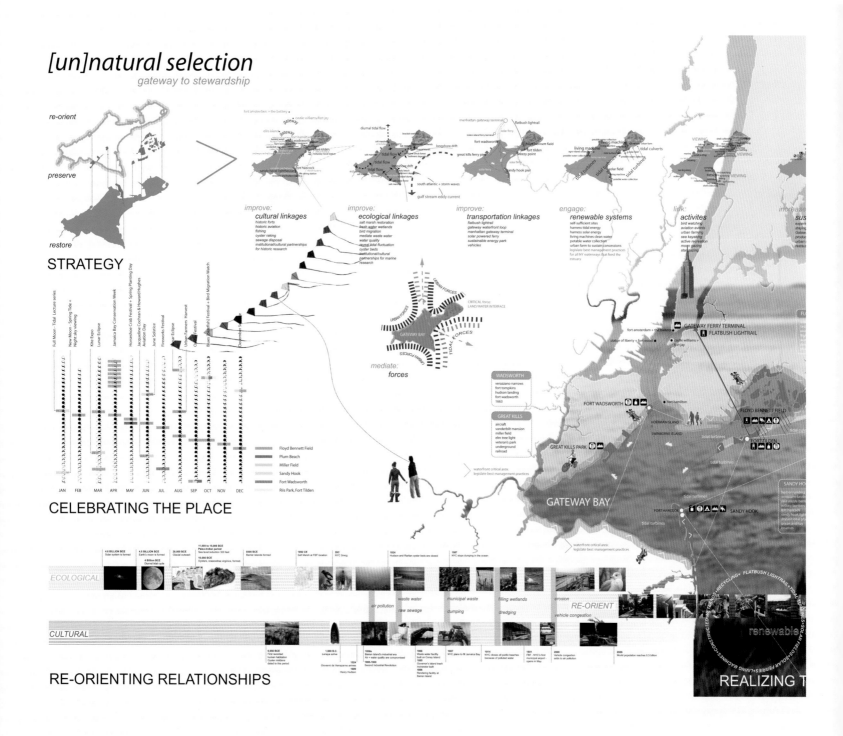

re-orient

preserve

restore

STRATEGY

improve: **cultural linkages**
historic forts
historic aviation
fishing
oyster raking
sewage disposal
institutional/cultural partnerships
for historic research

improve: **ecological linkages**
salt marsh restoration
fresh water wetlands
bird migration
mediate waste water
water quality
river tidal fluctuation
oyster beds
institutional/cultural
partnerships for marine
research

improve: **transportation linkages**
flatbush lightrail
gateway waterfront loop
manhattan gateway terminal
solar powered ferry
sustainable energy park
vehicles

engage: **renewable systems**
self-sufficient sites
harness tidal energy
harness solar energy
living machines clean water
potable water collection
urban farm to sustain concessions
legislate best management practices
for all NY waterways that feed the
estuary

link: **activites**
bird watching
aviation events
urban farming
sea kayaking
active recreation
moon gazing
stargazing

CELEBRATING THE PLACE

mediate:
forces

RE-ORIENTING RELATIONSHIPS

ECOLOGICAL

CULTURAL

RE-ORIENT

REALIZING T

Details of **[Un]natural Selection**
W Architecture and Landscape Architecture, *New York, NY*

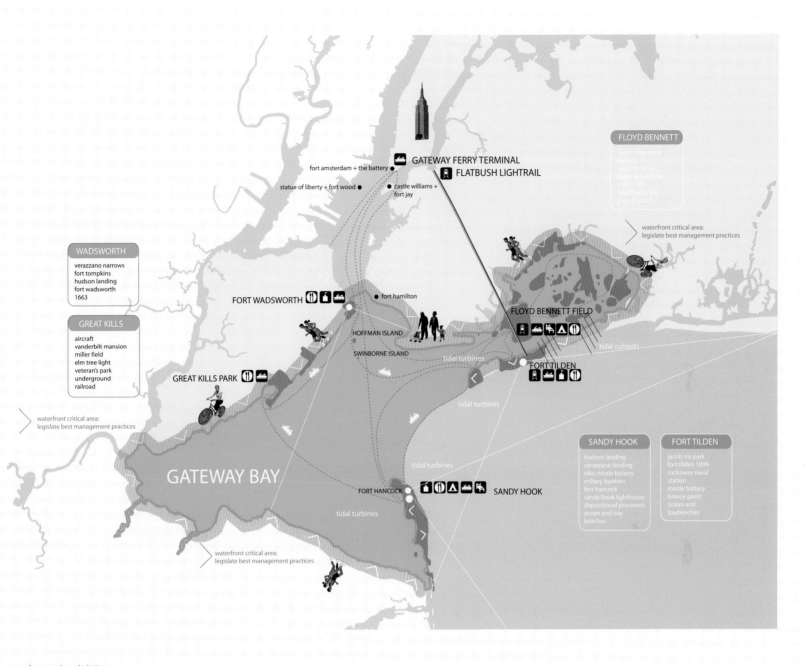

GATEWAY FERRY TERMINAL
FLATBUSH LIGHTRAIL

fort amsterdam + the battery

FLOYD BENNETT

statue of liberty + fort wood   castle williams +
                                                 fort jay

WADSWORTH
verazzano narrows
fort tompkins
hudson landing
fort wadsworth
1663

                                                                    waterfront critical area:
                                                                    legislate best management practices

FORT WADSWORTH   fort hamilton

GREAT KILLS
aircraft   HOFFMAN ISLAND   FLOYD BENNETT FIELD
vanderbilt mansion
miller field   SWINBORNE ISLAND
elm tree light   tidal culverts
veteran's park   tidal turbines
underground
railroad   FORT TILDEN

GREAT KILLS PARK   tidal turbines

waterfront critical area:
legislate best management practices

                                                                    SANDY HOOK   FORT TILDEN
GATEWAY BAY   tidal turbines   hudson landing   jacob riis park
                                                                     verazzano landing   fort tilden 1899
                                                                     nike missile battery rockaway naval
                                                                     military bunkers   station
                                              FORT HANCOCK   fort hancock   missile battery
                                                          SANDY HOOK sandy hook lighthouse breezy point
                                                                     depositional processes ocean and
                                tidal turbines   ocean and bay   baybeaches
                                                                     beaches

                      waterfront critical area:
                      legislate best management practices

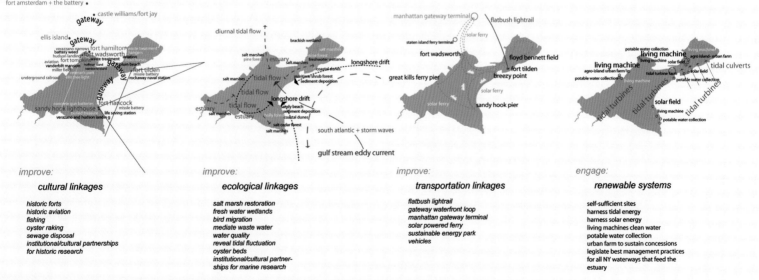

improve:

cultural linkages

historic forts
historic aviation
fishing
oyster raking
sewage disposal
institutional/cultural partnerships
for historic research

improve:

ecological linkages

salt marsh restoration
fresh water wetlands
bird migration
mediate waste water
water quality
reveal tidal fluctuation
oyster beds
institutional/cultural partnerships for marine research

improve:

transportation linkages

flatbush lightrail
gateway waterfront loop
manhattan gateway terminal
solar powered ferry
sustainable energy park
vehicles

engage:

renewable systems

self-sufficient sites
harness tidal energy
harness solar energy
living machines clean water
potable water collection
urban farm to sustain concessions
legislate best management practices
for all NY waterways that feed the
estuary

These entries emphasize the role of transit, wayfinding, and public access in revitalizing Gateway.

a grid to green

A Grid to Green   > page 125

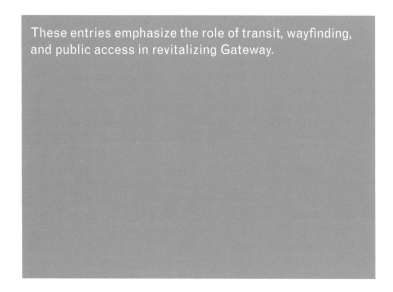

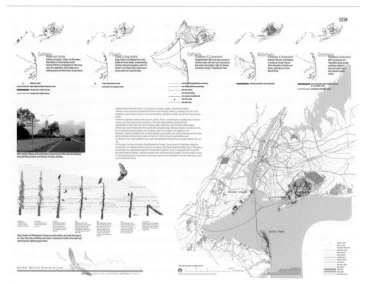

Gateway Waterway Greenway Pathway Flyway   > page 126

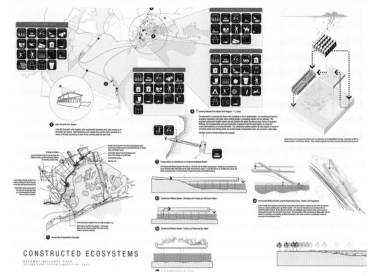

CONSTRUCTED ECOSYSTEMS

Constructed Ecosystems   > page 127

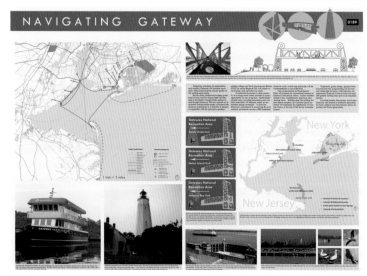

NAVIGATING GATEWAY

Navigating Gateway   > page 128

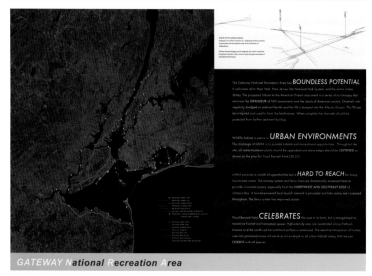

GATEWAY National Recreation Area

Untitled   > page 129

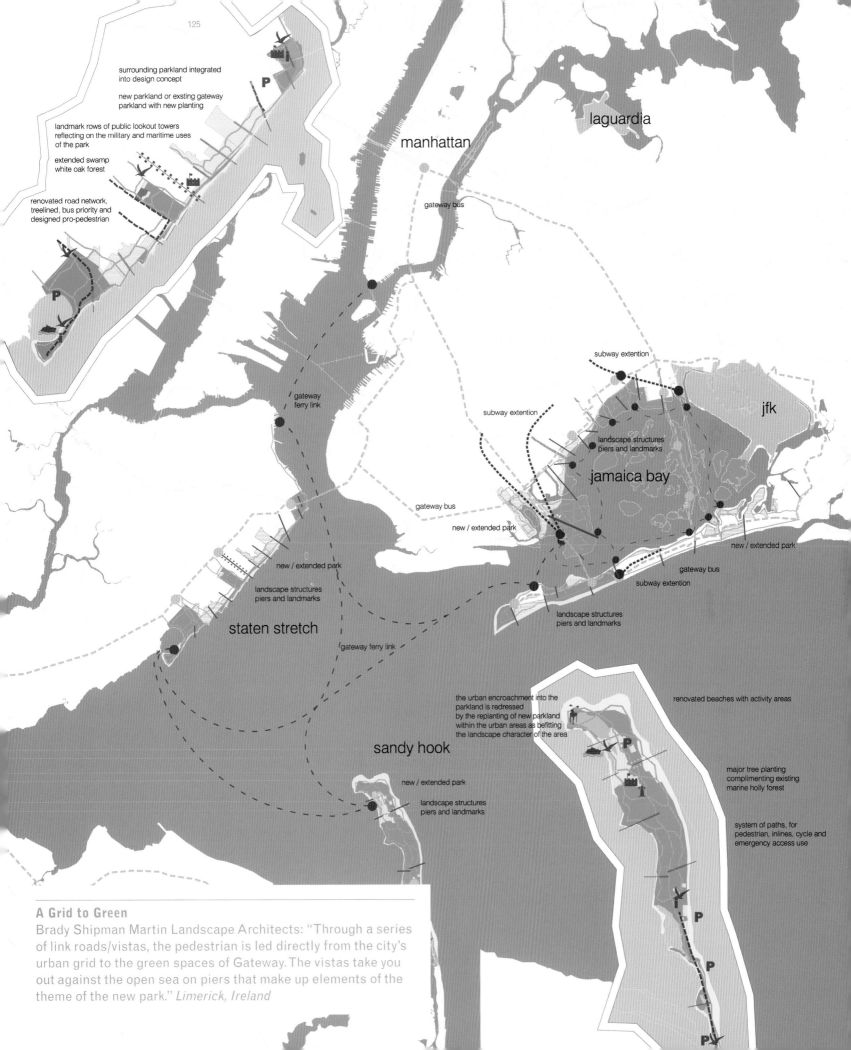

125

manhattan

laguardia

gateway bus

subway extention

subway extention

jfk

gateway
ferry link

landscape structures
piers and landmarks

jamaica bay

gateway bus

new / extended park

new / extended park

subway extention

gateway bus

new / extended park

landscape structures
piers and landmarks

landscape structures
piers and landmarks

staten stretch

gateway ferry link

the urban encroachment into the
parkland is redressed
by the replanting of new parkland
within the urban areas as befitting
the landscape character of the area

renovated beaches with activity areas

sandy hook

new / extended park

landscape structures
piers and landmarks

major tree planting
complimenting existing
marine holly forest

system of paths, for
pedestrian, inlines, cycle and
emergency access use

surrounding parkland integrated
into design concept

new parkland or exsting gateway
parkland with new planting

landmark rows of public lookout towers
reflecting on the military and maritime uses
of the park

extended swamp
white oak forest

renovated road network,
treelined, bus priority and
designed pro-pedestrian

A Grid to Green

Brady Shipman Martin Landscape Architects: "Through a series
of link roads/vistas, the pedestrian is led directly from the city's
urban grid to the green spaces of Gateway. The vistas take you
out against the open sea on piers that make up elements of the
theme of the new park." *Limerick, Ireland*

Staten Island

Jamaica Bay

Sandy Hook

TATION

5   10 MILES
1 INCH EQUALS 2 MILES

CHITECTURE PLANNING AND PRESERVATION

ORIGINAL DATA SOURCE:
WETLAND - NATIONAL WETLANDS INVENTORY, 2006
GATEWAY BOUNDARY - NATIONAL PARK SERVICE, 2006
AIRPORT - NEW YORK CITY TAX LOT - PLUTO DATA, 2004
SUBWAY, BUS, BIKE ROUTE - NEW YORK CITY DEPARTMENT OF TRANSPORTATION
MAJOR ROADS AND RAILROAD - ENVIRONMANTAL SYSTEMS RESEARCH INSTITUTES (ESRI), 2006

+   FERRY STOP
- - - FERRY LINE
·   SUBWAY STA
——   SUBWAY LIN
——   BUS ROUTE
····· BIKE ROUTE
——   INTERSTATE
——   STATE ROUT
——   US ROUTE
——   SHORE PKW
+-+-+ RAILROAD
       AIRPORT
       WETLAND
       GATEWAY NR

Gateway Waterway Greenway Pathway Flyway
K+L: Melanie Kramer, Svetlana Lavrentieva: "A network of pathways connects these areas for cyclists, drivers, and pedestrians,
including those on public transport, and the increased ferry connections. The nodes where pathways intersect become opportunities for bike rental, drop off and meeting places, wayfinding,
and information dissemination." *Toronto, ON, Canada*

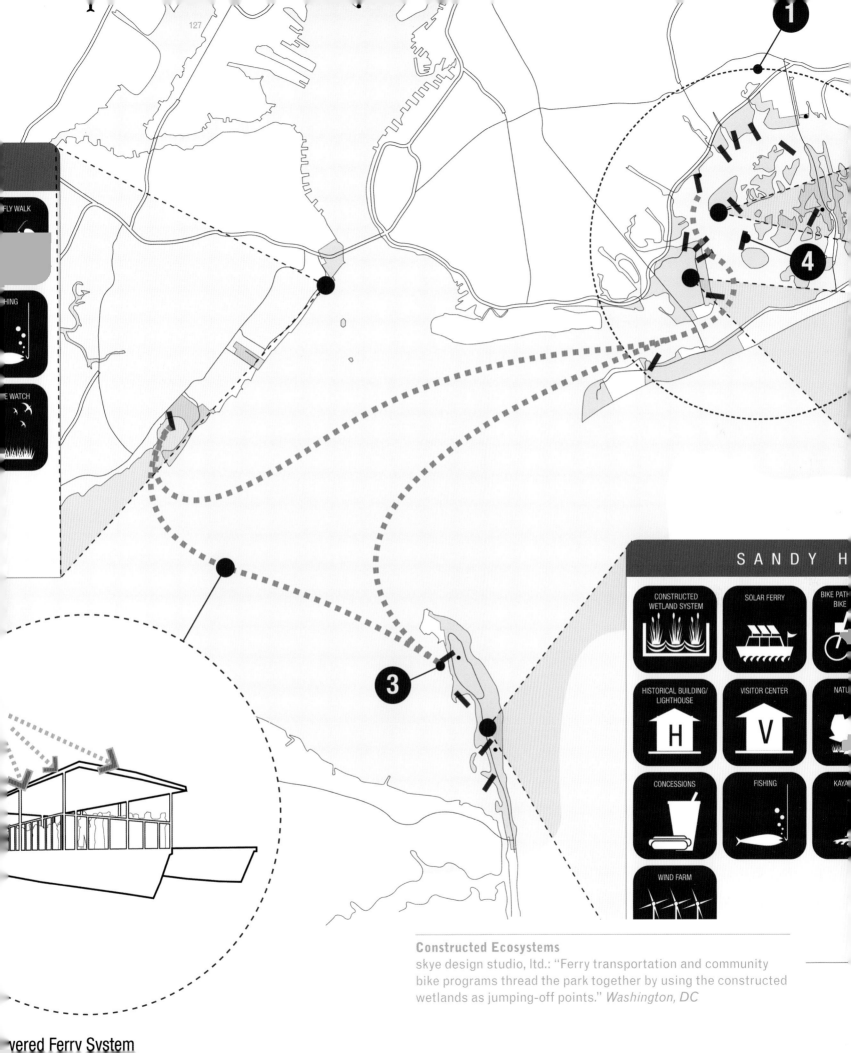

FLY WALK

HING

E WATCH

1

4

3

SANDY H

CONSTRUCTED
WETLAND SYSTEM

SOLAR FERRY

BIKE PATH
BIKE

HISTORICAL BUILDING/
LIGHTHOUSE

H

VISITOR CENTER

V

NATU

CONCESSIONS

FISHING

KAYA

WIND FARM

Constructed Ecosystems
skye design studio, ltd.: "Ferry transportation and community
bike programs thread the park together by using the constructed
wetlands as jumping-off points." *Washington, DC*

vered Ferry System

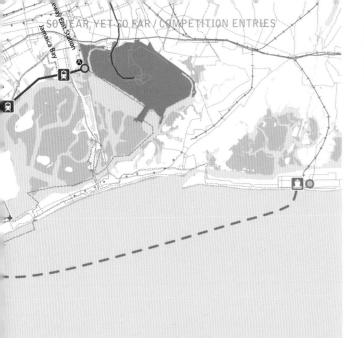

A light rail, starting at a new MTA subway stop on the A-line just south of Howard Beach and ending at a new stop on the B- and D-lines south of S posed along the eastern shore of Staten Island. Pedestrian overpasses modeled after the Marine Parkway Bridge will provide access for local resi

Guided by principles of sustainability and mobility, Gateway will stimulate recreation while preserving the natural quality of the existing open space.

Bicycle paths, pedestrian bridges, green boat service, and low-impact light rail lines add to the limited transportation options to and through Gateway. This new network of alternative transportation modes will extend the Gateway experience to a diversity of people. In conjunction with the community gardens,

ecology village and Parks Improvement District (P.I.D.) an annual Regional Fair will exhibit rural ecology and agriculture to locals.

An extensive ecosystem in close proximity to a large urban center provides a unique opportunity for new programs. HarborQuest aquatic tours, recycling/composting and wetland restoration will educate visitors on sustainable design techniques. To illustrate Gateway's commitment to preserving the environment, permeable runways, LEED compliant

EXISTING TRANSPORTATION

+ FERRY STOP
- - - FERRY LINE
· SUBWAY STATION
SUBWAY LINE
BUS ROUTE
BIKE ROUTE
INTERSTATE
STATE ROUTE
US ROUTE
SHORE PKWY
RAILROAD
AIRPORT
WETLAND
GATEWAY NRA

PROPOSED TRANSPORTATION

🚈 LIGHT RAIL STATION
⚓ GREENBOAT DOCK
━━ LIGHT RAIL LINE
━━ GREENBOAT SERVICE
- - - GREENBOAT LIMITED SERVICE
━━ BIKE PATH
◯ CONNECTION TO EXISTING SUBWAY
◯ CONNECTION TO EXISTING GREENWAY
◯ CONNECTION TO EXISTING RAIL LINE

les

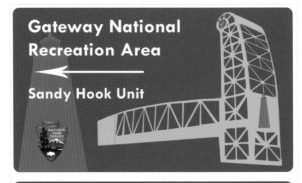

Gateway National Recreation Area

← Sandy Hook Unit

Gateway National Recreation Area

← Staten Island Unit

staten

m

Gateway National Recreation Area

← Jamaica Bay Unit

New J

Gateway currently lacks adequate signage and an effective marketing scheme. Park activities should be advertised through similar organizations throughout NYC, including museums, recreational organizations, and groups that advocate waterfront access, environmental and historic preservation, and education. Additional advertising can be shown in airports, on the subway, and train stations.

To help develop a cohesive network among the 3 units The visitor centers will also serve as the starting points

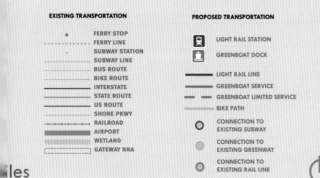

PROPOSED FERRY STOP
PROPOSED FERRY LINE
PROPOSED SUBWAY STOP
PROPOSED SUBWAY LINE
PROPOSED BIKE ROUTE
GATEWAY NRA BOUNDARY EXTENSION
PROPOSED HUMAN-POWERED BOAT LAUNCH
FLEXIBLE TRAIL SYSTEM

EXISTING FERRY STOP
EXISTING FERRY LINE
EXISTING SUBWAY STOP
EXISTING SUBWAY
EXISTING BUS LINE
EXISTING BIKE ROUTE
EXISTING MAJOR ROAD
EXISTING GATEWAY NRA BOUNDARY

←

Navigating Gateway

PrattGrads: Christina Ficicchia, Christine Fitzgerald, Eleni Glekas, Justin Kray, Vlada Smorgunov: "Gateway currently lacks adequate signage and an effective marketing scheme…the new signage will clearly identify each significant destination of Gateway." *Astoria, NY*

↑

Untitled

Joshua Anderson, Sohith Perera, Joann Green: "The subway system and ferry lines are dramatically increased here to provide increased access, especially from the northwest and southeast edge of Jamaica Bay. A human-powered boat launch network is provided and bike routes are increased throughout. The ferry system has improved access." *Indianapolis, IN*

Shifting Ground

We need to begin to think about nature as having many possible states, not one perfect state but many possible states. Some are more desirable than others. And like it or not, as human beings we are stuck in the position of having to make decisions because of our technological power. But if something has no first state, then what does it mean to restore?
— Daniel Botkin, professor emeritus, University of California, Santa Barbara, Department of Ecology, Evolution, and Marine Biology

In contrast to the solid bedrock outcroppings of Manhattan, which support skyscraper foundations and miles of city grid, Gateway National Recreation Area occupies a constantly shifting terrain. Gateway's 57 miles of shoreline have long been subject to geological forces, tidal flows, and urban impacts that make the park a remarkably dynamic place. Only 39 percent of Gateway is currently on solid ground; the remaining 61 percent is a fluid expanse of aquatic wilderness, open water, and fluctuating states in between. This evolving landscape also represents the front line for the increasing encroachment of rising tides predicted in the coming century, as climate change brings higher sea levels around the world. Already marked by a dramatic loss of wetlands, Gateway's shores offer both a cautionary tale and an opportunity to rethink our relationship with the water's edge.

Gateway's geological profile (set at the apex of a perpendicular bend in the Atlantic coastline of the United States and at the mouth of New York's Hudson River and New Jersey's Raritan River) was crafted during the last glacial advance in the Pleistocene era, approximately 15,000 years ago. Glaciers carved out the major features of the region's current topography and deposited sand and silt as they retreated. Since then the park's landscape has evolved through a series of dynamic changes, brought about by slow but steady sea level rise, natural shifts in ocean currents, and barrier island geomorphology. Ongoing fluvial processes from the Hudson River, and myriad impacts due to human settlement in the region, have also shaped the park's terrain.

The park's location within a coastal estuary makes its shoreline a confluence of ceaseless natural forces. The water throughout the park is a mix of freshwater and seawater. The lighter freshwater from the Hudson and Raritan rivers flows on top of the Atlantic Ocean's salt-laden seawater, creating a stratified condition characteristic of estuarine environments. Both the outer harbor and Jamaica Bay have a semidiurnal tidal cycle—two high waters and two low waters each day—putting this landscape in constant flux. During low tide, extensive areas of beaches, mudflats, and salt marshes throughout the park are exposed, providing rich habitat for waterfowl and ample recreational and educational opportunities for visitors. During high tide these areas are submerged, and marshes serve as reliable breeding grounds for diverse estuarine organisms, including multiple species of fin and shellfish.

Gateway's landscape is also being shaped via natural erosion and sedimentation processes. Littoral currents and changing tides deposit sand throughout the harbor, in particular at the barrier islands of Sandy Hook and Breezy Point. A naturally high sediment load from the Hudson River watershed—made even higher in the past two centuries as upstream vegetation has been replaced by urban and agricultural development—deposits additional glacial till and other soils into Jamaica Bay, and in some cases smothers aquatic vegetation or prevents the natural tidal cleansing or "flushing" of contaminants from the bay.

In addition to natural processes, the last two centuries of human settlement and urban development have made an equally dramatic impact on the landscape surrounding Gateway. As New York City developed into an industrial and commercial port, it became common practice to dredge channels in the harbor for navigational purposes, construct impermeable bulkheads and seawalls at the bay's edge, and fill marshes with soil or sand. Off the coast of Staten Island, Swinburne and Hoffman islands were constructed entirely from fill in 1870 and 1873. Intended to be regional quarantine centers, their creation required the deepening and widening of navigation channels in the harbor to allow access to the islands.[1]

Jamaica Bay has also been significantly reshaped to meet the needs of the city around it. The earliest fill project in the bay occurred around 1810 with the expansion of Barren Island, which became a municipal-waste landfill from 1852 to 1916, and was later expanded even further to accommodate Floyd Bennett Field (1930–31). This filling alone reduced the width of the bay's primary inlet by 50 percent.[2] The sandy soil of Jamaica Bay was used as fill not only for the construction of Floyd Bennett Field but also for John F. Kennedy International Airport (1943–48), located on the bay's eastern perimeter. The deep channels and borrow pits that were dredged for these projects altered the natural exchange of sediment and water in the bay to such an extent that mitigation of the resulting imbalances is still a focus of operations today by the U.S. Army Corps of Engineers.[3]

1891

1898

1910

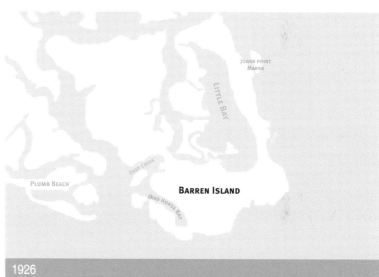

1926

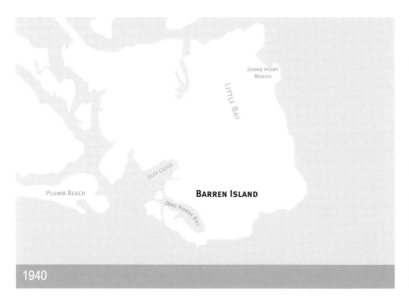

1940

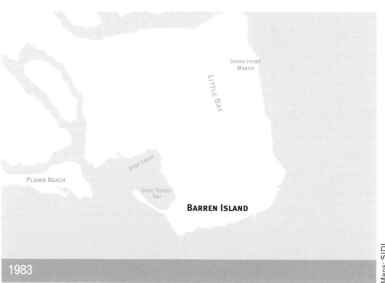

1983

Floyd Bennett Field, 1891–1983

In recent years, Jamaica Bay has experienced an accelerating loss of wetlands: from 1924 to 1974, the annual rate of loss was 10 acres; today the rate of loss is estimated to have jumped to a staggering 50 acres per year. No single reason has been isolated for this alarming rate of disappearance. Recent research indicates that a combination of water pollution, nutrient imbalance, sediment starvation from urbanization and dredging, biotic influences, wave action caused by watercraft, and sea level rise have all contributed to their decline.[4]

Gateway's vanishing marshlands are a matter of concern not just for the loss of natural habitat, but also for the region's ever more vulnerable human population. Throughout New York Harbor, these wetlands play a crucial role in protecting coastal areas from the projected impacts of climate change. The combined threats of sea level rise, more frequent storms, higher rates of beach erosion, and saltwater intrusion put areas that are 6 feet or less above sea level at risk of severe damage or destruction due to flooding. Without the wetlands and barrier islands that provide a natural line of defense during storms, most of Lower Manhattan's shoreline, the coastal and island areas around Jamaica Bay, much of downtown Hoboken and Jersey City, and the south-shore beaches in Staten Island and the Rockaways will become increasingly at risk to such dangers.[5]

As stewards of Gateway's unique combination of publicly owned land and water, the National Park Service and the Army Corps of Engineers are in a powerful position to provide leadership for restoration and conservation efforts addressing the park's important estuarine environment. According to Andrew Darrell, director of the Environmental Defense Fund's Living Cities Program, "There are lots of other places in New York City where you can go kayaking and do all sorts of recreational activities, but there is no other place in New York where you can really engage with the basic climate and ecological conditions of our time."[6] At a time of widespread concern about the fate of coastal cities, Gateway is uniquely poised to provide safe opportunities for public engagement with this dynamic edge condition, and to educate visitors about the complex and constantly evolving relationship between a city and its surrounding waters.

The competition entry Mapping the Ecotone by Ashley Scott Kelly and Rikako Wakabayashi directly addresses Gateway's condition as a ceaselessly changing landscape that is part land and part water. Through a single design gesture that can be repeated in locations throughout the park, the proposal suggests new ways that visitors might both experience and develop an awareness about the significance of climate change and its impacts on our national landscapes. The select competition entries that follow

similarly tackle the relationship between solid ground and open water, exploring ways that Gateway might successfully occupy its shifting terrain.

ENDNOTES

Epigraph Daniel Botkin, keynote presentation, Nature Now: The Urban Park as Cultural Catalyst conference, Columbia University GSAPP, October 14, 2006.

1 Jennifer Johnson, "Brought Up in the Bay," in *Beyond Manhattan: New York's Other Islands*, Columbia University Graduate School of Journalism, http://www.nyc24.org/2003/islands/zone7/broadhistory.html.

2 Mary Beth Betts, "Masterplanning: Municipal Support of Maritime Transport and Commerce 1870–1930s," in Kevin Bone, ed., *The New York Waterfront: Evolution and Building Culture of the Port and Harbor* (New York: Monacelli Press, 1997), 64.

3 See New York City Department of Environmental Protection, "Jamaica Bay Watershed Protection Plan: Interim Report," September 1, 2006, 4.

4 Gateway National Recreation Area and Jamaica Bay Watershed Protection Plan Advisory Committe, "An Update on the Disappearing Salt Marshes of Jamaica Bay, New York," August 2, 2007, 1–7.

5 Vivien Gornitz, "Climate Change and a Global City: An Assessment of the Metropolitan East Coast Region," Columbia University Center for Climate Systems Research, June 8, 2000, 7–9.

6 Andrew Darrell, statement during the Envisioning Gateway competition jury, May 12, 2007.

Shoreline change and
wetland type

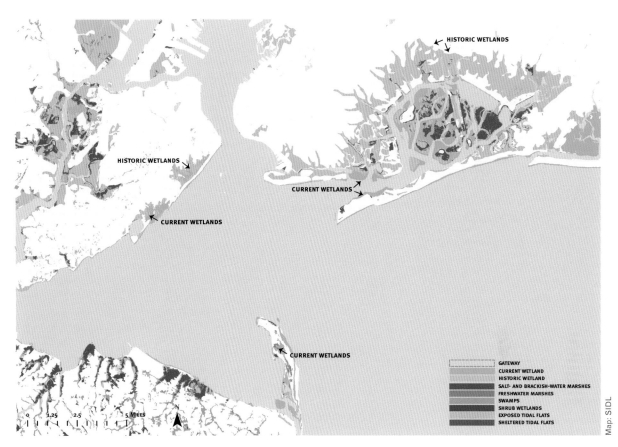

GATEWAY
CURRENT WETLAND
HISTORIC WETLAND
SALT- AND BRACKISH-WATER MARSHES
FRESHWATER MARSHES
SWAMPS
SHRUB WETLANDS
EXPOSED TIDAL FLATS
SHELTERED TIDAL FLATS

Map: SIDL

Jamaica Bay wetland types

GATEWAY
SALT- AND BRACKISH-WATER MARSHES
FRESHWATER MARSHES
SWAMPS
SHRUB-SHRUB WETLANDS
EXPOSED TIDAL FLATS
SHELTERED TIDAL FLATS

Map: SIDL

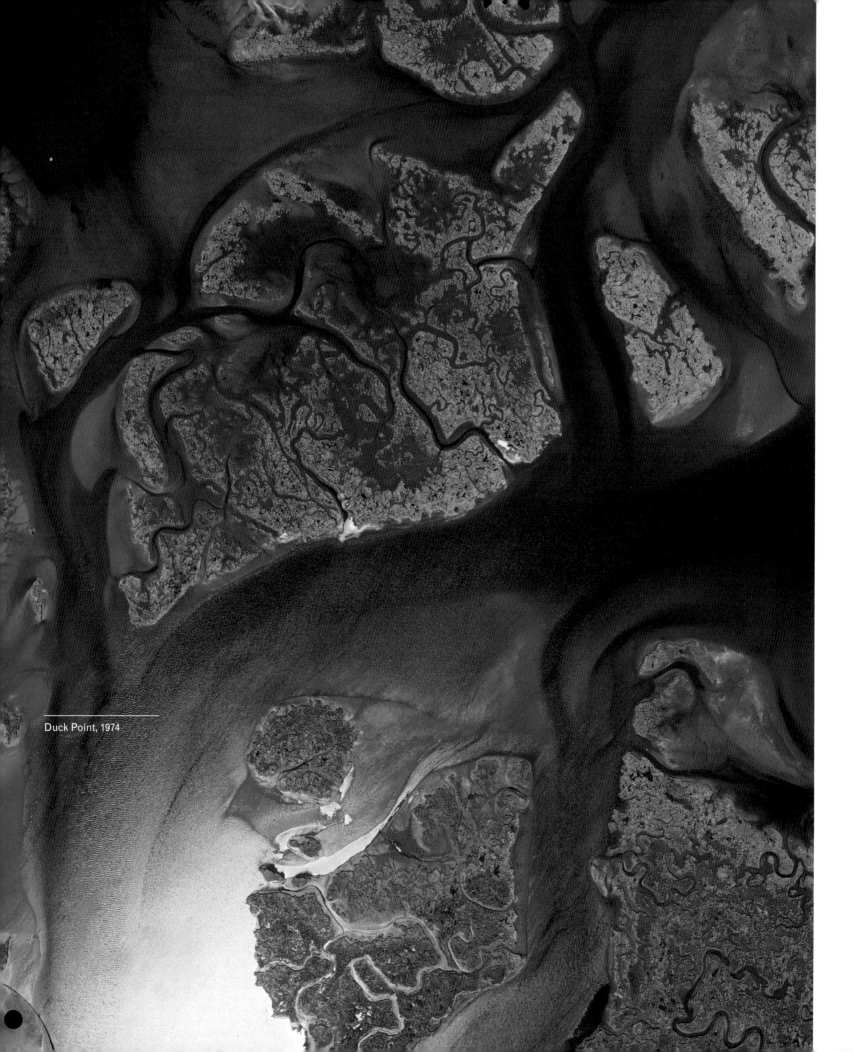

Duck Point, 1974

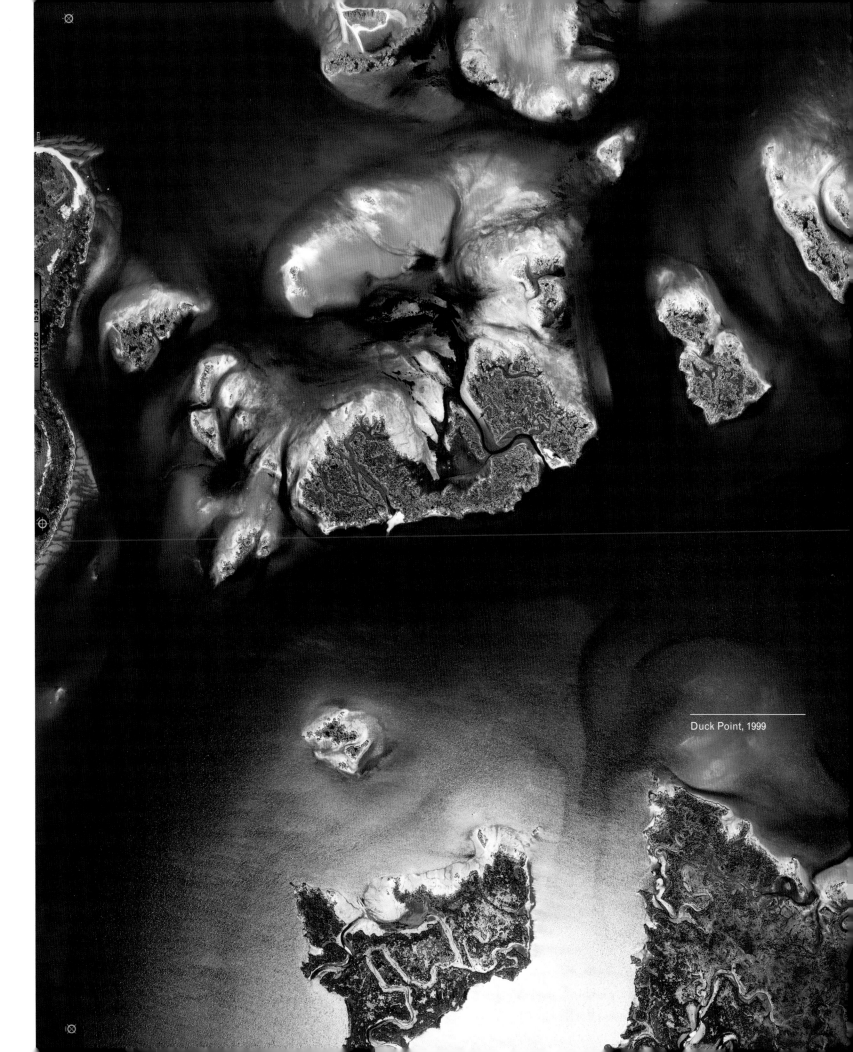

Duck Point, 1999

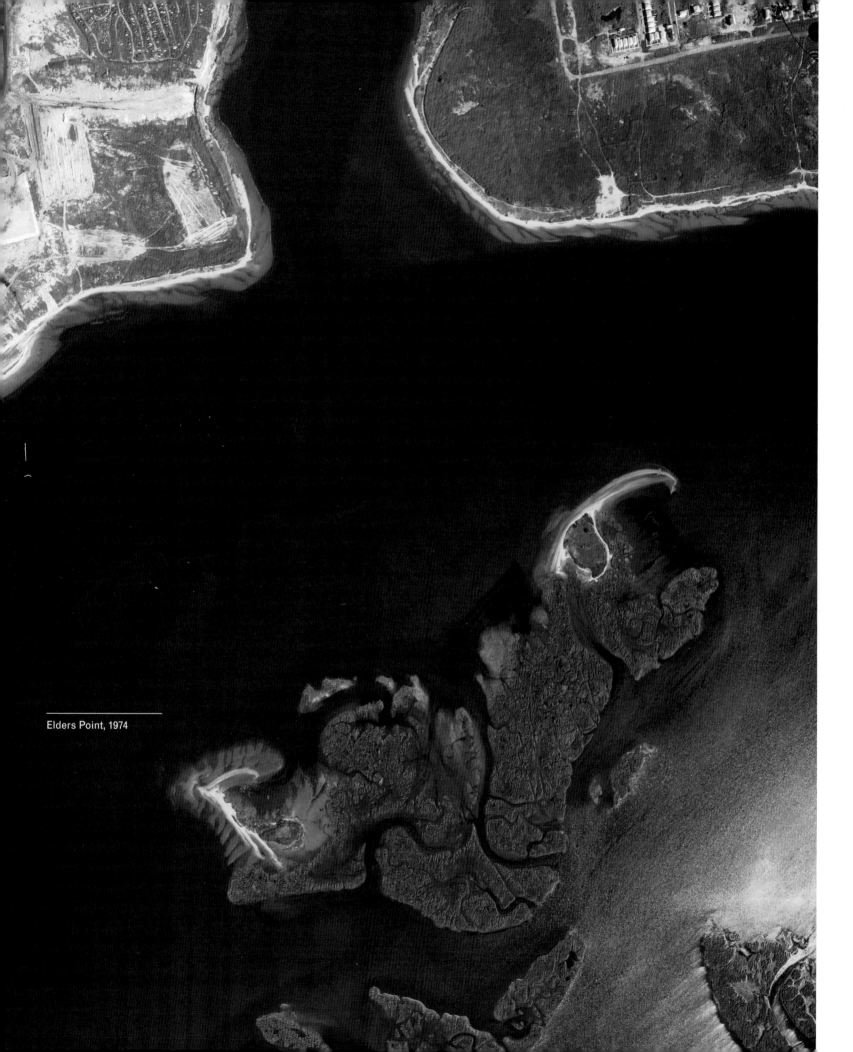

Elders Point, 1974

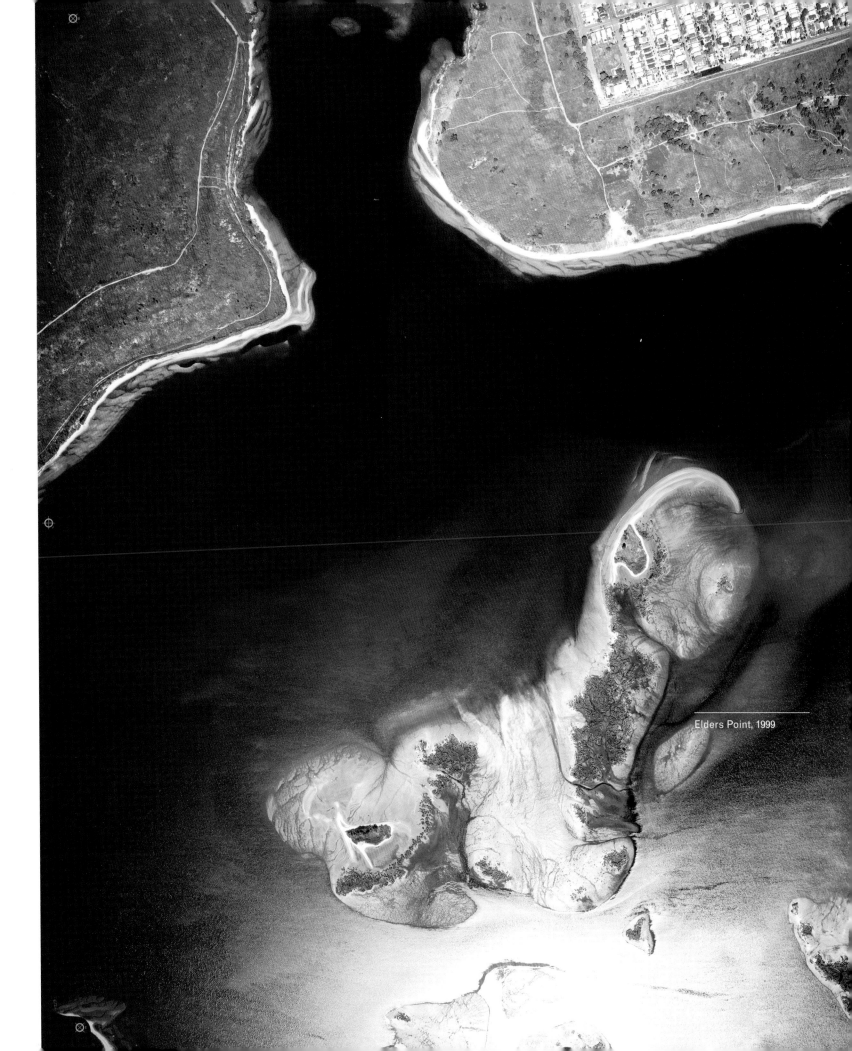

Elders Point, 1999

Mapping the Ecotone
Ashley Scott Kelly and Rikako Wakabayashi (Urban Found Architecture)

We propose an urban park that creates a microcosm of shifting habitats, programs, and landforms that capture the diversity of Gateway's ecotones, or zones of ecological tension. Our spatial and formal mapping of the ecosystem boundaries on Floyd Bennett Field enriches the visitor experience and heralds the concept of climate change as an immediately legible, urgent, human-scaled interaction of climate, water, and land.

Gateway must be made more accessible in terms of its idea. Any design to revitalize a 26,000-acre national park must have the capacity to shape many contradictory, disconnected sites within an urban context while retaining its legibility. The scale of experience is large, with the three-hundred-foot-wide runways at Floyd Bennett Field situated among an array of urban detritus. Mapping the Ecotone deploys strongly physical linear forms that trace changes in the landscape, imagining and making visible large-scale processes at the visitor experience's micro scale.

A channel is dug through the Rockaway Peninsula on an undeveloped tract of parkland at a width optimal to create an artificial natural disaster. Development along the coast has suspended this barrier island's natural landward movement and sediment over-wash from mid-Atlantic storms. This new corridor will help simulate hydrological effects, carrying much-needed salt and peat to Jamaica Bay and reanimating those processes made static by decades of urban dross, fill, and dredging.

A system of jetties and piers cut through Floyd Bennett Field dramatically reintroduces a landscape of tidal waterways. This array interfaces with the runways to create a multi-strand linear park with playing fields, hiking trails, algae blooms, and lookouts that stretch from the existing sports and visitor's center toward Jamaica Bay. The piers, along with their marshlands and landforms, create a highly visible, experiential public infrastructure similar to a viaduct, skyscraper, or other symbol of the city; they also help register and reframe our environmental doubts and insecurities.

Disturbances, rather than equilibrium, are necessary to shape the development and long-term sustainability of biotic communities. Tidal flows may appear cyclic or seasonal, but in the case of a nor'easter storm for example, cannot be forecast. Consider the Environmental Protection Agency's (EPA) predictions on sea level rise and natural tidal fluctuations, coupled at around 12 feet, and that much of the site levels off at an elevation just under this. Nature at its tipping point is made visible and accessible to park visitors: just as we incorporate imminent tension into the design of the jetty system, at some point this habitat, and those of the entire region, may violently shift.

Extending from the high ground of Flatbush Avenue, the piers are elevated at points above any predicted water level. The design responds, copes, and most importantly foreshadows how it may evolve and remain resilient through construction and forty to eighty years of plant growth and change, if and when the impact of global sea level rise is realized.

A system of jetties, marshlands, and tides, in addition to rising sea levels, defines where the ecotone line will be drawn, it inscribes the way people map boundaries, and communicates these concepts at a human scale. The design establishes a sense of place, a monumental artifact prepared to mark the future of our "natural" environment. It is a complex landscape, actively constructed, yet naturally passive, that re-conceptualizes a national park at Gateway where urban decay, renewal, and refuge can coexist.

MAPPING THE
GATEWAY NATIONAL RECREATION ARE

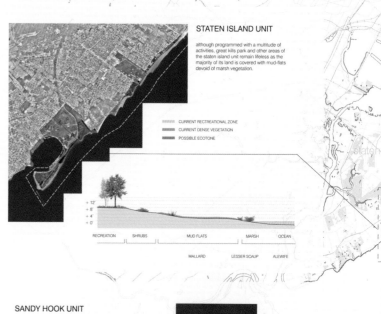

STATEN ISLAND UNIT

although programmed with a multitude of activities, great kills park and other areas of the staten island unit remain lifeless as the majority of its land is covered with mud-flats devoid of marsh vegetation.

CURRENT RECTREATIONAL ZONE
CURRENT DENSE VEGETATION
POSSIBLE ECOTONE

+ 12'
+ 8'
+ 4'
+ 0'

RECREATION | SHRUBS | MUD FLATS | MARSH | OCEAN

MALLARD | LESSER SCAUP | ALEWIFE

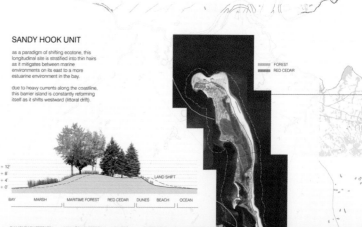

SANDY HOOK UNIT

as a paradigm of shifting ecotone, this longitudinal site is stratified into thin hairs as it mitigates between marine environments on its east to a more estuarine environment in the bay.

due to heavy currents along the coastline, this barrier island is constantly reforming itself as it shifts westward (littoral drift).

FOREST
RED CEDAR

+ 12'
+ 8'
+ 4'
+ 0'

LAND SHIFT

BAY | MARSH | MARITIME FOREST | RED CEDAR | DUNES | BEACH | OCEAN

DIAMONBACK TERRAPIN | MONARCH BUTTERFLY | SNAKES | GHOST CRAB | BLACK SEA BASS
BLACK DUCK | RED FOX | OSPREY | SAND PIPER | SEA GULLS

ECOTONE

FLOYD
BENNETT
FIELD

JFK

(possible canal to
JFK for shipping
thoroughfare)

HOFFMAN ISLAND

SWINBURNE ISLAND

BREEZY POINT

JAMAICA BAY
WILDLIFE REFUGE

SALINITY/ FRESH-WATER SOURCES
— SEWER OUTFALL
— WATER TREATMENT CONTROL
— MARSH (ECOTONE)

AMBROSE CHANNEL

new un-dredged jetty
satisfies the estuarine
marsh ecosystem's need
for a /natural disaster/

soil is moved into rockaway
inlet to fill years of dredging
that trapped sedementation

SANDY
HOOK

MAPPING THE ECOTONE

This project creates a highly visible, experiential public infrastructure that responds
to the shifting ecosystem of Jamaica Bay and defines a new vision of the relationship
between nature and people. Though within New York City, it is a stretch to call this
an urban park in the context of Manhattan. Gateway must be made more accessible
in terms of its idea.

On a marginal landscape with great biotic diversity, we believe that people should be
educated that ecosystems are in necessary flux, a cycle increasingly complex with
today's global climate shifts. Capturing the diversity of Gateway's ECOTONES, or
zones of ecological tension, we propose an urban park that creates a microcosm of
shifting habitats, program and landforms. These ecotones then operate at the larger
scale of Jamaica Bay's salt-marshes to reanimate those processes made static by
decades of urban dross, fill and dredging.

Great cities have a hard edge, a definite sense of place and identity. This designed
strategy of jetties and piers, marshlands, tides and rising sea levels defines where
the ecotone line will be drawn – the way people map boundaries and communicate
them at a more human scale. In doing so, we establish a sense of place prepared to
mark the future of our 'natural' environment. We're approaching the notion of a
complex landscape, actively constructed, naturally passive, and which reconceptual-
izes the national park where urban decay, renewal and refuge can coexist.

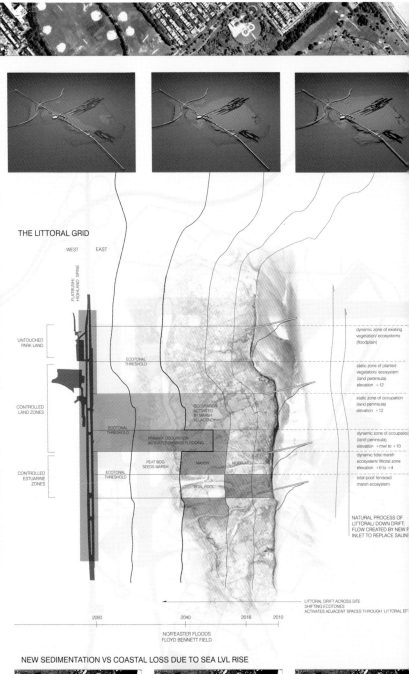

THE LITTORAL GRID

WEST　　EAST

FLATBUSH HIGHLAND SPINE

UNTOUCHED
PARK LAND

ECOTONAL
THRESHOLD

CONTROLLED
LAND ZONES

OCCUPATION
ACTIVATED
BY MARSH
ADJACENCY

ECOTONAL
THRESHOLD

PRIMARY OCCUPATION
ACTIVATED BY MASS FLOODING

CONTROLLED
ESTUARINE
ZONES

ECOTONAL
THRESHOLD

PEAT BOG
SEEDS MARSH

MARSH

MUDFLAT

TIDAL POOL

dynamic zone of existing
vegetation/ ecosystems
(floodplain)

static zone of planted
vegetation/ ecosystem
(land peninsula)
elevation +12

static zone of occupation
(land peninsula)
elevation +12

dynamic zone of occupation
(land peninsula)
elevation +mwl to +10

dynamic tidal marsh
ecosystem/ littoral zone
elevation +0 to +4

tidal pool/ terraced
marsh ecosystem

NATURAL PROCESS OF
LITTORAL/ DOWN DRIFT/
FLOW CREATED BY NEW
INLET TO REPLACE SALIN

2080　　　　2040　　　　2016　　2010

LITTORAL DRIFT ACROSS SITE
SHIFTING ECOTONES
ACTIVATES ADJACENT SPACES THROUGH 'LITTORAL EF

NOR'EASTER FLOODS
FLOYD BENNETT FIELD

NEW SEDIMENTATION VS COASTAL LOSS DUE TO SEA LVL RISE

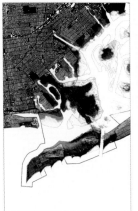

DIURNAL AND LUNAR TID

WETLAND 2

Mapping the Ecotone
Ashley Scott Kelly and Rikako Wakabayashi
Brooklyn, NY

+9'
+8'
+7'
+6'
+5'

PEAT MOSS

MARSH BIOTOPE
HEAVY METAL UPTAKE

SPRING TIDE

MHHW

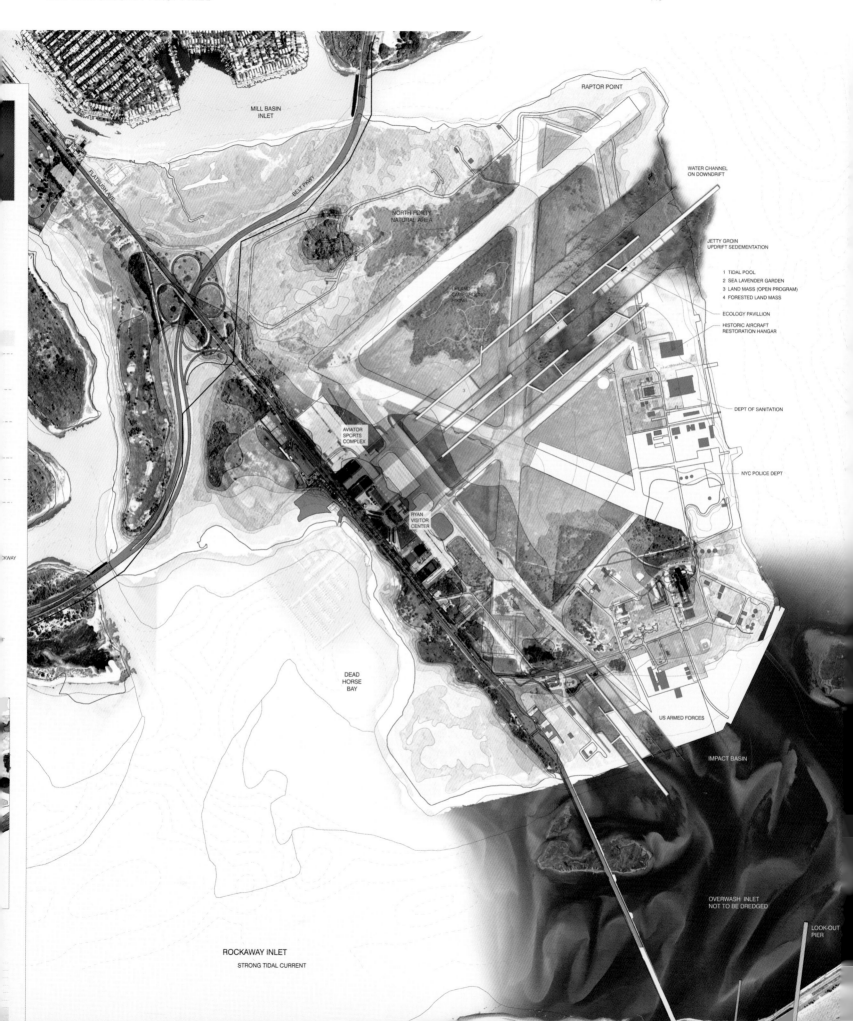

RAPTOR POINT

MILL BASIN
INLET

WATER CHANNEL
ON DOWNDRIFT

BELT PKWY

FLATBUSH AVE

NORTH FORTY
NATURAL AREA

JETTY GROIN
UPDRIFT SEDEMENTATION

1 TIDAL POOL
2 SEA LAVENDER GARDEN
3 LAND MASS (OPEN PROGRAM)
4 FORESTED LAND MASS

UPLAND
CAMPGROUND
HIKING

ECOLOGY PAVILLION

HISTORIC AIRCRAFT
RESTORATION HANGAR

DEPT OF SANITATION

AVIATOR
SPORTS
COMPLEX

NYC POLICE DEPT

RYAN
VISITOR
CENTER

CKWAY

DEAD
HORSE
BAY

US ARMED FORCES

IMPACT BASIN

OVERWASH INLET
NOT TO BE DREDGED

LOOK-OUT
PIER

ROCKAWAY INLET

STRONG TIDAL CURRENT

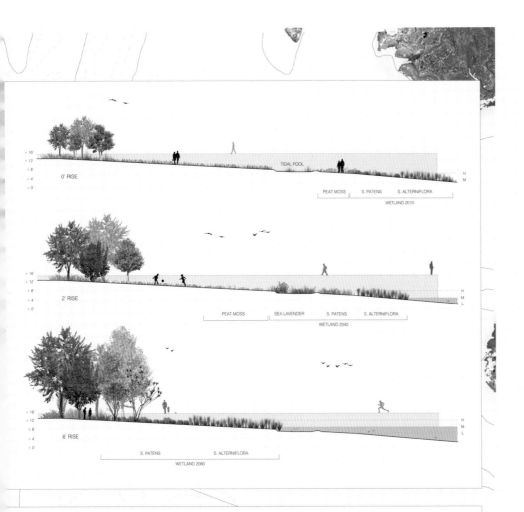

+ 16'
+ 12'
+ 8'
+ 4'
+ 0'

0' RISE

TIDAL POOL

H
M

PEAT MOSS　S. PATENS　S. ALTERNIFLORA
WETLAND 2010

+ 16'
+ 12'
+ 8'
+ 4'
+ 0'

2' RISE

H
M
L

PEAT MOSS　SEA LAVENDER　S. PATENS　S. ALTERNIFLORA
WETLAND 2040

+ 16'
+ 12'
+ 8'
+ 4'
+ 0'

6' RISE

H
M
L

S. PATENS　　S. ALTERNIFLORA
WETLAND 2080

NEGATIVE EFFECT

The Netherlands's Deltawerken, as an engineering feat for flood control, had several impacts on the ecosystem of the entire region. Though comparatively these projects serve different purposes, Deltawerken may provide a model for what to expect when drastic man-made shifts attempt to control natural systems.

POSITIVE EFFECT

If and when the diminishing salt-marsh ecosystem is restored to Jamaica Bay, there are likely to be similar effects to life which may have adapted to this microclimate over the past few decades. This is to be expected, as the entire system as an ecotone straddles a fluctuating boundary between land and water.

Mapping the Ecotone
Ashley Scott Kelly and Rikako Wakabayashi
Brooklyn, NY

These entries find inspiration in the
park's dynamic landscape and anticipate changes
in its ecological and hydrological form.

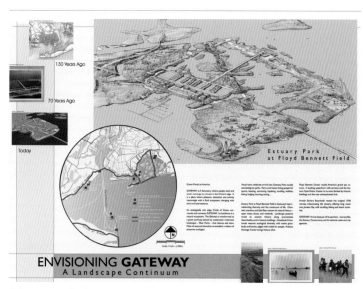

A Landscape Continuum

> page 143

Changing Scenery

> page 144

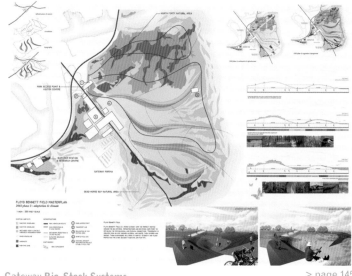

Gateway Bio-Stock Systems

> page 145

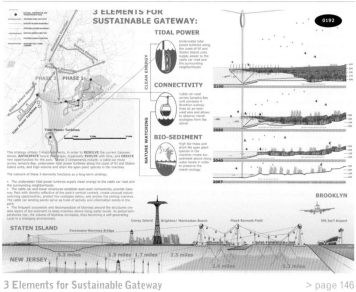

3 Elements for Sustainable Gateway

> page 146

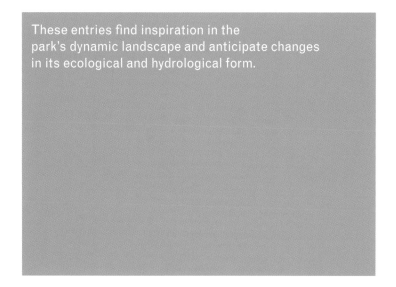

Deconstruction / Construction

> page 147

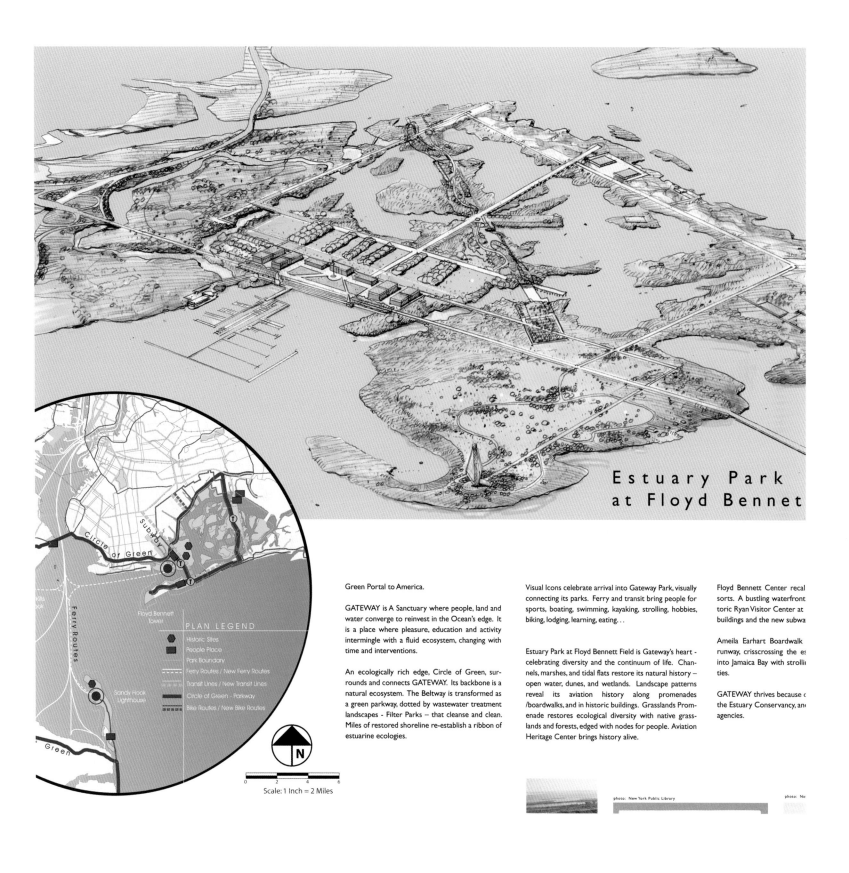

Estuary Park
at Floyd Bennet

PLAN LEGEND

- ⬣ Historic Sites
- ■ People Place
- Park Boundary
- Ferry Routes / New Ferry Routes
- Transit Lines / New Transit Lines
- Circle of Green - Parkway
- Bike Routes / New Bike Routes

Scale: 1 Inch = 2 Miles

Green Portal to America.

GATEWAY is A Sanctuary where people, land and water converge to reinvest in the Ocean's edge. It is a place where pleasure, education and activity intermingle with a fluid ecosystem, changing with time and interventions.

An ecologically rich edge, Circle of Green, surrounds and connects GATEWAY. Its backbone is a natural ecosystem. The Beltway is transformed as a green parkway, dotted by wastewater treatment landscapes - Filter Parks – that cleanse and clean. Miles of restored shoreline re-establish a ribbon of estuarine ecologies.

Visual Icons celebrate arrival into Gateway Park, visually connecting its parks. Ferry and transit bring people for sports, boating, swimming, kayaking, strolling, hobbies, biking, lodging, learning, eating. . .

Estuary Park at Floyd Bennett Field is Gateway's heart - celebrating diversity and the continuum of life. Channels, marshes, and tidal flats restore its natural history – open water, dunes, and wetlands. Landscape patterns reveal its aviation history along promenades /boardwalks, and in historic buildings. Grasslands Promenade restores ecological diversity with native grasslands and forests, edged with nodes for people. Aviation Heritage Center brings history alive.

Floyd Bennett Center recal
sorts. A bustling waterfront
toric Ryan Visitor Center at
buildings and the new subwa

Ameila Earhart Boardwalk
runway, crisscrossing the e
into Jamaica Bay with strolli
ties.

GATEWAY thrives because
the Estuary Conservancy, an
agencies.

A Landscape Continuum
Mundus Bishop Design, Inc.: "Channels, marshes, and tidal flats restore its natural history: open water, dunes, and wetlands."
Denver, CO

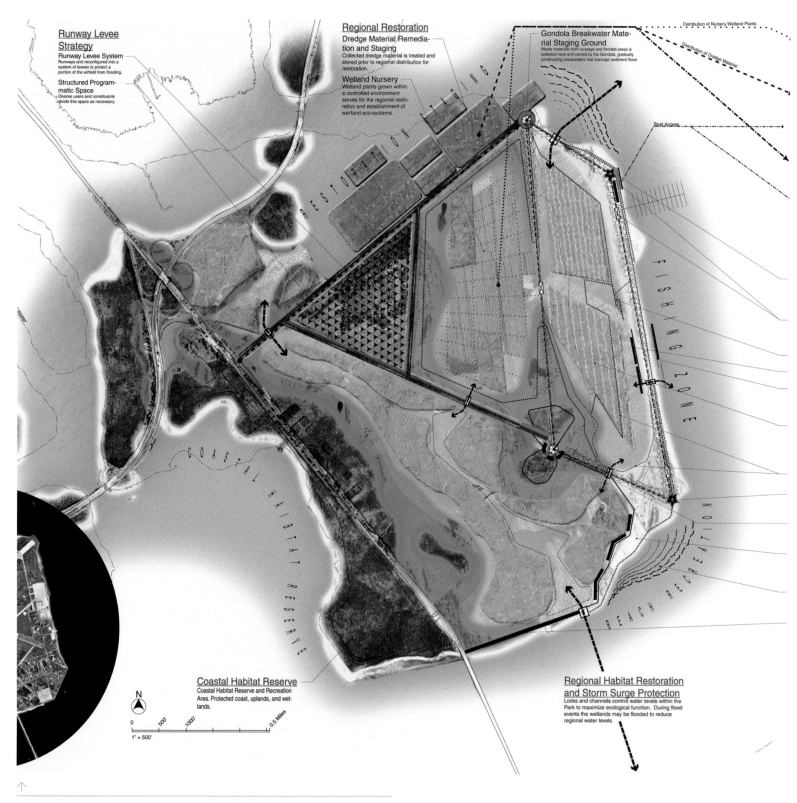

Runway Levee Strategy

Runway Levee System
Runways and reconfigured into a system of levees to protect a portion of the airfield from flooding.

Structured Programmatic Space
Diverse users and constituents divide this space as necessary.

Regional Restoration

Dredge Material Remediation and Staging
Collected dredge material is treated and stored prior to regional distribution for restoration.

Wetland Nursery
Wetland plants grown within a controlled environment serves for the regional restoration and establishment of wetland eco-systems.

Gondola Breakwater Material Staging Ground
Waste materials from runways and flooded areas is collected here and carried by the Gondola, gradually constructing breakwaters that intercept sediment flows

Distribution of Nursery Wetland Plants

Distribution of Dredge Material

Boat Access

RESTORATION STAGING

FISHING ZONE

COASTAL HABITAT RESERVE

BEACH RECREATION

Coastal Habitat Reserve
Coastal Habitat Reserve and Recreation Area. Protected coast, uplands, and wetlands.

Regional Habitat Restoration and Storm Surge Protection
Locks and channels control water levels within the Park to maximize ecological function. During flood events the wetlands may be flooded to reduce regional water levels.

N

0   500'   1000'   0.5 Miles

1" = 500'

Changing Scenery

SWA Group–LA: "Gateway is only a representative within the large network of NPS lands that are increasingly influenced by global environmental crises. As a general directive, the landscape management in the twenty-first century must reconsider the operative potential of its natural resources and recognize how it serves or suffers within a greater environmental context." *Los Angeles, CA*

Gateway Bio-Stock Systems

Adam Rothwell, Stephen Suen, Taku Suzuki, Erika Uribe: "Topography is created from on site crushed material and waste, then covered and seeded. These earthworks will bring in habitat diversity and flood protection for other Gateway habitats and for NYC." *London, UK*

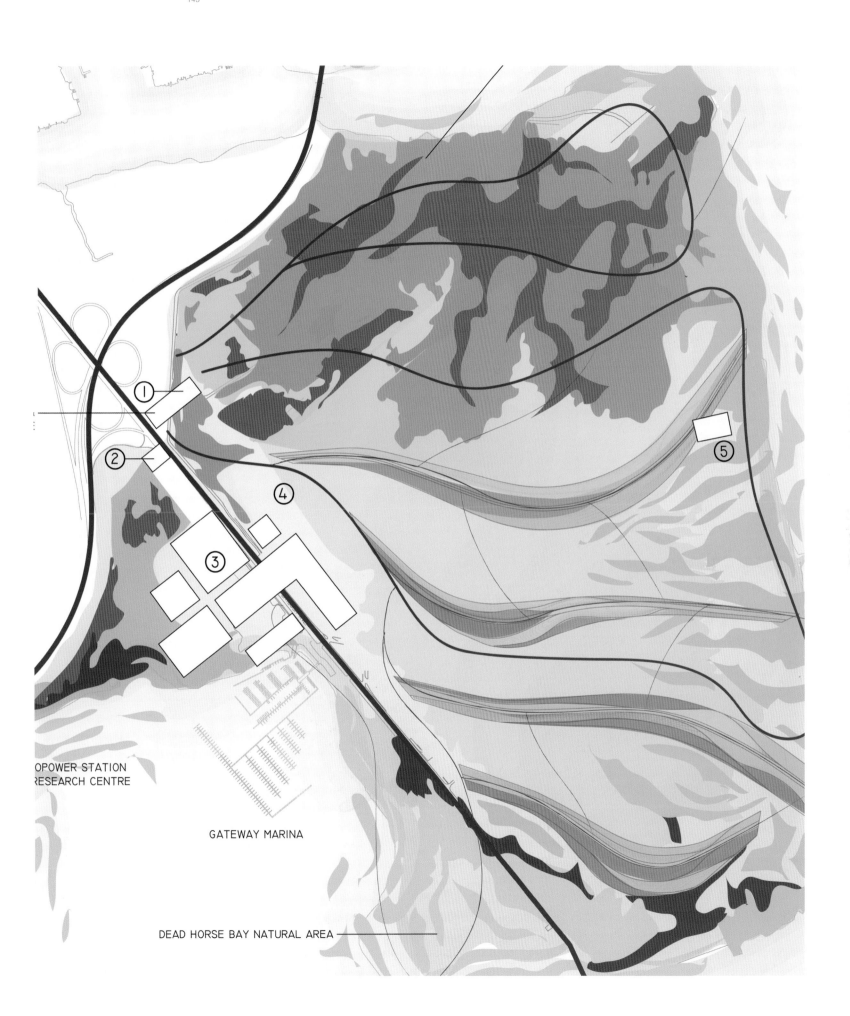

①

②

④

③

⑤

OPOWER STATION
RESEARCH CENTRE

GATEWAY MARINA

DEAD HORSE BAY NATURAL AREA

TIDAL POWER

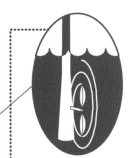

CLEAN ENERGY

Underwater tidal power turbines along the coast of NJ and Staten Island units supply power to the cable car road and the surrounding neighborhoods

CONNECTIVITY

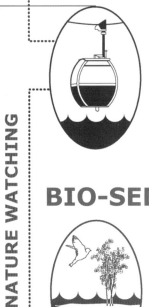

NATURE WATCHING

Cable car road across Jamaica Bay unit connects 4 Brooklyn subway lines on an east-west axis and allows to observe marsh ecologies from the above

BIO-SEDIMENT

High bio-mass and short life span plant species in the marshes create bio-sediment above rising water levels in order to preserve the marsh ecology

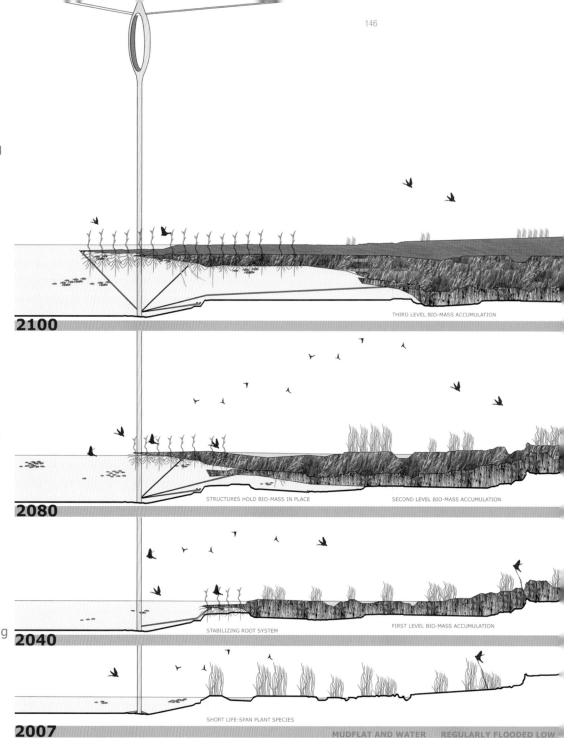

2100 THIRD LEVEL BIO-MASS ACCUMULATION

2080 STRUCTURES HOLD BIO-MASS IN PLACE   SECOND LEVEL BIO-MASS ACCUMULATION

2040 STABILIZING ROOT SYSTEM   FIRST LEVEL BIO-MASS ACCUMULATION

2007 SHORT LIFE-SPAN PLANT SPECIES   MUDFLAT AND WATER   REGULARLY FLOODED LOW

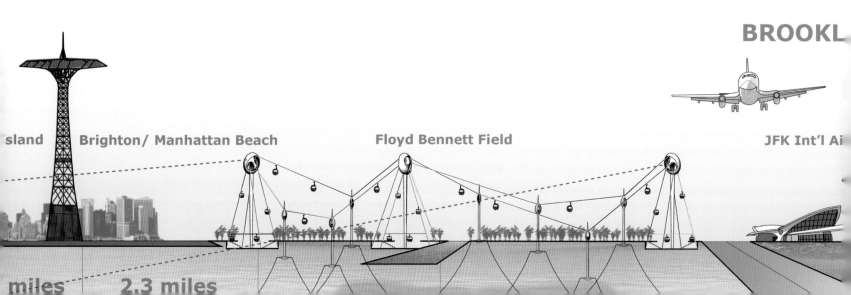

BROOKL

Island   Brighton/ Manhattan Beach   Floyd Bennett Field   JFK Int'l Ai

miles   2.3 miles

←

3 Elements for Sustainable Gateway
Olga Drobinina, Ximena Valle: "The frequent succession and decomposition of biomass around the structures creates layers of biosediment to keep marshes above rising water levels. As global temperatures rise, the volume of biomass increases, thus becoming a self-generating cycle in a changing environment."
Berwyn, PA

↓

Deconstruction / Construction
Chihiro Shinohara: "Deconstruction of runways will occur consistently on site. Deconstruction of immense and monotonous runways also means construction of more human-scale, usable areas at the same time. The inhabitable deconstruction edge and tidal spectacle, as depicted below, can be one of the main attractions in the park. Concrete taken out from the runways is transported to other parts of the park to construct raised walkways." *Charlottesville, VA*

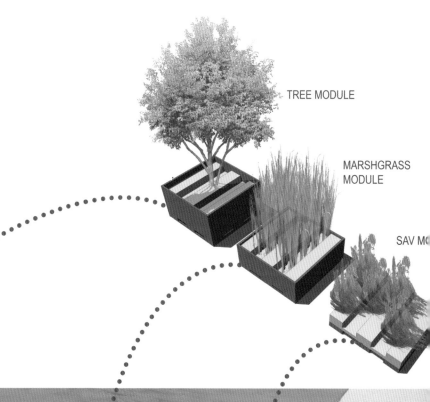

TREE MODULE

MARSHGRASS MODULE

SAV MO

Eco-Harbor

Jamaica Bay is an ecological gem—it may be stressed, altered, even compromised—but if you commune with its waters you can't not sense its latent natural vitality. New York City is fortunate to have a functioning urban aquatic wilderness on its shores.
—John Waldman, professor of biology, Queens College, NY

Gateway is part of a dynamic harbor that is a globally important reservoir of ecological diversity. Lying at the mouth of the Hudson River, the park contains an array of estuarine habitats that teem with life. Even in this highly urbanized corner of the United States, these resource-rich areas provide natural nurseries for myriad species of birds, fish, and mammals, and serve as one of the last remaining breeding and feeding grounds for horseshoe crabs, sandpipers, and diamondback terrapins. With its capacity to support dunes, grasslands, wetlands, and forests, Gateway also offers a refuge for endangered plant communities such as the maritime holly forest at Sandy Hook, itself a crucial habitat for rare butterflies and birds. Though often under stress, these interconnected ecological systems remain one of Gateway's principal attractions—a haven for both wildlife and the nature-starved residents of New York City.

Among naturalists, Gateway is most renowned as one of the nation's best bird-watching locations, and its wealth of avian life draws birders from all over. As a node on the Atlantic flyway, the shores of Gateway are an annual stopover for 330 species as they migrate through the area. At various times throughout the year, the Jamaica Bay Wildlife Refuge is alive with warblers, coastal shorebirds, waterfowl, and butterflies, and its more than 9,000 acres are also part of extensive efforts to restore once-decimated avian populations. The osprey, for instance, was once all but extinct due to environmental toxins and loss of habitat, but platform nests like those built in Gateway have helped the species rebound. Nearby Breezy Point offers important nesting grounds for the threatened piping plover, along with other species such as the American oystercatcher and black skimmer. Floyd Bennett Field's 140-acre grassland habitat, maintained since 1985, is home to the Savannah sparrow and the bobolink, rare breeders in the area—not to mention Peregrine falcons and kestrels—while Swinburne and Hoffman Islands, now bird sanctuaries, host hundreds of double-crested cormorant nests, and are an important site for ornithological research into this once-threatened species.

Though Gateway's estuarine landscapes still boast an extraordinary diversity of avian life, adverse effects resulting from human activity have reduced these marshes to half their former size, and had severe impact on resident populations of fish and shellfish. Today, along with a variety of fiddler and blue claw crabs, clams, and mussels, the bay seasonally hosts striped bass, bluefish, flounder, and other game fish. While many concerns about their consumption remain, given the known presence of marginally toxic sediments in the water, the area nonetheless draws enthusiastic groups of anglers. Due to its relatively shallow waters—averaging about 10 feet deep—the bay warms early in the spring, luring all manner of marine life, and, like all estuaries, its grounds serve as nurseries for younger fish and as safe harbor for fish of prey.

The flora surrounding the harbor have fared worse than its marine life, bearing little resemblance today to the landscape's pre-settlement state. Gateway's legacy of dredging and filling, along with encroaching urban development, have supplanted much of the area's original coastal terrain, with its dunes, swales, grasses, and mosaic of beach heather, pitch pines, and wild rose.[1] Further inland was a maritime forest, with its understory of poison ivy, wild sarsaparilla, and chokeberry, and further still, the forest itself, dominated by American holly, sassafras, and black gum. Beyond that lay the region's more characteristic upland forests, largely composed of oak, pine, chestnut, and maples.[2]

Little is left of such botanical riches, but Gateway preserves some of the most important native landscapes that remain. In these small but magnificent swatches of nature, Gateway offers a glimpse both of the past and a potential future. The dynamism of its rookeries, waters, and thickets points toward the area's rebirth as an ecological generator—one whose power as both a place and an idea can be harnessed for the common good.

The competition entry Reassembling Ecologies by North Design Office proposes to repair and rebuild Gateway's deteriorating aquatic and terrestrial environment by concentrating human use to one area of the park. At Floyd Bennett Field, all public recreational activities and uses would be built along one of the historic runways, allowing the rest of the site to be replanted and restored to mimic a more "wild" state. The proposal further calls for a redefinition of the park's mission to reflect a contemporary awareness of environmental stewardship and the special character of ecological and historical sites. In the same spirit, the competition submissions that follow prioritize the restoration and enhancement of Gateway's ecological resources.

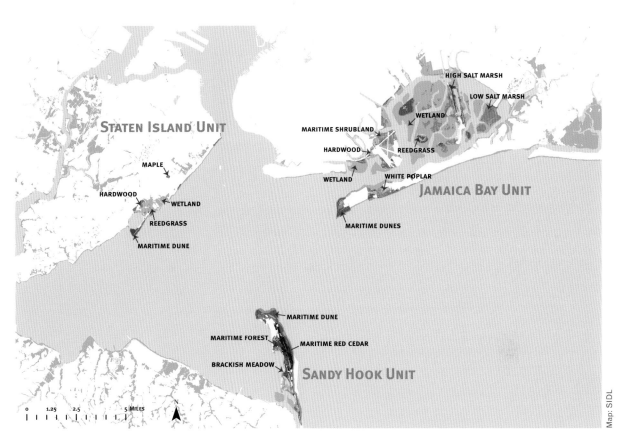

Map: SIDL

Vegetation types

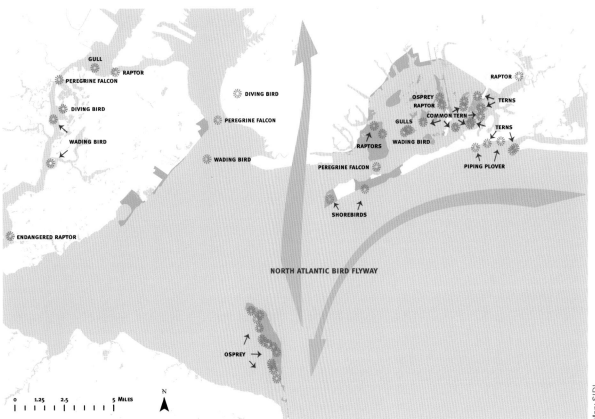

Bird nesting grounds of rare
and endangered species

Map: SIDL

ENDNOTES

Epigraph John Waldman, e-mail message to the editors, August 3, 2009.

1 Henry W. Art, *Ecological Studies of the Sunken Forest, Fire Island National Seashore* (Boston, MA: National Park Service Northeast Regional Office, 1976).

2 Alexander R. Brash, "New York City's Primeval Forest: A Review Characterizing the Type Specimen," in *The Natural History of New York City Parks and Great Gull Island*, edited by A. Deutsch (New York: The Linnaean Society of New York and Ann Arbor, MI: Edward Brothers, Inc., 2007), 55–78.

Bird species at Gateway

Bird species at Gateway

Bird species at Gateway

Bird species at Gateway

Bird species at Gateway

Fish species at Gateway

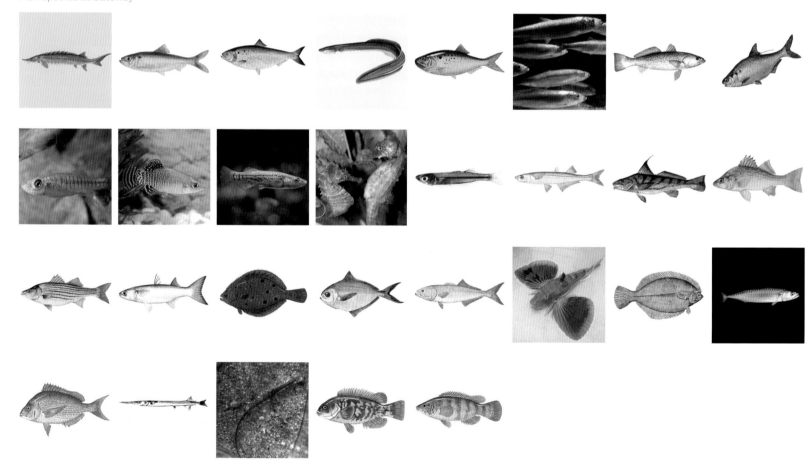

Vegetation types at Gateway

Invertebrate species at Gateway

Maritime mammal species at Gateway

Reassembling Ecologies
Pete North and
Alissa North
(North Design Office)

The Reassembling Ecologies proposal is based on an intense understanding of existing conditions and in-depth knowledge of optimal conditions for strengthened aquatic and terrestrial ecologies in and around Gateway National Recreation Area. Running parallel with this is the need for a stronger definition of activities for park users, through an enhanced structure that allows for sensitive ecologies and recreation to coexist.

The concentration and intensification of recreation along a central spine in Floyd Bennett Field, utilizing the historic runway, is the primary reorganizing strategy. Liberating tracts of land that currently have sprawling and ill-defined uses, the concentrated activity enables larger tracts of sensitive terrestrial ecologies to flourish, while the condensed programs allow amenities to be maintained at the highest standards. The new spine of activity is reinforced with a linear landform, constructed of material relocated from the retired airstrips, and performs multiple functions: gateway, sound barrier, viewing platform, seating, and protection from future sea-level rise.

In the various sites that comprise Gateway, habitat restoration is intensified, smaller habitat pockets are connected in an effort to strengthen them, and access to sensitive areas is restricted. Increased monitoring targets invasive species, which are reduced when advantageous for ecological health. Water quality is improved by re-engineering the connection through Breezy Point, allowing saltwater to flow into the bay to reduce the rampant Phragmites or reeds. Constructed wetlands at JFK Airport are mandated to phytoremediate toxic runoff, while water pollution control plants are improved and combined sewers are phased out. Wetlands are reconstructed at every available water edge, and the material excavated from these projects is used to level aquatic borrow pits. Through the use of specific species of vegetation, phytoremediation occurs with bio-islands in the bay, and on land with selected plants able to remediate toxins. A new phytoremediation facility is created to dry, compost, or ash

plants that have accumulated toxins and the metals are recovered and sold for profit. Considering future sea level rise, best management practices are phased in around Gateway. Bioswales are created along streets and highway medians, school yard greening programs are fostered, incentives for industrial eco-parks are provided, and where land is being submerged by sea level rise, a federal strategy is developed to purchase this shoreline.

Walking tours of Lenape tribe settlements, historic trail markers, archeological demonstration digs, and heritage seed programs on old cultivated fields are instituted. Access to and from Gateway is improved with ample buses and frequent stops. A future subway link is created with a stop at the heart of Floyd Bennett Field, pedestrian bridges are built to link neighborhoods to Gateway, and bike rental is available for the strengthened connected network of bike routes. On the water, boat docking is increased, self-propelled boat rental is available, and an all-year ferry service with local ferry taxi between the various parts of Gateway is instituted. A Gateway ferry tour to historic military sites is conducted, while airfield history is celebrated through annual events. Historic buildings are reprogrammed, while nondesignated buildings that cannot be adapted for new use are taken down, and their materials are stored on site for future building projects. In this sense Gateway serves as a precedent to initiate a new era of programming and design in National Parks through zero-footprint activities, transportation, and constructions.

Reassembling Ecologies attempts to repair and rebuild the deteriorating aquatic and terrestrial ecologies in and around Gateway through the rethinking and reorganizing of territories and infrastructures to better accommodate future uses and ecological flows. Strengthening both recreational and ecological functions, Reassembling Ecologies provides a precedent-setting rethinking for Gateway National Recreation Area such that intensive recreation can exist within flourishing ecologies.

an Visitor Center

REASSEMBLING**ECOLOGIES**

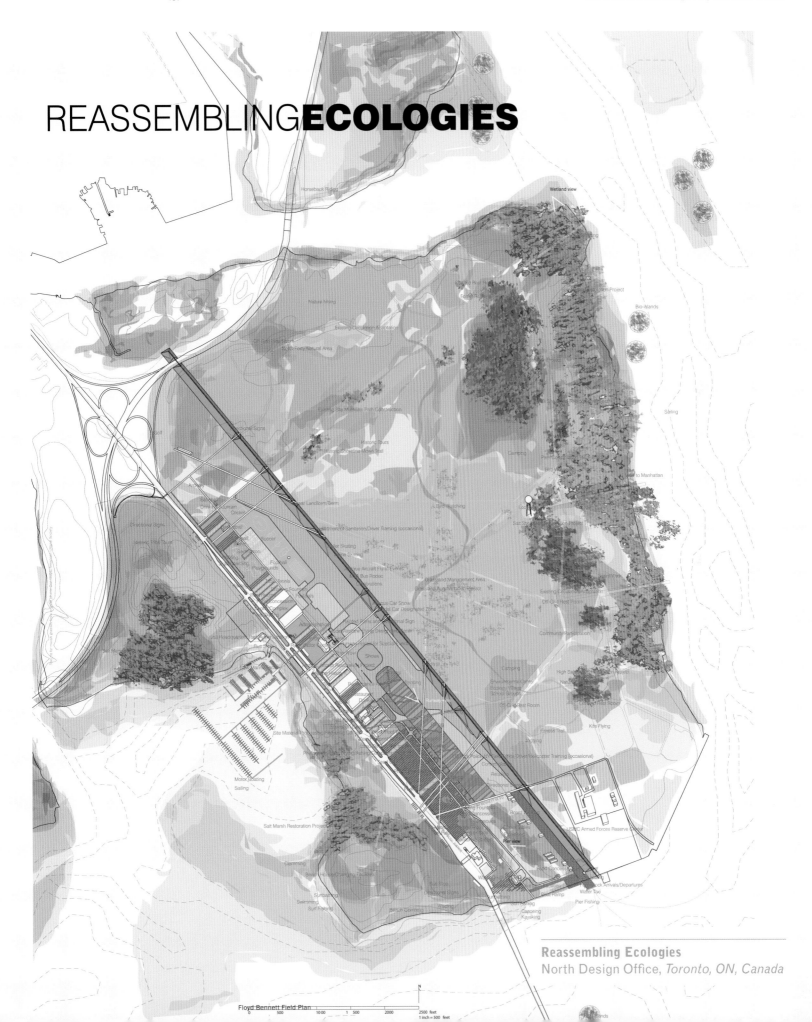

Floyd Bennett Field Plan

0   500   1000   1500   2000   2500 feet
1 inch = 500 feet

Reassembling Ecologies
North Design Office, *Toronto, ON, Canada*

ENVISIONING**GATEWAY**
REASSEMBLING**ECOLOGIES**

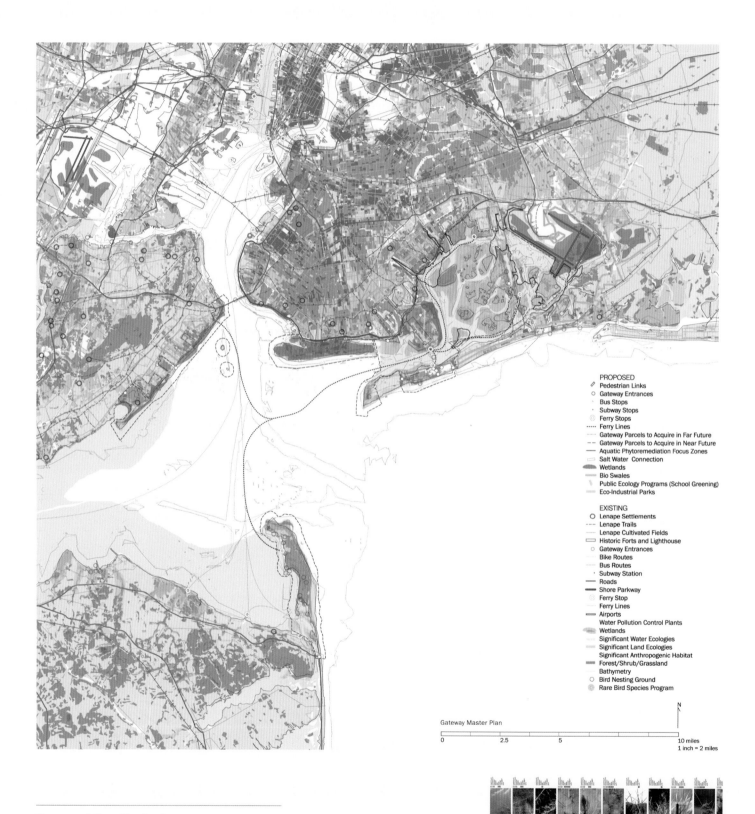

PROPOSED
◿ Pedestrian Links
○ Gateway Entrances
▪ Bus Stops
· Subway Stops
⊙ Ferry Stops
---- Ferry Lines
········· Gateway Parcels to Acquire in Far Future
-- - Gateway Parcels to Acquire in Near Future
— Aquatic Phytoremediation Focus Zones
▭ Salt Water Connection
▬ Wetlands
═ Bio Swales
╲ Public Ecology Programs (School Greening)
▭ Eco-Industrial Parks

EXISTING
○ Lenape Settlements
--- Lenape Trails
— Lenape Cultivated Fields
▭ Historic Forts and Lighthouse
○ Gateway Entrances
— Bike Routes
— Bus Routes
· Subway Station
— Roads
▬ Shore Parkway
Ferry Stop
— Ferry Lines
▬ Airports
Water Pollution Control Plants
▬ Wetlands
Significant Water Ecologies
Significant Land Ecologies
Significant Anthropogenic Habitat
▬ Forest/Shrub/Grassland
Bathymetry
○ Bird Nesting Ground
◉ Rare Bird Species Program

Gateway Master Plan

0   2.5   5   10 miles
1 inch = 2 miles

Reassembling Ecologies
North Design Office, *Toronto, ON, Canada*

Reassembling Ecologies

The *Reassembling Ecologies* proposal for Envisioning Gateway is based on an intense understanding of existing conditions and in-depth knowledge of optimal conditions for strengthened aquatic and terrestrial ecologies in and around the Gateway National Recreation Park. Running parallel with this is the need for a stronger definition of programs and activities for park users and an enhanced structure that allows for sensitive ecologies and recreation to coexist. Reassembling Ecologies attempts to repair and rebuild the deteriorating aquatic and terrestrial ecologies in and around Gateway through the rethinking and reorganizing of territories and infrastructures to better accommodate future uses and ecological flows.

The concentration and intensification of active recreation along a central spine in Floyd Bennett Field, utilizing the existing historic central runway, is the reorganizing strategy. The goal with this move is to liberate vast tracts of land that currently have sprawling, ill-defined, uses. Intensifying activity and concentrating its footprint enables larger tracts of sensitive terrestrial and aquatic ecologies to flourish with minimal disturbance. The central spine of activity is reinforced with a linear landform. The landform, constructed of material relocated from on-site (primarily the asphalt and concrete from the retired airstrips), performs multiple functions including; gateway to park on a local and regional scale, sound barrier, viewing platform, seating, link through site and as protection from future sea-level rise.

Reassembling Ecologies strengthens both recreational and ecological functions and provides a precedent setting rethinking for Gateway National Recreation Park such that intensive recreation can exist within flourishing ecologies.

Vegetation / Habitats

Continue habitat restoration projects and research
Use Floyd Bennett Field as a nursery to vegetate NYC
Sell plants at a discount to increase vegetation on private property
Monitor invasive species and reduce distribution when advantageous for ecological health
Concentrate active programs to open up more areas for ecological restoration
Connect even the smallest areas of habitat and continue to expand them
Restrict access to sensitive areas and provide ample education opportunities
Involve adjacent communities as habitat stewards

History / Program

Lenape tribe settlements walking tours and archeological demonstration digs
Institute a heritage seed program on available lands of old Lenape cultivated fields
Street marking program for old trails
Ferry loop tour to historic military sites within Gateway
Airfield history through a variety of celebratory programs
Condense programming strategy such that all amenities can be maintained at the highest standards
Develop private partnerships to help fund restoration efforts if necessary
Take down old, non-designated, buildings that cannot be adapted for new use and store materials on site for future building projects
Use Gateway as a precedent to initiate a new era of design and building in National Parks through Zero Footprint constructions

Flooding

Implement Best Management Practices
Bio-swales along streets (particularly those prone to flooding)
School yard greening programs
Green highway medians
Industrial Eco-Parks
Consider a federal strategy for purchasing shoreline due to sea level rise
Incorporate these new lands as part of Gateway NRA

Access

More buses and more frequent stops
Future subway stop to the heart of Floyd Bennett Field
Pedestrian bridges to link neighborhoods to Gateway
Better bike routes and connections, with bike rental
More places to dock a boat and more self propelled boat rental
All year ferry service with local ferry taxi between the various parts of Gateway NRA

Water Health / Toxicity

Re-engineer connection through Breezy Point to allow saltwater flow into Jamaica Bay
Water with higher salt content will reduce rampant growth of Phragmities
Mandate constructed wetland creation at JFK airport to detain and phytoremediate toxic runoff into bay
Continue to improve water pollution control plants
Phase out combined sewers
(Re)Construct wetlands at every available water's edge
Use cut from these projects to level aquatic borrow pits
Phytoremediate with bio-islands (floating mats of vegetation) and on land with plants able to remediate toxins in bay (see list of some suggested plants)
Create new phytoremediation facility at Floyd Bennett Field to dry, compost, or ash plants that have accumulated toxins
In the case of plants that have accumulated metals, recover metal and sell for profit

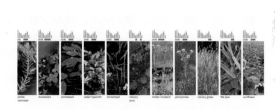

These entries engage ecological processes and species restoration to rethink the park's role in the surrounding region.

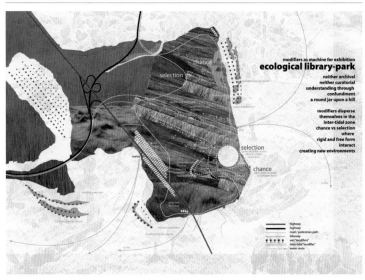

Ecological Modifiers

> page 161

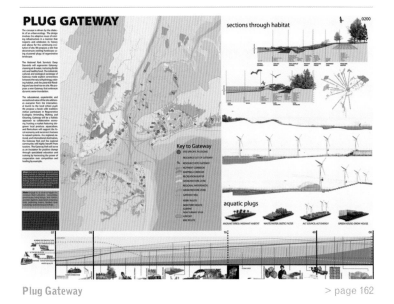

Plug Gateway

> page 162

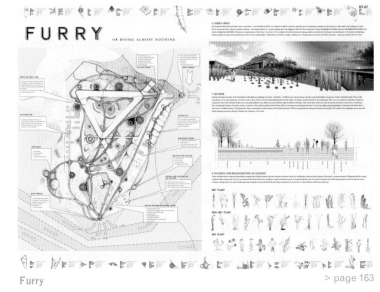

Furry

> page 163

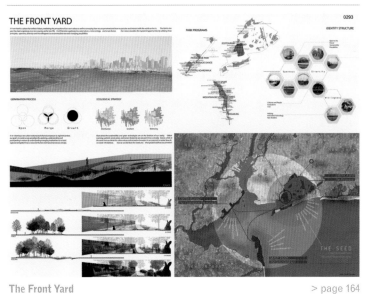

The Front Yard

> page 164

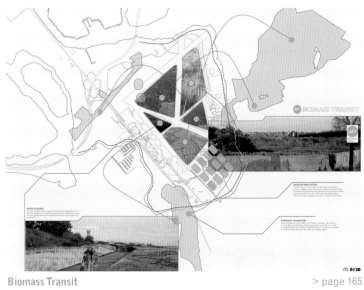

Biomass Transit

> page 165

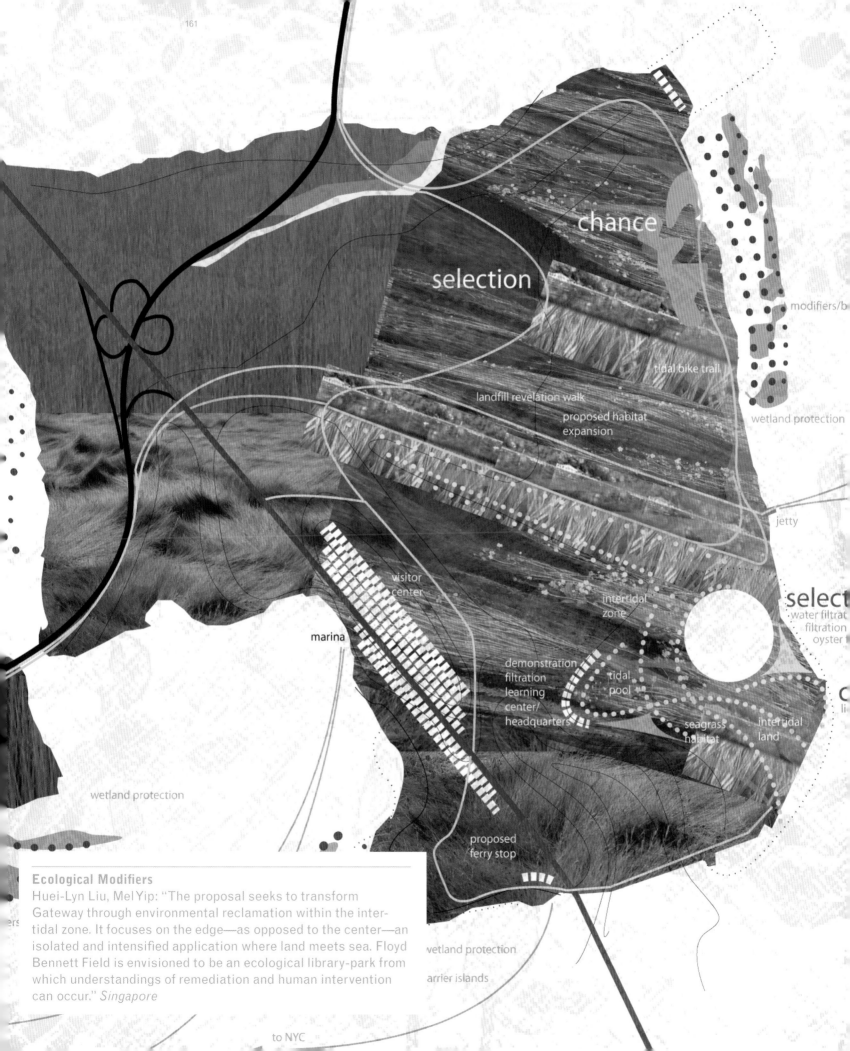

chance

selection

modifiers/b

tidal bike trail

landfill revelation walk

proposed habitat
expansion

wetland protection

jetty

visitor
center

intertidal
zone

select

water filtrat
filtration
oyster f

marina

demonstration
filtration
learning
center/
headquarters

tidal
pool

seagrass
habitat

intertidal
land

c
li

wetland protection

proposed
ferry stop

Ecological Modifiers

Huei-Lyn Liu, Mel Yip: "The proposal seeks to transform
Gateway through environmental reclamation within the intertidal zone. It focuses on the edge—as opposed to the center—an
isolated and intensified application where land meets sea. Floyd
Bennett Field is envisioned to be an ecological library-park from
which understandings of remediation and human intervention
can occur." *Singapore*

vetland protection

arrier islands

to NYC

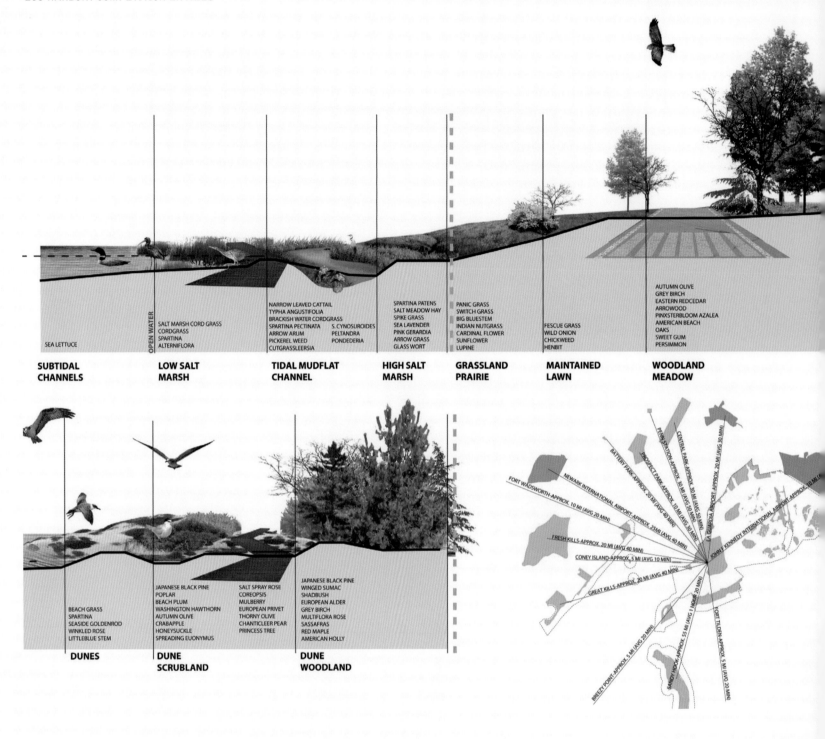

SEA LETTUCE

SUBTIDAL CHANNELS

OPEN WATER

SALT MARSH CORD GRASS
CORDGRASS
SPARTINA
ALTERNIFLORA

LOW SALT MARSH

NARROW LEAVED CATTAIL
TYPHA ANGUSTIFOLIA
BRACKISH WATER CORDGRASS
SPARTINA PECTINATA   S. CYNOSUROIDES
ARROW ARUM   PELTANDRA
PICKEREL WEED   PONDEDERIA
CUTGRASSLEERSIA

TIDAL MUDFLAT CHANNEL

SPARTINA PATENS
SALT MEADOW HAY
SPIKE GRASS
SEA LAVENDER
PINK GERARDIA
ARROW GRASS
GLASS WORT

HIGH SALT MARSH

PANIC GRASS
SWITCH GRASS
BIG BLUESTEM
INDIAN NUTGRASS
CARDINAL FLOWER
SUNFLOWER
LUPINE

GRASSLAND PRAIRIE

FESCUE GRASS
WILD ONION
CHICKWEED
HENBIT

MAINTAINED LAWN

AUTUMN OLIVE
GREY BIRCH
EASTERN REDCEDAR
ARROWOOD
PINXSTERBLOOM AZALEA
AMERICAN BEACH
OAKS
SWEET GUM
PERSIMMON

WOODLAND MEADOW

BEACH GRASS
SPARTINA
SEASIDE GOLDENROD
WINKLED ROSE
LITTLEBLUE STEM

DUNES

JAPANESE BLACK PINE
POPLAR
BEACH PLUM
WASHINGTON HAWTHORN
AUTUMN OLIVE
CRABAPPLE
HONEYSUCKLE
SPREADING EUONYMUS

SALT SPRAY ROSE
COREOPSIS
MULBERRY
EUROPEAN PRIVET
THORNY OLIVE
CHANTICLEER PEAR
PRINCESS TREE

DUNE SCRUBLAND

JAPANESE BLACK PINE
WINGED SUMAC
SHADBUSH
EUROPEAN ALDER
GREY BIRCH
MULTIFLORA ROSE
SASSAFRAS
RED MAPLE
AMERICAN HOLLY

DUNE WOODLAND

Plug Gateway
TypicalState: Jason Addington, Anthony Corso, Matt Fordham, Ryan Wilson: "Sections through habitat." *Chicago, IL*

Furry
M+: Kenneth Yeung, Urtzi Grau: "Defining an element that presupposes minimum intervention and adapts to the different conditions of Gateway—the pile—we take advantage of its capacity to stabilize terrains, promote bivalve shellfish restoration, and absorb temporary constructions and activities." *Princeton, NJ*

4. PILES, DOTS

Instead of projecting into the landscape, we deducted from it, hoping that we could reverse the argument. Defining an element that presupposes minimum intervention and adapts to the different conditions of Gateway - the pile -, we take advantage of its capacity to **stabilize terrains**, promote **bivalve shellfish restoration** and adsorb **temporary constructions and activities**; the smallest footprint - repeated enough times in different densities - will solve ecological, historical, recreational and educational requirements.

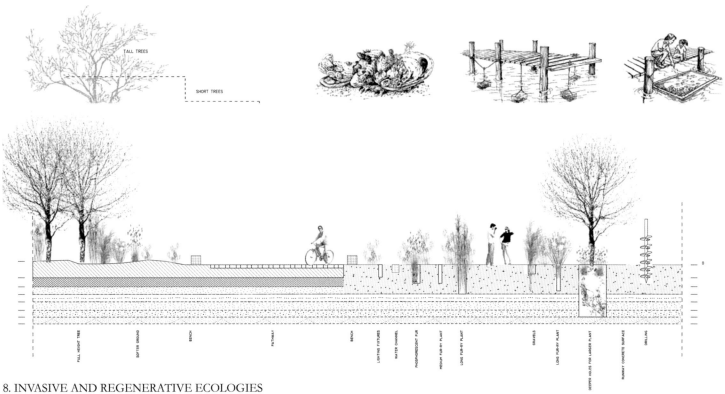

8. INVASIVE AND REGENERATIVE ECOLOGIES

Nodes and Bands house variations park pavilions resulting from a hybrid structures that joint tensegrity structures (Hard), low-technologies (Soft), perennial vegetation (Permanent), seasonal ecosystems (Temporal) with the existing conditions (Water and ground). They are the framework that allows the invasive recycling of vegetal and animal systems. Evolving through time they will connect forming a circuit while their programs can be develop into variety of themes, mixing scenic views with scientific panoramas along the journey and effectively, becoming a mechanism of coexistence of natural habitats and intensive urban uses.

WET PLANT

SEMI WET PLANT

DRY PLANT

0-2 YEARS

2-5 YEARS

5-10 YEARS

10-20 YEARS

↑

The Front Yard
EDAW Limited: "In revisioning a new urban national park that encompasses its regional context, our goal is to create a new paradigm for exploring, understanding, and participating in nature." *Hong Kong*

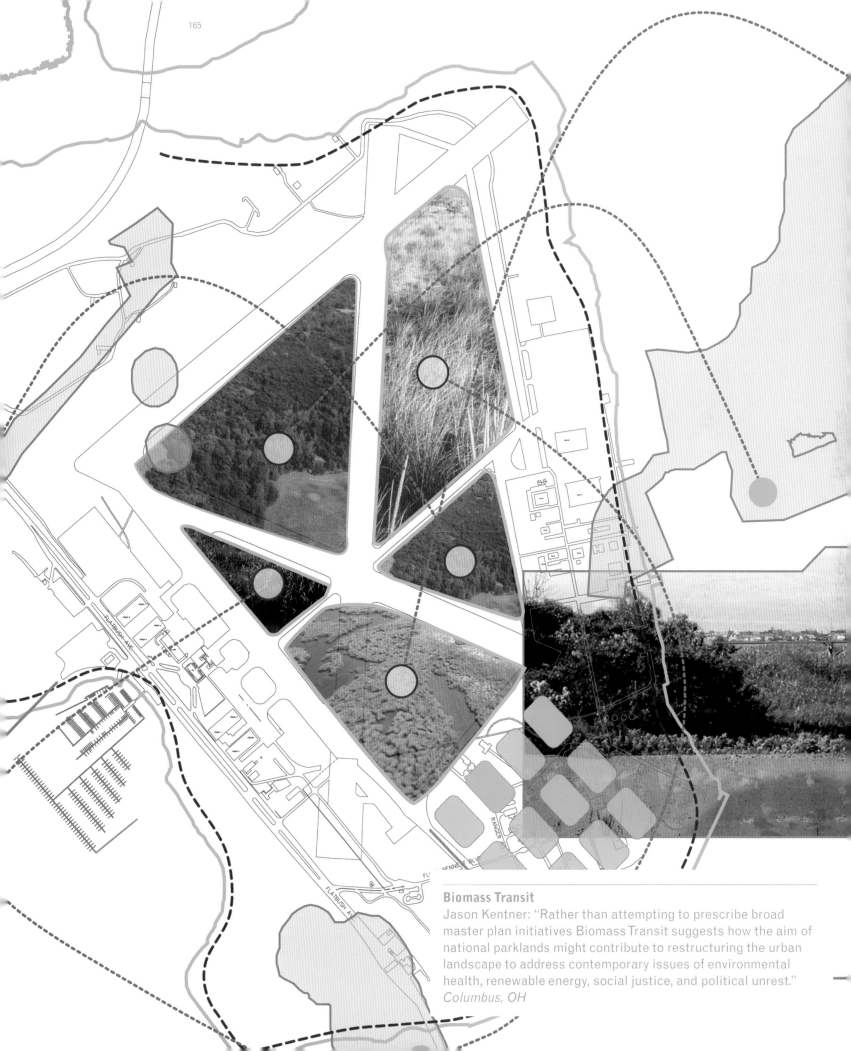

Biomass Transit
Jason Kentner: "Rather than attempting to prescribe broad master plan initiatives Biomass Transit suggests how the aim of national parklands might contribute to restructuring the urban landscape to address contemporary issues of environmental health, renewable energy, social justice, and political unrest."
Columbus, OH

Down in the Dumps

Restoration of Jamaica Bay is key to realizing the vision of a world class harbor estuary, in which a vibrant and sustainable ecosystem coexists with a thriving port. Countless partners and stakeholders collaborate in service of this vision, working hard to improve water quality, revive critical fish and wildlife habitat, and enable the millions of people living within the watershed to access the treasure that is Jamaica Bay.
—Col. John R. Boulé II, Commander, New York District,
　 U.S. Army Corps of Engineers

From Staten Island to JFK International Airport, nearly every square acre of Gateway has been altered by infrastructure. The area's former role as a dumping ground for liquid, solid, and hazardous waste is of particular concern. Gateway is significantly impacted by NYC's wastewater treatment system, a network of sewer mains, settling tanks, and sludge digesters that has dramatically changed local drainage patterns. Every day 320 million gallons of water flow from Jamaica Bay into the Hudson-Raritan Estuary, of which an estimated 60 percent consists of treated sewage from nearby water pollution control plants. Although cleansed of harmful bacteria, this water contains high levels of nitrogen and other organic matter that contribute to algal blooms, threatening the bay's aquatic life. When heavy rains overwhelm the capacities of the city's waste treatment plants, raw sewage is dumped directly into Jamaica Bay from virtually all directions. The problem is exacerbated by the region's impervious highways, airplane runways, and parking lots that surround the park's shores and diminish the wetlands that once provided a natural cleansing of these pollutants.

Treated sewage and untreated stormwater are not the only types of waste that have impacted the park's waters. Salt marshes located on both sides of Old Mill Creek near the Spring Creek Towers (formerly Starrett City) have long served as dumping grounds for human and municipal refuse. Edgemere Landfill, located on Gateway's eastern border, was home to 7,000 drums of hazardous materials that had been buried illegally in the 1970s, leaching unknown quantities of toxins into the groundwater. Landfills like Edgemere have made Jamaica Bay a hotspot for the detrimental effects of these dumping practices, and samples of its waters reveal dangerous levels of a number of toxic chemicals.

The heavy presence of transportation infrastructure around Gateway has added to the load of pollutants entering the harbor's waters. JFK Airport alone has annually discharged millions of gallons of de-icing chemicals into Jamaica Bay, prompting regulatory scrutiny of the airport's practices. In 2010, the U.S. Army Corps of Engineers announced that it would begin cleaning up the tainted areas, preparing them for recreational use. The remediation of these sites and others around the harbor will continue to impact Gateway for decades to come.

In addition to the city's waste, fill and construction debris have long been dumped into the marshes, and most of what is left of the original shoreline has been hardened with bulkheads. Indeed much of Gateway's current topography has been shaped by the demands of urban infrastructure. Its presence along the Staten Island shore, for example, owes a debt to an infrastructural project that never was: the South Shore Parkway envisioned by Robert Moses was abandoned in the 1960s. Much of this property subsequently became state parkland or part of Gateway, a testament to the powerful urban forces that continue to shape the land.

More recently, public and private stakeholders have helped reshape Gateway's fate as a dumping ground, turning old landfills into ecological assets. In 2009, New York City's Department of Environmental Protection completed a $200 million ecological rehabilitation of the Fountain Avenue and Pennsylvania Avenue landfill sites, topping off the former dumps with native grasses, shrubs, and trees to create 400 acres of Northeastern coastal woodland. Landfills like these have begun to be seen holistically as places where damaged natural systems can be nurtured back to life.

Ultimately, Gateway must accommodate a variety of human demands and infrastructural needs within this crucially productive estuarine habitat. Wastewater plants, transportation infrastructure, and other urban impacts that have accumulated on the site over centuries have been a major part of Gateway's history and will continue to shape its landscapes and constitutive ecological systems.

The competition entry H2grOw, by Hayley Eber and Frank Gesualdi, takes a futuristic approach to two of these infrastructural impacts. First, with its floating hydroponic pods, H2grOw launches a uniquely constructive new technology by introducing a bionic interface that would clean up and restore the waters of Jamaica Bay. Second, with their vegetative "skins" the pods would augment Gateway's landscape by adding acres of habitat commensurate with that now being lost. This entry's creative solution for the fragile estuarine environment highlights key issues for balancing the bay's ecological heritage with the infrastructural demands placed on it. The competition entries that follow similarly propose advanced technologies and innovative strategies to mitigate—or accommodate—Gateway's infrastructural legacy.

Jamaica Bay fill
and landfills

MANMADE FILL

MANMADE FILL

FRESH CREEK LANDFILL
(EST 1923, CLOSING DATE UNKNOWN)

HAWTHORNE CREEK LANDFILL
(1938-1989)

FOUNTAIN AVENUE LANDFILL
(1961-1985)

PENNSYLVANIA AVENUE LANDFILL
(1956-1979)

IDLEWILD
CONSTRUCTION WASTE
LANDFILL (1970-1979)

MANMADE FILL

MANMADE FILL

EDGEMERE LANDFILL
(1938-1989)

BARREN ISLAND LANDFILL
(1900-1914)

KNOWN ILLEGAL DUMPING

MANMADE FILL

NATURAL FILL

MANMADE FILL

NATURAL FILL

NATURAL FILL

SHORELINE CHANGE

HISTORIC WETLAND

-76   378

ELEVATION IN METERS

Map: SIDL

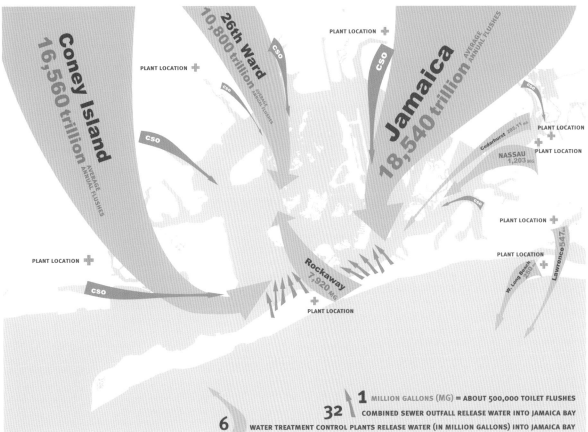

Water treatment plants

Coney Island
16,560 trillion
AVERAGE
ANNUAL FLUSHES

26th Ward
10,800 trillion
AVERAGE
ANNUAL FLUSHES

Jamaica
18,540 trillion
AVERAGE
ANNUAL FLUSHES

PLANT LOCATION

PLANT LOCATION

CSO

CSO

CSO

CSO

CSO

PLANT LOCATION

Cedarhurst 255.11 MG

NASSAU
1,203 MG

PLANT LOCATION

PLANT LOCATION

CSO

PLANT LOCATION

PLANT LOCATION

CSO

Rockaway
7,920 MG

PLANT LOCATION

W. Long Beach 259 MG

Lawrence 547 MG

PLANT LOCATION

1 MILLION GALLONS (MG) = ABOUT 500,000 TOILET FLUSHES

32 COMBINED SEWER OUTFALL RELEASE WATER INTO JAMAICA BAY

6 WATER TREATMENT CONTROL PLANTS RELEASE WATER (IN MILLION GALLONS) INTO JAMAICA BAY

Map: SIDL

ENDNOTE
Epigraph Col. John R. Boulé II, e-mail message to the editors, September 29, 2009.

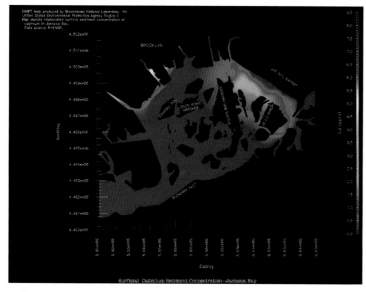

a. Cadmium (toxic metal)

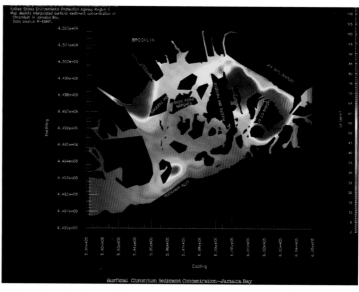

b. Chromium (toxic metal)

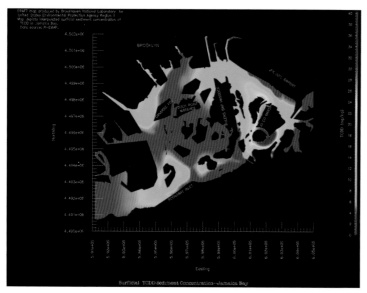

e. Dioxin (organic metalcompound)

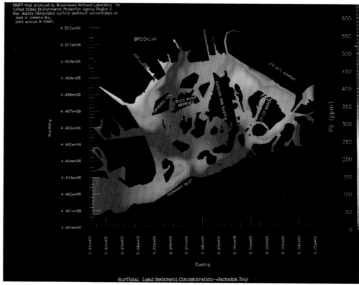

f. Lead (toxic metal)

Metal levels in Jamaica Bay, 1998

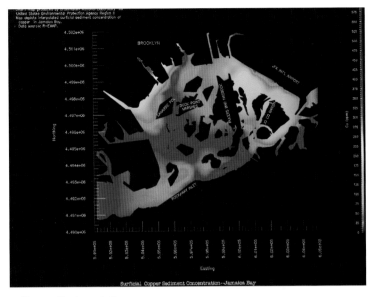

c. Copper (toxic metal)

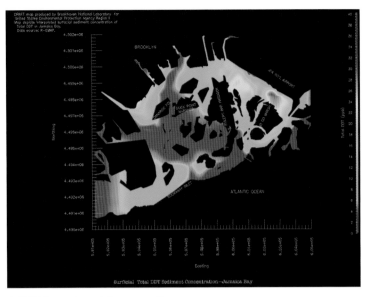

d. DDT (organic metalcompound)

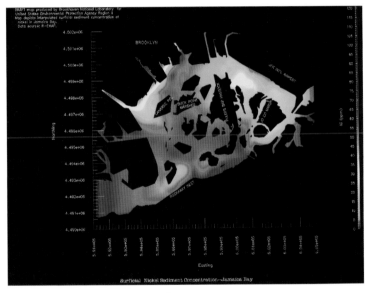

g. Nickel (organic metalcompound)

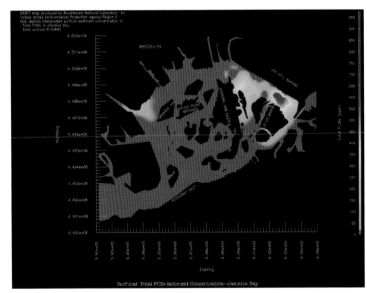

h. PCB (organic metalcompound)

H2grOw
Hayley Eber and Frank Gesualdi (EFGH)
with assistance by David Rhoese

Gateway National Recreation Area is 61 percent water. As a network of landmasses spread across a vast fluid terrain, Gateway has the unique opportunity to engage in and celebrate the potential of this aquatic landscape.

In response to this environment, H2grOw draws on techniques of floater hydroponics, exploring the possibilities of using water as a resource for planting, transportation, energy harnessing, food production, and recreation. A fleet of mobile Hydro Pods, each measuring 75 feet by 140 feet, is deployed across Gateway's network of islands and peninsulas. Each pod is a hydroponic ecosystem grown completely without soil. This new landscape is supported primarily on a pontoon ring structure, beneath which hangs a semi-permeable membrane housing all essential nutrients.

The large array of mobile landscape "particles" allows for unlimited reconfigurations and combinatorial complexity. All robust ecosystems depend on a balance of conditions to maintain a dynamic equilibrium; H2grOw provides a level of responsiveness and adaptability suitable for the natural rhythms of Gateway. The landscape units self-sort and cluster to form diverse combinations of both similar and dissimilar plant species and environments. It is this continuous, slow process of mixing that allows Gateway, as a living ecosystem, to constantly reinvent itself. It is its very instability that allows it to remain vital and thriving. Gateway National Recreation Area is envisioned here as a differential environment that harnesses change and leverages flux.

Floyd Bennett Field, acting as the public and programmatic center of Gateway, is a microcosm of the entire network of islands in the park. The hardscapes of the existing field are flooded, allowing the Hydro Pods to circulate through the site. The newly formed, water-bound landmasses of Floyd Bennett Field support a variety of recreational and cultural programs that are destinations along the vast circuit of ecologies that comprise Gateway. A park-wide visitor's center,

a nature reserve, recreational meadows, sports fields, concert and festival venues, nature trails, and an adopt-a-pod headquarters are among the new programs and amenities of the main park site.

Gateway, as one of the first national urban parks to be re-imagined in the twenty-first century, has an obligation to lead by example in the rethinking of our country's coastlines as global sea levels continue to rise. In this precarious environment, whereby human inhabitation is increasingly threatened by the natural landscape, we need to rethink our relationship to water. In this context, hydroponic landscapes allow for both the stability necessary to foster thriving plant and animal communities, and the level of flexibility crucial to successfully adapt to changing and unstable conditions. It is the blurred boundary between solid ground and fluid terrain that makes this possible.

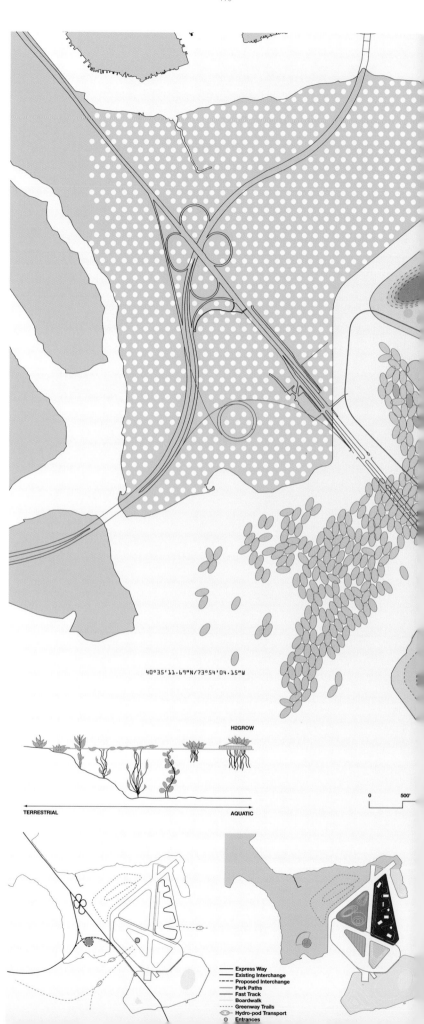

40°35'11.69"N/73°54'04.15"W

H2GROW

TERRESTRIAL   AQUATIC

0   500'

— Express Way
— Existing Interchange
--- Proposed Interchange
— Park Paths
— Fast Track
— Boardwalk
···· Greenway Trails
⬡ Hydro-pod Transport
○ Entrances

40°35'45.91"N/73°52'19.11"W

h2gr0w

Gateway National Recreation Area is comprised of 61% water. As a network of landmasses spread across a vast fluid terrain, GNRA has the unique opportunity to engage in and celebrate the potential of this aquatic landscape.

H2grOw is a conceptual systems design project that draws on techniques of floater hydroponics[1], exploring the possibilities of using water as a resource for planting, transportation, energy harnessing, food production and recreation. A fleet of mobile Hydro Pods, measuring 75' x 140', is deployed across Gateway's network of islands and peninsulas. Each pod is a hydroponic eco-system grown completely without soil. This new landscape is supported primarily on a pontoon ring structure, beneath which hangs a semi permeable membrane housing all essential nutrients.

Sorting Landscape: The principles of data sorting are applied to this large array of mobile landscape "particles", allowing for unlimited reconfigurations and combinatorial complexity. As all robust ecosystems depend on a balance of conditions to maintain a dynamic equilibrium, H2grOw provides a level of responsiveness suitable for the natural rhythms of Gateway. The landscape units self-sort and cluster to form diverse combinations of both similar and dissimilar plant species and environments.

Floyd Bennett Field, acting as the public and programmatic center of Gateway, is a microcosm of the entire network of islands in the park. The hardscapes of the existing field are flooded, allowing the Hydro Pods to circulate through the site. The newly formed water bound landmasses of FBF support a variety of recreational and cultural programs that are destinations along the vast circuit of ecologies that comprise Gateway.

[1]Hydroponics (literally "water working") refers to a method for growing plants in a nutrient solution without soil. The science of hydroponics proves that soil isn't required for plant growth but the elements, minerals and nutrients that soil contains are. A hydroponic solution provides the exact nutrients needed for plants in precisely correct ratios.

Disclaimer: Almost any terrestrial plant will grow with hydroponics, but some will do better than others.

40°35'06.07"N/73°52'35.47"W

3000'

r Aviation Unit	Poker Club	Boardwalks
ps Base	Arts + Play Area	Woodland Trails
tries Launch Area	Children's Exhibits	Cycling
	Petting Zoo	Inline Skating
leadow	Outdoor Films	Motorcycling
	Festivals	Nature Trails
reenhouses	Concerts	Parking-Park Helix
	Political Rallies	Drive-In IMAX
	Visitor Center	
	Adopt-A-Pod Headquarters	
	Donor Recognition Garden	
	Library	
	Deck / Outlook	
ball Fields	Shake Shack	
	Land Sailing	
	Camping	
b	Bird / Butterfly Watching	
	Star-gazing	
	Radio Relaying	
	Canoeing	
	Tilted Sun Deck	
	Beach Volley Ball	
	Wave Pool	
	Fishing Piers	
	Crystal Pools	
	Kavak Piers	

0   2 mi   4 mi   6 mi

H2gr0w
Frank Gesualdi and Hayley Eber
New York, NY

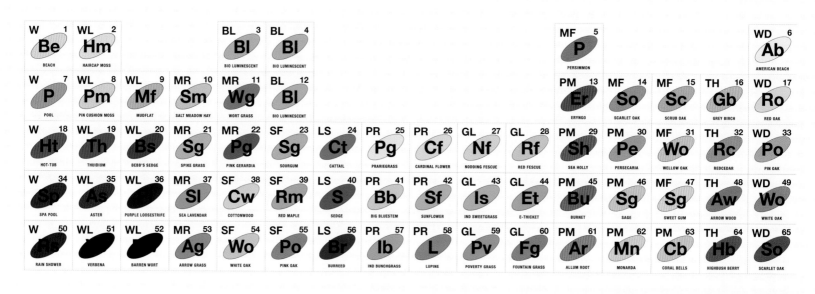

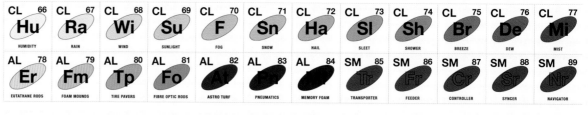

↖ ↑
_____

Details of H2gr0w Frank Gesualdi and
Hayley Eber, _New York, NY_

These entries deploy regenerative technologies and remediation strategies to restore Gateway's physical and environmental fabric.

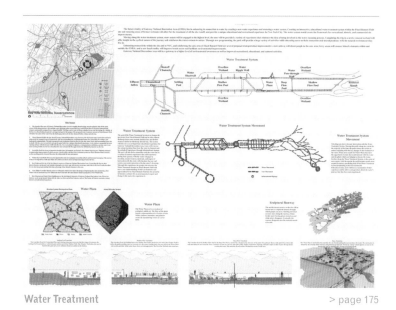

Water Treatment

> page 175

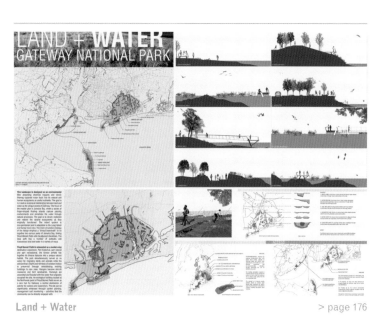

Land + Water

> page 176

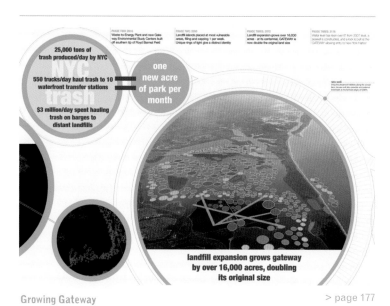

Growing Gateway

> page 177

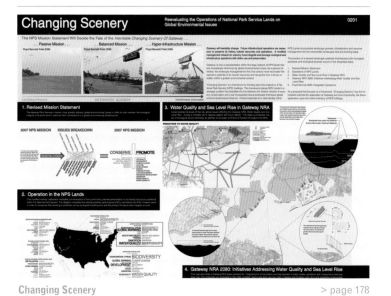

Changing Scenery

> page 178

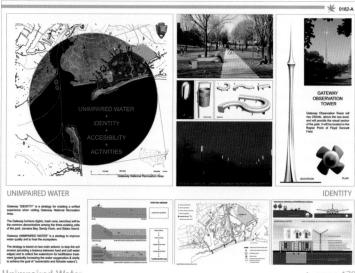

Unimpaired Water

> page 179

Water Treatment System

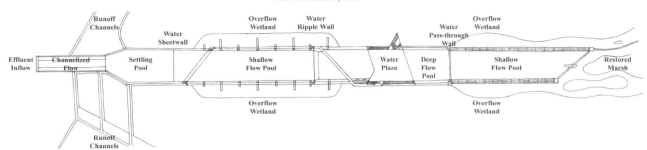

Water Treatment System Movement

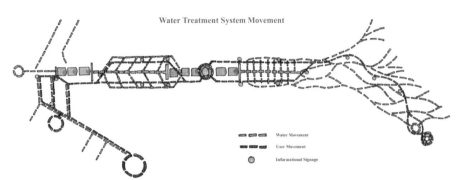

Water Treatment System

The goal of the Water Treatment System is to cleanse the greywater from Floyd Bennett Field and to take effluent discharge from areas around Jamaica Bay and further cleanse it before its discharge into the bay. The system will also serve as an important educational experience for Gateway National Recreation Area. Users will traverse the system learning about how the water is cleansed and its ecological importance through informational signage. The user will also feel a connection with the water due to a variety of sensory experiences they will experience during their journey with the water. Changes in elevation, sound, textures, materials, and degree of interaction with the water will stimulate the user and create a personal connection with the water's cleansing. Through this experience, the people who traverse the Water Treatment System on Floyd Bennett Field will have a new understanding of their environment and appreciation for it. Floyd Bennett Field has the potential to become a catalyst for an environmental respect and change in the users who experience it.

Water Movement

User Movement

Informational Signage

Water Treatment System Movement

This diagram shows the user interaction with the Water Treatment System. Moving linearally along the system for the majority of the time, the path crosses the system at points coinciding with the key changes in the treatment of the water. When users reach the Water Plaza they have the opportunity to slow down and interact with the water and the plants which are helping to cleanse the water. Further along the Water Treatment System, at the point of convergence with the marsh, the path becomes much more organic in nature, paralleling that of the Water Treatment System terminating at the Environmental Education Center, users will have a summation of their experience and be able to ask questions about the water's journey that they have just experienced.

Settling Pool Transition

The transition from the Channelized Flow representing urban greywater into the first stage of treatment, the Settling Pool is marked by a vertical descent and the start of the Window Wall. The Window Wall allows the user to look into the pool and see the sediment which has settled on the bottom.

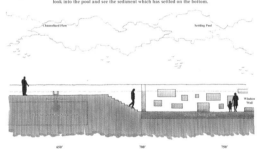

Shallow Flow Transition

The transition from the Settling Pool to the Shallow Flow Pool is marked by the end of the Window Wall as well as the path ascending stairs as it crosses over the water. Looking back, the user will see the Water Sheetwall, a glass partition which water sheets down as it changes pools. The Overflow Wetlands also start here.

Deep Flow Transition

The transition from the Shallow Flow Pool to the Deep Flow Pool is marked by a change in the character of the path. The path goes from a wide path with a short, thin wall seperating the user from the Water Treatment System to a narrow path with a taller, thicker, much more imposing wall and a tight corridor to pass through before crossing the water. The end of the first Overflow Wetland also occurs in this area.

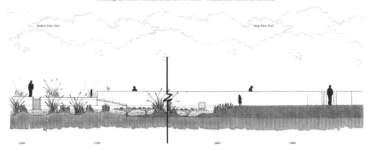

Plaza Transition

The Water Plaza is marked by the ascention of a set of stairs placing the user out above the water. The water plaza is shaped by the crossing of the runways and pedestrian promenade. It features a large wetland planter, as seen in the foreground, and an amphitheatre, as seen in the background.

Water Treatment

Richard Rudnicki: "Creating an interactive, educational water treatment system within the Floyd Bennett Field site and restoring areas of former wetlands will allow for the treatment of all the site runoff, and provide a unique educational and recreational experience for New York City." *Central, SC*

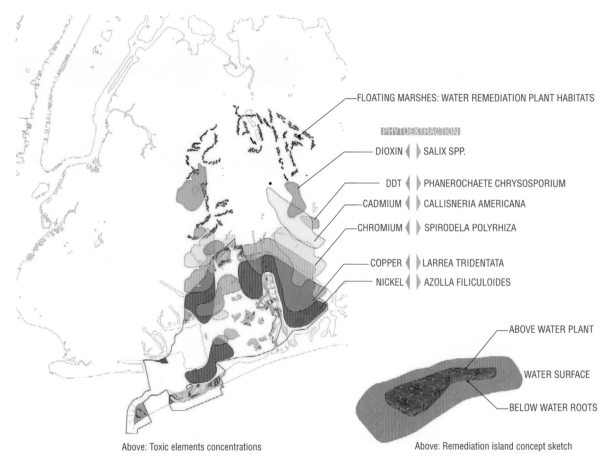

FLOATING MARSHES: WATER REMEDIATION PLANT HABITATS

PHYTOEXTRACTION

DIOXIN ◀ ▶ SALIX SPP.

DDT ◀ ▶ PHANEROCHAETE CHRYSOSPORIUM

CADMIUM ◀ ▶ CALLISNERIA AMERICANA

CHROMIUM ◀ ▶ SPIRODELA POLYRHIZA

COPPER ◀ ▶ LARREA TRIDENTATA

NICKEL ◀ ▶ AZOLLA FILICULOIDES

ABOVE WATER PLANT

WATER SURFACE

BELOW WATER ROOTS

Above: Toxic elements concentrations

Above: Remediation island concept sketch

ANALYSIS

PHYTOREMEDIATION describes de polluting contaminated water with plants which contain, degrade or eliminate metals and various other contaminants. The results are a clean, efficient, inexpensive and non-environmentally disruptive process minimizing the use of additional resources.

Our floating remediation islands & marshes seek to not only restore the balance of mass eroded from gateway but to restore water quality from its current polluted state.

The concept is to develop growth patterns based on various plant species that counteract the specific types of contamination in the polluted locations creating harvestable plant biomass.

↑

Land + Water

82.m: Ayvind Karlsen, Jonathan Lundstrom, Mounir Tawadrous: "Our floating remediation islands and marshes would restore both the balance of mass eroded from Gateway and the water quality from its current polluted state." *Philadelphia, PA*

→

Growing Gateway

office42: "Gateway will be the flagship of sustainable urbanism with microlandfills along its coast, utilizing a new waste-to-energy (WTE) plant, and existing waterfront garbage transfer stations in the five boroughs." *Los Angeles, CA*

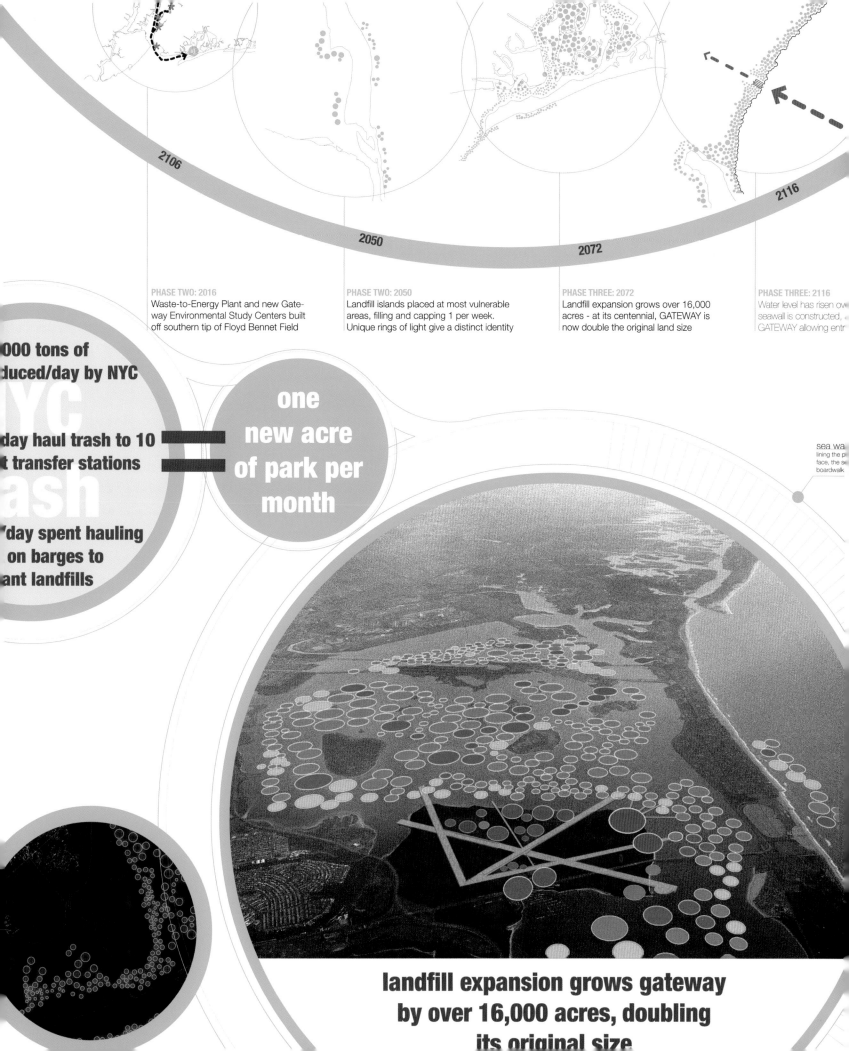

2106

2050

2072

2116

PHASE TWO: 2016
Waste-to-Energy Plant and new Gateway Environmental Study Centers built off southern tip of Floyd Bennet Field

PHASE TWO: 2050
Landfill islands placed at most vulnerable areas, filling and capping 1 per week. Unique rings of light give a distinct identity

PHASE THREE: 2072
Landfill expansion grows over 16,000 acres - at its centennial, GATEWAY is now double the original land size

PHASE THREE: 2116
Water level has risen ov
seawall is constructed,
GATEWAY allowing entr

000 tons of
duced/day by NYC

day haul trash to 10
transfer stations

one new acre of park per month

day spent hauling
on barges to
ant landfills

sea wa
lining the p
face, the s
boardwalk

landfill expansion grows gateway by over 16,000 acres, doubling its original size

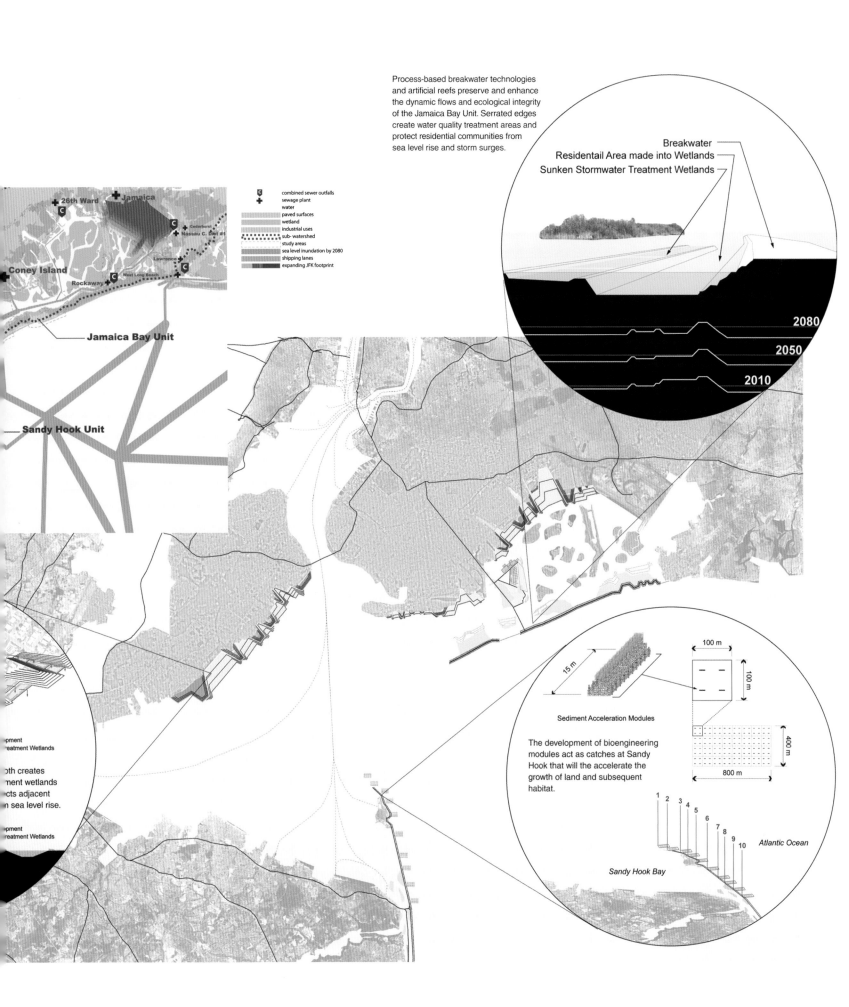

Process-based breakwater technologies and artificial reefs preserve and enhance the dynamic flows and ecological integrity of the Jamaica Bay Unit. Serrated edges create water quality treatment areas and protect residential communities from sea level rise and storm surges.

Breakwater
Residentail Area made into Wetlands
Sunken Stormwater Treatment Wetlands

2080
2050
2010

combined sewer outfalls
sewage plant
water
paved surfaces
wetland
industrial uses
sub- watershed
study areas
sea level inundation by 2080
shipping lanes
expanding JFK footprint

26th Ward   Jamaica
Cedarhurst
Nassau C. Dist #1
Lawrence
Coney Island
Rockaway   West Long Beach

Jamaica Bay Unit

Sandy Hook Unit

...pment
...eatment Wetlands

...oth creates
...ment wetlands
...cts adjacent
...n sea level rise.

...pment
...reatment Wetlands

100 m
15 m
100 m
400 m
800 m

Sediment Acceleration Modules

The development of bioengineering modules act as catches at Sandy Hook that will the accelerate the growth of land and subsequent habitat.

1 2 3 4 5 6 7 8 9 10

Atlantic Ocean

Sandy Hook Bay

stormwater collection and biofiltration stations.

stormwater collection from highway

stormwater collection from JFK airport parking and runways, to avoid direct discharge of oil/gasoline to Jamaica Bay water

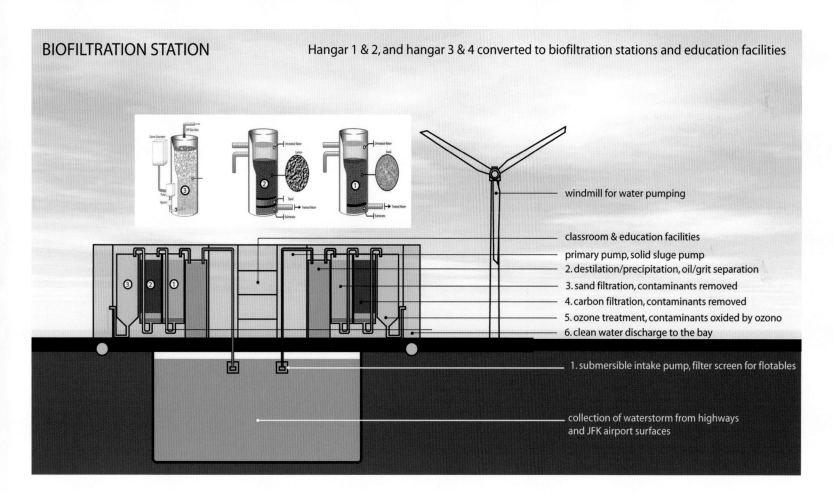

BIOFILTRATION STATION

Hangar 1 & 2, and hangar 3 & 4 converted to biofiltration stations and education facilities

windmill for water pumping

classroom & education facilities

primary pump, solid sluge pump

2. destilation/precipitation, oil/grit separation

3. sand filtration, contaminants removed

4. carbon filtration, contaminants removed

5. ozone treatment, contaminants oxided by ozono

6. clean water discharge to the bay

1. submersible intake pump, filter screen for flotables

collection of waterstorm from highways and JFK airport surfaces

Changing Scenery

SWA Group–LA: "Close analysis of two key issues affecting Gateway NRA, water quality and sea level rise, reveals a complex set of regional causes and future effects. This step summarizes one set of ecological issues that need to be addressed at all scales throughout the NRA." *Los Angeles, CA*

Unimpaired Water

Paula Tomisaki: "The strategy is based on two main actions: to stop the soil erosion (providing a balance between hard and soft edges) and to collect the stormwater for biofiltration treatment (gradually increasing the water oxygenation and clarity) to create 'swimmable and fishable waters.'" *New York, NY*

Past as Prologue

The New York Harbor has always been a zone of meeting and negotiation. There freshwater meets the salty sea, the land slides into the ocean, and the city edges into wilderness. Cultures also have met here—the Lenape and the Dutch, the Dutch and the British, the British and the American, the nativist and the immigrant, the New Yorker and the tourist. When one looks across Jamaica Bay, one is cognizant not only of a moment of time, but of the fabric of time stretching forward and back, as various and unrelenting as the tide.
— Eric W. Sanderson, Founder of the Mannahatta Project,
  Wildlife Conservation Society

Gateway National Recreation Area is comprised of layers of history, from Lenape Indian sites to military outposts to runways that saw record-breaking around-the-world flights. The park's landscape reflects this varied history and, through its nearly 400 existing structures and interpretive exhibits, tells a broader story of America's rise as an international power. Though perhaps among the lesser-known dimensions of the park, these fragments from the past form an essential element of Gateway's identity. If placed within a larger vision for the park as a cultural resource, layers of human history could contribute even more powerfully to Gateway's multifaceted role as a regional destination.

From the time of the region's earliest inhabitants, the grounds of Gateway provided a foundation for the rise of New York as a place of human settlement. Its rivers and streams delivered fresh water; its forests supplied building material and fuel; the mouth of the Hudson River offered a natural harbor; and marshes supported large populations of fish and game. Gateway encompasses the tribal homelands of the Lenape people, who took advantage of these natural riches and were found throughout the park's current borders. Though few tangible links remain to their time in the area, their presence can be traced through shells of the quahog clam—used by the Lenape for making wampum—that can still be found along the Sandy Hook shore.

As European settlers arrived, Gateway's location at the entrance to New York Harbor made it an important navigation point for sailors heading toward Gotham's increasingly lucrative shores, piers, and wharves. Close to forty years after the Dutch consolidated their colonies at the southern tip of Manhattan, the British forcibly took control in 1664, embarking on major trading efforts that set New York City on the rise as a global economic hub. While under British rule, New York supplied rum, lumber, and agri-

cultural products to Europe and quickly expanded its role in international trade. After the American Revolution, a growing class of merchants strategically used the city as a link between three of the most dynamic regions of the nineteenth century: the cotton-producing South, the agricultural Midwest, and England's manufacturing Midlands. These traders prospered by shipping cotton and wheat east while funneling labor, capital, and manufactured and cultural goods west. The opening of the Erie Canal in 1825 assured this position, and by the 1900s New York City had become one of the world's major international ports.

During this period of the city's growth and transformation, new infrastructures were added to secure the harbor and ensure stable conditions for its growing mercantile activities. The first of the era's major navigational efforts was the Sandy Hook Lighthouse, lit in 1764. Built at the request of merchants to facilitate safe passage of goods into port, the structure still stands as the oldest working lighthouse in the United States, and remains a popular point of interest as a designated National Historic Landmark. In addition to the lighthouse, a network of forts was built to defend the harbor from invasion, expanding gradually over a period of more than three centuries. Fort Wadsworth, the oldest of Gateway's three remaining forts, was built at the narrowest point in the mouth of the Hudson River, now in the shadow of the Verrazano-Narrows Bridge. Active from 1650, the fort was the longest continuously serving military site in the U.S. at the time of its closure in 1995, and is now maintained, like the lighthouse, by the National Park Service. To defend against threats posed by increasingly larger ships and longer-range guns, Forts Hancock and Tilden, active respectively since 1776 and 1917, were built beyond the mouth of the harbor. Fort Hamilton, begun in 1825, remains an active military site serving the Army National Guard and the United States Army Reserve.

Along with navigational and military sites, Gateway's landscape features the history of immigration in America. During the late nineteenth century, millions of immigrants began to arrive in New York, compelled for economic, political, religious, and other reasons to seek new opportunity in the United States. With some came contagious diseases, and in an effort to limit their spread, strategically located harbor islands were enlarged and developed to quarantine those who were sick or potential carriers of disease. Two artificial islands within Gateway were part of this network: Swinburne Island received infected individuals directly from Ellis Island, the main immigration processing center, and Hoffman Island received individuals who had come in contact with those who were infected. As immigration declined, the islands were repurposed for national defense, with Swinburne used as a Coast

Lenape trails and
settlements

Map: SIDL

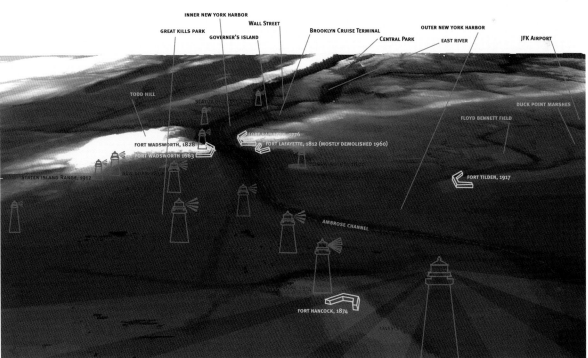

Historic lighthouses and
forts of New York Harbor

Map: SIDL

Guard base and Hoffman serving the U.S. Maritime Service. The NPS now manages both islands as part of the Staten Island unit, maintaining them as sanctuaries for cormorants, egrets, herons, and other birds of the harbor.

Other Gateway landmarks celebrate the region's history of innovation in aviation and New York City's role as a portal between the United States and the world. Occupying the present-day location of Jacob Riis Park, Rockaway Naval Air Station was the point of departure for the NC-4 flying boat on May 8, 1919, when it began the first-ever completed transatlantic flight. Floyd Bennett Field opened in 1931 as New York City's first municipal airport, and it became the landing or takeoff point for many record-breaking feats. Amelia Earhart, Wiley Post, and Douglas "Wrong Way" Corrigan were but a few of the famous aviators who used the airfield. During World War II, after new airplanes were built in Midwestern factories, they were delivered to Floyd Bennett Field, where they were checked, sorted, marked, and then sent off to war. The field's administration building now serves as a visitor center, and the complex includes several original structures along with a historic aircraft restoration project.

Despite Gateway's richly layered human history, to date few of its historical contexts have been fully documented or interpreted for visitors. Moreover, without a larger vision for the park's cultural assets, little funding has been made available for the preservation of historic landscapes and structures. As time continues to take a toll on these fragile links to the past, Gateway's cultural heritage should be considered an integral part of its physical and ecological footprint, and one equally deserving of protection for the benefit of future generations.

The competition entry Landmarks, Seamarks, Ciphers, by a team from Virginia Tech, focuses on the historical identity of Gateway through a series of earthworks and landmarks on the site of Floyd Bennett Field. Much of Floyd Bennett would become open grassland, with elevated mounds and meadows marking the sea level at different times throughout geologic history. Another series of "lines" made from thin earthwork channels and paths would be created in the grassland, with the length of each line representing the elevation of other parks and monuments within the national park system. Historic, current, and emerging site conditions are layered on top of one another in this proposal, revealing the strands of natural and human history that together form the place we know as Gateway today.

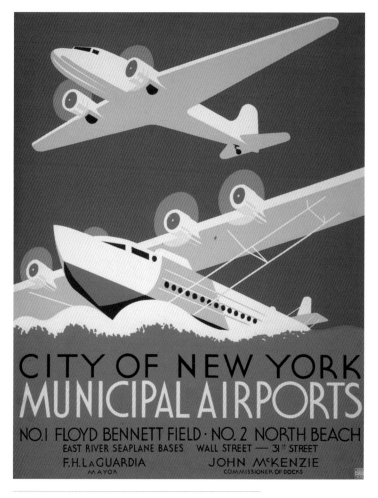

Works Progress Administration Poster

ENDNOTES
Epigraph Eric W. Sanderson, interview with the editors, February 10, 2009.

Floyd Bennett Field Control Tower, 1943

Lighthouse at Fort Hancock, Sandy Hook, NJ, 1937

Battery at Fort Wadsworth, Fort Tilden, NY, 1946

Landmarks, Seamarks, Ciphers

Laurel McSherry, Terry Surjan, and Rob Holmes (Virginia Polytechnic)

In the physical, topological fact, there are very likely all the prejudices about what a landscape is supposed to be; there is bias from literature, from the building-up of conventional images, from a rehearsing of names, compounding fragments of data.
—Paul Vanderbilt

Our work, a field guide to the landscapes of Gateway, provides a series of physical markers and tangible connections to vanished, inaccessible, and emerging site conditions. Three types of markings, integrated into the visitor experience, guide the revival of local and regional landscape knowledge and act as organizing elements within and across the site: landmarks, seamarks, and ciphers.

Landmarks

Unlike other national parks that celebrate nature in raw settings, Gateway is a landscape of accumulation—topographically, spatially, and culturally. Juxtaposing the remote with the familiar, the proposed landmark field brings the breadth of the nation's park system within reach of a local urban public, inviting visitors to explore the native and the manufactured—on the ground and in their imagination. In our proposal, twenty paths of differing lengths stretch eastward from Floyd Bennett Field's historic runway and spatially index elevations above sea level of other iconic parks, monuments, preserves, and memorials within and across the American landscape. Stone cairns mark the terminus of each path and situate landscape referents relative to each other and the latitude/longitude of Lower New York Bay (for example, Old Faithful Geyser in Yellowstone National Park, Wyoming, elevation 130 feet). Shade trees planted nearby make variations in path lengths discernable from a distance to the park visitor.

Seamarks

Within Gateway, existing seamarks—land-based or floating navigational structures used by mariners—present innumerable variations on a single theme, including cans, lights, bells, buoys, caissons, and beacons. The proposed seamark field continues this critical form of site inscription.

Combining the cardinal (generic) with the circumstantial (idiosyncratic), sixty-two seamarks "anchor" Floyd Bennett Field from the Belt Parkway to the Rockaway Inlet, and guide visitors as they wander through sites in various stages of ecological succession. An intentionally subtle feature in the landscape, the seamark field traces the former route of the Irish Channel, which vanished during the construction of Floyd Bennett Field and Flatbush Avenue. Defined by elevations identical, though inverted, to those of the former channel, this new midden (a mounded landform succeeding a pre-Columbian dump) serves as index of the site's historic bathymetry. It also creates a datum within and beyond the site, and a surrogate for the experience of an otherwise inaccessible historic landscape form. Piled incrementally from Ambrose Channel dredge, the proposed midden combines the temporal and topographic fullness suggested by its cultural namesake. Visitors arriving from Flatbush Avenue would pass though portions of this prehistoric dumping ground, while motorists along the Belt Parkway would see it on the horizon before entering Gateway.

Ciphers

Typically ciphers are used to obscure the familiar. Our third type of marking reverses this relationship, making the inaccessible less so. Organized in panels of commemorative postage stamps (ciphers) honoring a place or event, the proposed series would illustrate (front) and describe (back) the influence of select regional conditions on unit-level events, for example geology, hydrology, vegetation, wildlife, history, ecology, and architecture. Combining evocative imagery with narrative text, these commemorative stamps enable a wider reading of natural and cultural resources across Gateway and precipitate their appreciation, conservation, restoration, and use. Postal services throughout the world issue commemoratives, often holding first-day-of-issue ceremonies at locations connected with their subjects. The first U.S. commemoratives, issued in conjunction with Chicago's Columbian Exposition (1893), were followed by those marking the Louisiana Purchase Exposition (1904), the New York World's Fair (1939), and the creation of Everglades National Park (1947). As sites of public tribute and civic pride, Gateway's commemorative ciphers would launch with a first-day-of-issue ceremony at the Ryan Visitor Center and conclude with a combined Gateway/Yellowstone commemoration on the common anniversary of their founding.

ENDNOTES
Epigraph Paul Vanderbilt, *Between the Landscape and Its Other* (Baltimore, MD: The Johns Hopkins University Press, 1993), 1.

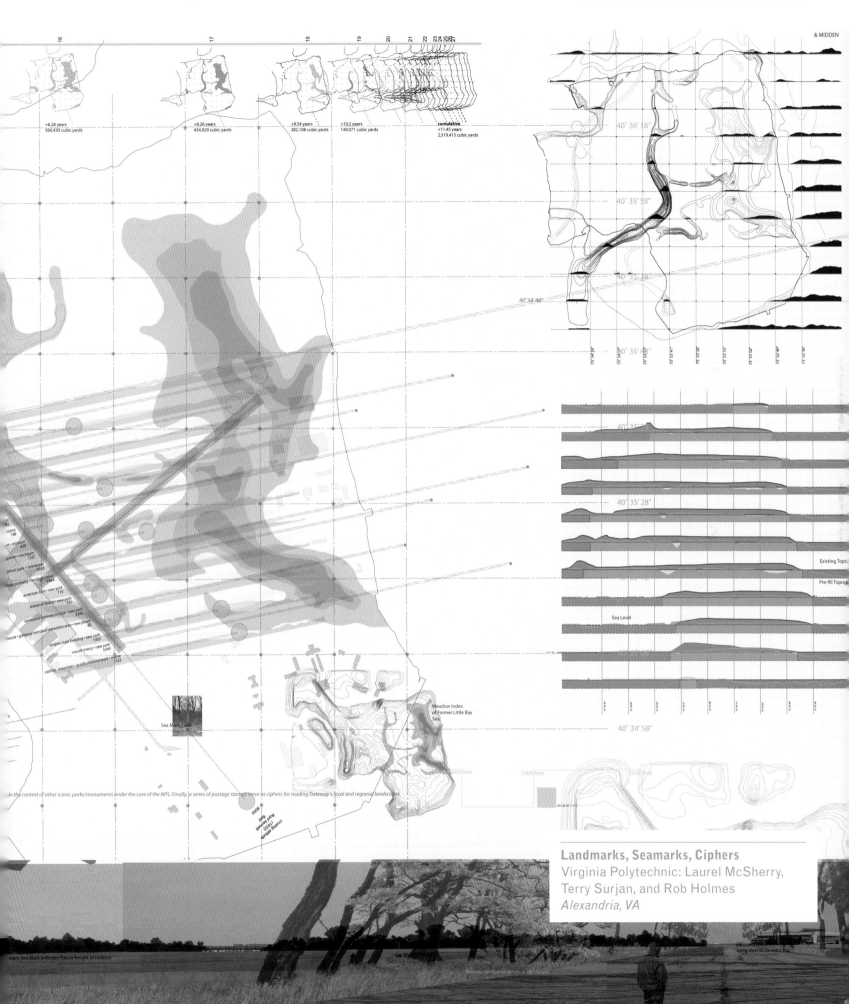

Landmarks, Seamarks, Ciphers
Virginia Polytechnic: Laurel McSherry,
Terry Surjan, and Rob Holmes
Alexandria, VA

"at the maps cuts up, the story runs across."

Michel de Certeau, *The Practice of Everyday Life*

WATERS

of Gateway. This issue describes some of the ways water presents itself within the units of Gateway and the influence of hydrology on topography, wildlife and settlement patterns. This 12-stamp plate, covering portions of Brooklyn, Queens, Staten Island and Sandy Hook, illustrates the contribution of drainage patterns to the look, shape, and ecology of a regional landscape.

BOUNDARIES

of Gateway. This issue describes the different ways the landscapes of Gateway are bounded (natural, cultural, political). This 12-stamp plate, covering portions of Brooklyn, Queens, Staten Island and Sandy Hook, illustrates the contribution of measuring conventions to the look, shape, and ecology of the regional landscape.

HABIT

describes the
and neighborin
plate, covering
Island and Sandy
natural and c

BARROWS / MIDDENS

Gateway National Recreation Area contains the channel of a substantial international harbor port, used since 1626. It is a landscape subjected to both natural and anthropogenic fill and dredging. This 12-stamp plate, covering portions of Brooklyn, Queens, Staten Island and Sandy Hook illustrates contribution of topography to the look, shape, and ecology of a regional landscape.

SOILS

Gateway National Recreation Area is comprised of beaches, wetlands, and the channel of a substantial international harbor port, used since 1626. The of Gateway have been subject both to natural and anthropogenic fill and dredging. This 12-stamp plate, covering portions of Brooklyn, Queens, Staten Island and Sandy Hook, illustrates contribution of soils to the look, shape, and ecology of a regional landscape.

Great Kills Park
Frederick Douglass Memorial Pa

Buildings to Remain
Foundations to Reuse

Historic (1932) Runway &
Tree Landmarks

the landscapes of Gateway, provides tangible connections to pre-existing, ongoing, and emerging site conditions. Three types of markings are suggested to guide the revival of local and regional landscape knowledge: landmarks, seamarks and ciphers. Located every 1000 feet along cardinal directions, sixty-two seamark

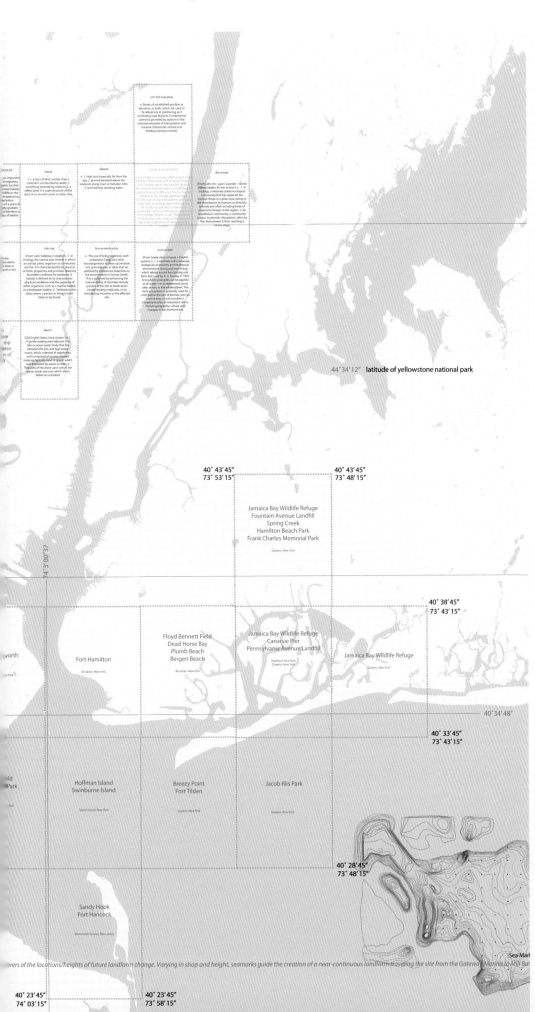

Landmarks, Seamarks, Ciphers
Virginia Polytechnic: Laurel McSherry,
Terry Surjan, and Rob Holmes
Alexandria, VA

These entries looked to the past and to Gateway's historic relics for clues to its future.

Broken Lands

> page 189

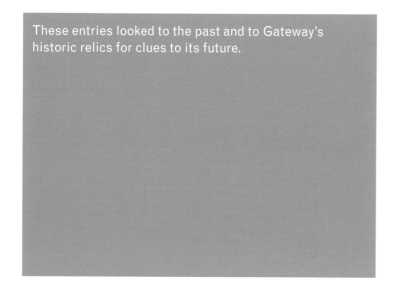

Gateway: A Sustainable Idea Landscape

> page 190

Edge Effects

> page 191

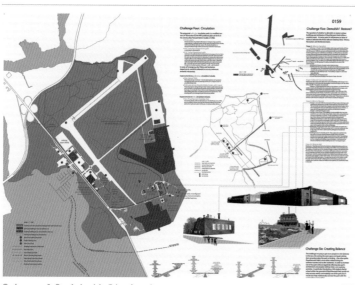

Constructed Ecosystems

> page 192

Reemergence

> page 193

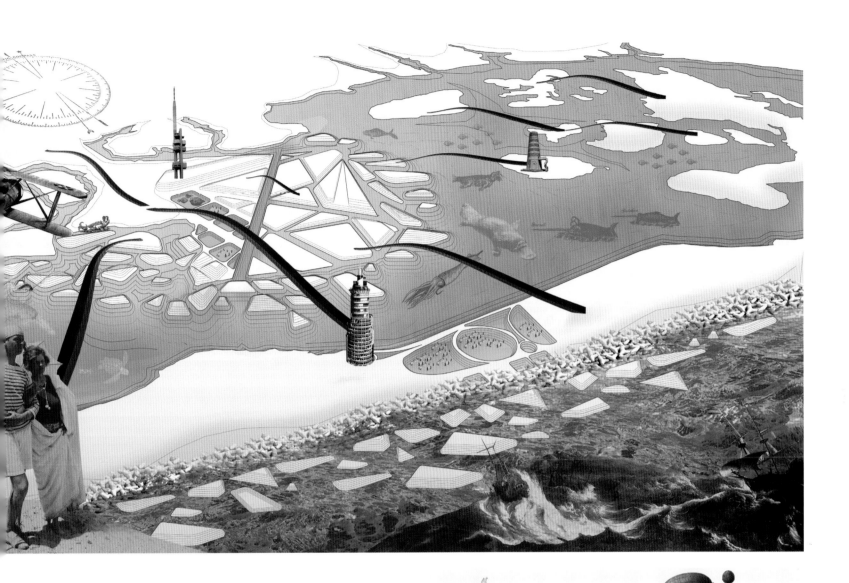

Broken Lands
Claire Agre, Liat Margolis, Darlene Montgomery: "Once upon
a time, the sea levels rose so high that the people of coastal
cities had to adopt an amphibious culture, living with and in
water. To protect their land, they created inland pools and barrier
islands by cut and fill so that tidal energy was dissipated. They
called these islands 'avant-garde': a front line of storm defense."
Somerville, MA

Challenge Four: Circulation

The proposed vehicular circulation path is a modified version of "Alternative D", the NPS preferred plan set forth in the Jamaica Bay Transportation Studies of 2006.

- **Visitor paths**
  Identical to those described in Alternative D. However they would be augmented by a weekend shuttle service within the park for those arriving by ferry and without vehicular access. The shuttle should be an environmentally friendly vehicle powered by biodiesel or natural gas.
- **NYC Sanitation Department path**
  As described in Alternative D
- **NYC Police Department path**
  Contrary to the path described in Alternative D, we propose that the Police continue to use the Southernmost entrance to the park. We recommend this path over the one set forth in Alternative D because this path has less negative effects on the sensitive grassland management area of the park and would interfere less with hikers, bikers and most visitors. Reducing visible municipal traffic will make the experience for visitors more 'park like'. As for the concerns that the police currently drive too quickly through the Southern portion of the park.... well..... call the police!

In cases of emergency, the Police and Sanitation departments would be allowed to use any entrances and exits neccessary.

Improvements to pedestrian circulation include:
- **New Nature Trails**
  Removing runways 12-30 and 1-19 and replacing them with grassland management areas and new plantings will result in a large increase in accessible hiking trails.
- **Pathways connecting the Visitor Center with nature**
  Previously, anyone visiting the Ryan Visitor Center would need to then get back into their car and drive to the portion of the park they wanted to see. By simply connecting the Visitor Center to the hiking trails, more people will be able to leave their cars behind and travel the park by foot. Thus reducing traffic and making the park feel more accessible.

Improvements to bike circulation include:
- **New Floyd Bennett Field Bike Trail**
  Connecting directly with the Belt Parkway in the Northeast corner of the park (a lockable entrance) and with the existing Flatbush Avenue bike path in the Southwest corner of the park. Its scenery will be diverse.

Challenge Five: Demolish? Rest

The question of whether to demolish or restore various buildings and attributes of Floyd Bennett Field will be a sensitive topic. At some point, it will become an issue of balance between the three relevant Gateway ideas: His Recreation and the Environment.

Stage 1: What to Demolish
- Runways 1-19 and 12-30: We propose removing a good portion of the runways and replacing them with new grassland management, natural planti and hiking areas. While the runways are historically relevant and interesting, t existence poses long term maintenance challenges. In Africa, there are desert runways that provide great bird habitats, but here in Brooklyn, the deserted a generally inaccessible runways are one of the main reasons why visitors feel a sense of abandonment and decay. Those runways currently open to car traffi safety issues because their width and length invites speeding which results in several accidents a year. In order to accommodate Ranger Pete McCarthy's ann fly-in of historic aircraft, Runway 6-24 will be maintained in its current FAA approved state.
- Building 85: Extreme disrepair and no historical value
- Building 98: No historical value. Located in the middle of a new grass management area. The maintenance facility that uses this building c moved to the existing maintenance facility near the HARP hangar.
- Building 272: No historical value. This building is subject to extreme high utility bills.
- Building 275: No historical value
- Several abandoned buildings new Reserve Center: No value

Stage I Sidenote: Construction debris
What to do with construction debris from removed buildings and runways? F park dedicated to environmental stewardship, it would be wrong to cart this c off to a landfill. Two options are proposed:
- Option A: Since Floyd Bennett Field is in fact sitting on an island of fill rubble, it seems only fitting that the construction debris be used to create a n topography for a portion of the new grassland management areas.
- Option B: (to be debated by environmentalists). Given that one of th issues contributing to the demise of wetlands in Jamaica Bay is the existence 'borrow pits' where sand was dredged to create JFK and channels, can the clea concrete runway debris be used to fill some of these pits? These borrow pits a sediment sinks and are causing the marsh islands to erode and disappear.

Stage II: What to Restore
- Hangars 1,2,3 and 4: With the renovation of these hangars into large greenhouses, preservation and the environment can work hand in ha The conversion will require few changes to the landmarked hangars than changing the roofs and replacing the large glass doors/window large steel and glass greenhouse would be constructed in between hangars 1 and 2 and Hangars 3 and 4.
- The Ryan Visitor Center: This building is in poor condition but has gre potential to act as the facility that provides visitors with a comprehen overview of Gateway as a whole. As with all buildings at Gateway, th Ryan Visitor Center should be renovated with the environmental challenges of the future in mind. For example, the building is overstr tured and could easily accommodate a green roof which would redu heating and cooling costs and reduce storm runoff. The three ample could accommodate offices for any enviorment organization that space and has goals similar to those of Gateway.
- Building 86: This old steam boiler plant could be easily renovated in home for the public "Gateway Rowing Club". It is located sufficiently to the water and visitors could reuse the parking lot of demolished building 272.
- Buildings 62, 72, 74, 129, 130, and 131: This compound would form th new home of the Ross Global Academy Charter School, or another similarly environment and culture focused charter school. The buildi consist of two historically significant structures in dire condition (62/ and four insignificant buildings in good condition. It will be up to the school to determine whether buildings 62 and 72 are beyond repair.

Stage III: What to Add
Restaurants: Floyd Bennett Field will not become a family destination until it provide the two things necessary for traveling with children: food and bathro The addition of a food court in the Aviation complex is a step in the right dire however more needs to be done. We propose adding two restaurant concess aires at Floyd Bennett Field. The first would be located at the Marina and wou provide easy meals for people arriving by ferry, visiting the greenhouses, com nity garden, golf complex or Ryan Visitor Center. The second concessionaire w be located in the HARP parking lot. The ideal food service for this location wo be similar to the "Shake Shack" in Madison Park in Manhattan; quick food with available picnic tables for visitors to HARP, the fishing beach, the model plane or the trails.

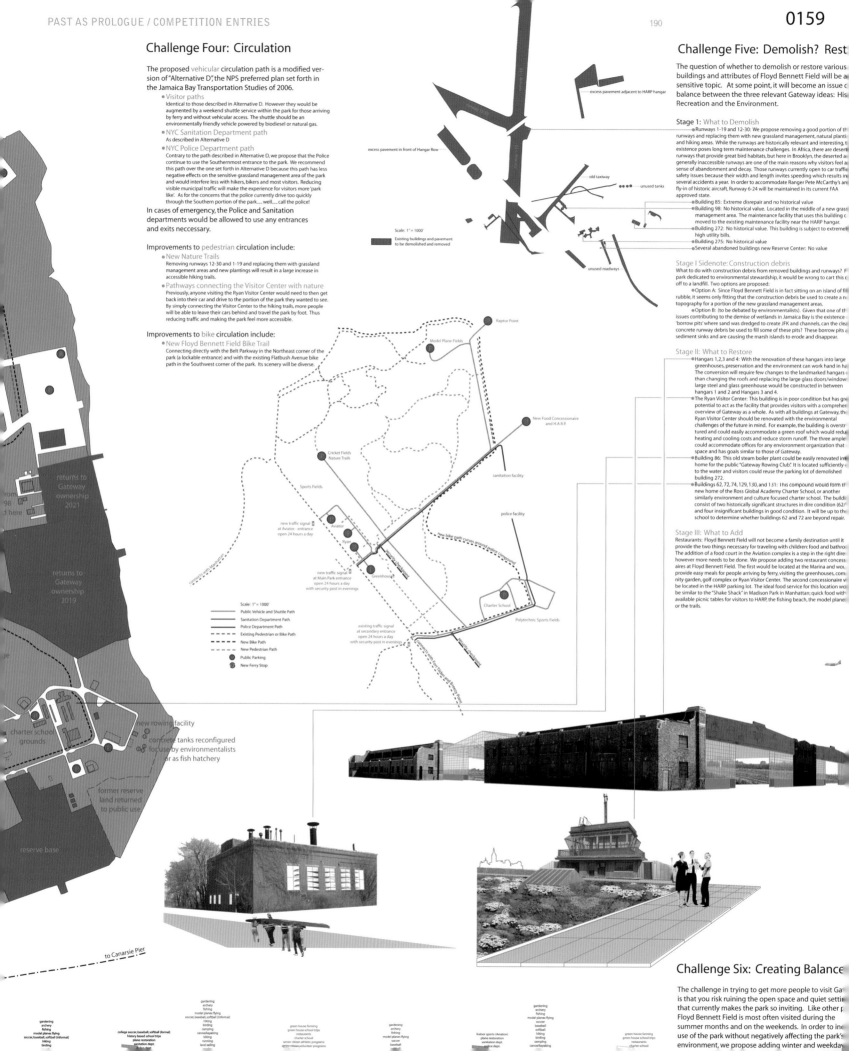

Map labels:
- excess pavement adjacent to HARP hangar
- excess pavement in front of Hangar Row
- old taxiway
- unused tanks
- unused roadways
- Existing buildings and pavement to be demolished and removed
- Scale: 1" = 1000'
- Raptor Point
- Model Plane Fields
- New Food Concessionaire and H.A.R.P.
- Cricket Fields Nature Trails
- sanitation facility
- Sports Fields
- police facility
- new bike path curves around police compound
- new traffic signal at Aviator - entrance open 24 hours a day
- Aviator
- Ryan
- new traffic signal at Main Park entrance open 24 hours a day with security post in evenings
- Greenhouse
- Charter School
- Polytechnic Sports Fields
- existing traffic signal at secondary entrance open 24 hours a day with security post in evenings
- connects with Manhattan
- connects with Tilden and Breezy Point
- connects with Manhattan
- returns to Gateway ownership 2021
- returns to Gateway ownership 2019
- charter school grounds
- new rowing facility
- concrete tanks reconfigured focus by environmentalists or as fish hatchery
- former reserve land returned to public use
- reserve base
- to Canarsie Pier

Legend:
- Scale: 1" = 1000'
- Public Vehicle and Shuttle Path
- Sanitation Department Path
- Police Department Path
- Existing Pedestrian or Bike Path
- New Bike Path
- New Pedestrian Path
- Public Parking
- New Ferry Stop

Challenge Six: Creating Balance

The challenge in trying to get more people to visit Gat is that you risk ruining the open space and quiet setti that currently makes the park so inviting. Like other p Floyd Bennett Field is most often visited during the summer months and on the weekends. In order to inc use of the park without negatively affecting the park's environment, we propose adding winter and weekda

Bottom activity lists:
- gardening / archery / fishing / model planes flying / soccer, baseball, softball (informal) / hiking / birding / camping / plane restoration / running / land sailing
- green house farming / green house school trips / restaurants / charter school / senior citizen athletic programs / senior citizen volunteer programs
- gardening / archery / fishing / model planes flying / soccer / baseball / softball / hiking / birding / camping / canoe/kayaking
- Indoor sports (Aviation) / plane restoration / sanitation dept. / police dept.
- green house farming / green house school trips / restaurants / charter school
- college soccer, baseball, softball (formal) / history based school trips / sanitation dept.
- gardening / archery / fishing / model planes flying / soccer / baseball / softball / hiking / birding / camping / canoe/kayaking

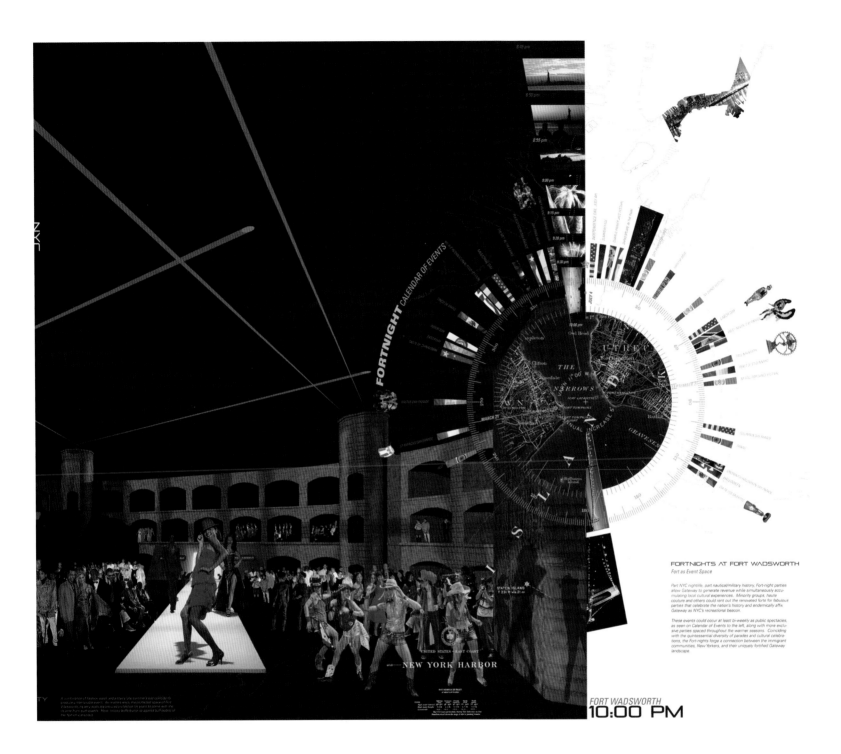

FORTNIGHTS AT FORT WADSWORTH
Fort as Event Space

Part NYC nightlife, part nautical/military history, Fort-night parties allow Gateway to generate revenue while simultaneously accumulating local cultural experiences. Minority groups, haute couture and others could rent out the renovated forts for fabulous parties that celebrate the nation's history and endemically affix Gateway as NYC's recreational beacon.

These events could occur at least bi-weekly as public spectacles, as seen on Calendar of Events to the left, along with more exclusive parties spaced throughout the warmer seasons. Coinciding with the quintessential diversity of parades and cultural celebrations, the Fort-nights forge a connection between the immigrant communities, New Yorkers, and their uniquely fortified Gateway landscape.

FORT WADSWORTH
10:00 PM

Gateway: A Sustainable Idea Landscape
Leander Grayson Krueger: "Gateway will retrofit existing buildings with green technologies, construct large public greenhouses to grow plants and produce, set aside land for organic farming, reduce impervious surfaces and therefore stormwater runoff, remove unwanted buildings, and provide more ecology-based education programs." *Stamford, CT*

Edge Effects
Case Brown: "To celebrate the larger Gateway experience, entryways are at each major fort. At Fort Wadsworth, major holiday festivities and party cruises terminating at the fort fund its renovation." *Clyde, NC*

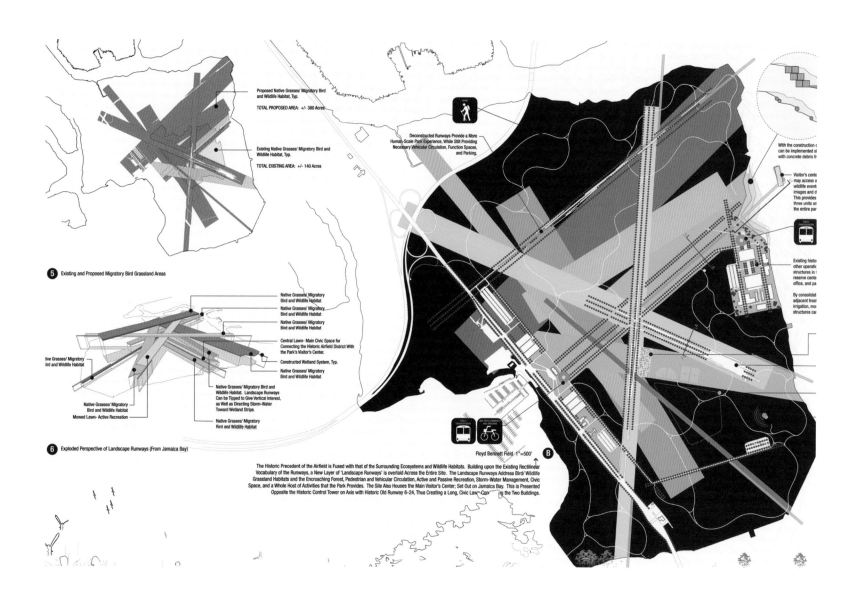

Proposed Native Grasses/ Migratory Bird
and Wildlife Habitat, Typ.

TOTAL PROPOSED AREA: +/- 380 Acres

Existing Native Grasses/ Migratory Bird and
Wildlife Habitat, Typ.

TOTAL EXISTING AREA: +/- 140 Acres

Deconstructed Runways Provide a More
Human-Scale Park Experience, While Still Providing
Necessary Vehicular Circulation, Function Spaces,
and Parking.

5 Existing and Proposed Migratory Bird Grassland Areas

Native Grasses/ Migratory
Bird and Wildlife Habitat

Native Grasses/ Migratory
Bird and Wildlife Habitat

Native Grasses/ Migratory
Bird and Wildlife Habitat

Central Lawn- Main Civic Space for
Connecting the Historic Airfield District With
the Park's Visitor's Center.

Constructed Wetland System, Typ.

Native Grasses/ Migratory
Bird and Wildlife Habitat

Native Grasses/ Migratory Bird and
Wildlife Habitat. Landscape Runways
Can be Tipped to Give Vertical Interest,
as Well as Directing Storm-Water
Toward Wetland Strips.

Native Grasses/ Migratory
Bird and Wildlife Habitat

ive Grasses/ Migratory
ird and Wildlife Habitat

Native Grasses/ Migratory
Bird and Wildlife Habitat

Mowed Lawn- Active Recreation

6 Exploded Perspective of Landscape Runways (From Jamaica Bay)

The Historic Precedent of the Airfield is Fused with that of the Surrounding Ecosystems and Wildlife Habitats. Building upon the Existing Rectilinear
Vocabulary of the Runways, a New Layer of 'Landscape Runways' is overlaid Across the Entire Site. The Landscape Runways Address Bird/ Wildlife
Grassland Habitats and the Encroaching Forest, Pedestrian and Vehicular Circulation, Active and Passive Recreation, Storm-Water Management, Civic
Space, and a Whole Host of Activities that the Park Provides. The Site Also Houses the Main Visitor's Center; Set Out on Jamaica Bay. This is Presented
Opposite the Historic Control Tower on Axis with Historic Old Runway 6-24, Thus Creating a Long, Civic Lawn Con... ng the Two Buildings.

Floyd Bennett Field 1"=500'   **B**

With the construction o
can be implemented si
with concrete debris fr

Visitor's cente
may access a
wildlife event
images and d
This provides
three units an
the entire par

Existing histo
other operatio
structures in t
reserve cente
office, and pa

By consolidat
adjacent trea
irrigation, mo
structures ca

Constructed Ecosystems
skye design studio, ltd.: "The history of the airfield is fused
with that of the surrounding ecosystems and wildlife habitats.
Building upon the runways' existing rectilinear vocabulary,
a new layer of 'landscape runways' is overlaid across the entire
site." *Washington, DC*

garland infrastructure

Reemergence
Civitas Inc.: "A garland infrastructure of dykes and jetties enables the emergence of land and new ecologies along the coastal edges. The detained sediment from urban runoff builds new islands with biofiltration gardens and habitats. Through tidal fluctuations, cleansed freshwater feeds and purifies the bay's ecology." *Denver, CO*

REFLECTIONS

THE URBAN PARK AS CULTURAL CATALYST
ROLF DIAMANT

In the fall of 1971, as I began my third year of college and started paying attention to career prospects, I happened to read a profile of the director of the National Park Service (NPS) at the time, George Hartzog. Written by John McPhee for *The New Yorker*, the profile was a revelation.[1] The story appealed to my youthful idealism as well as my love of the outdoors. The Hartzog that McPhee described was a man of action, a man who represented smart, effective, and personable government. He emerged from the profile larger than life—ranger and reformer rolled into one. At one moment he was directing operations in Yosemite, the next he was perched precariously in a helicopter over New York Harbor, sizing up what was to be one of the greatest urban parks in the world. As Hartzog would recall in an interview years later, "We felt that the Park Service had to be relevant to an urban environment…if we were to survive as an institution and as a resource for America."[2]

Here was a renaissance man, capable of bridging the two seemingly estranged worlds I found most appealing: nature and great cities. Whether it was Hartzog himself or the deft storytelling of McPhee, I was hooked.

The early 1970s was a time of widespread urban malaise. In response to racial unrest, poverty, and growing concern for municipal insolvencies and crumbling infrastructure, restoring the overall health of America's cities was cautiously being elevated to the status of national priority. Hartzog would make sure the NPS was not left out of the picture. In this context, the idea of using national assets to assist cities, including the national park system, began to gain traction in Congress. By the end of the 1970s, new national recreation areas were being established in and around Los Angeles, Atlanta, and Cleveland, in addition to Gateway in New York and New Jersey and Golden Gate, in the San Francisco Bay Area.

This was not the first time, nor the last, that the NPS would be deployed by Congress and the executive branch to respond to what was broadly perceived as a national crisis. In the 1930s Franklin D. Roosevelt tasked the fledgling agency—until then, largely eclipsed in size, appropriations, and influence by its longtime rival and predecessor, the U.S. Forest

George Hartzog, Director of the National Park Service
(1964–1972)

Tent on Glacier Bay, Glacier Bay National Park, AK

Marin County Headlands, Marin County, CA

President Franklin Delano Roosevelt with the Civilian Conservation
Corps at Shenandoah National Park, VA

Service—with assuming a key managerial role during the Great Depression. The Roosevelt administration directed the NPS to administer hundreds of Civilian Conservation Corps (CCC) camps to provide work for thousands of unemployed men. In addition to making extensive improvements to our national parks, the CCC under NPS supervision built state, county, and metropolitan parks, including most of the nation's state park system—nearly seven hundred areas. They also developed recreation demonstration areas in twenty-four states, most of which were to become regional or state parks.[3]

It can be said that the New Deal created the national park system as it is known today. Prior to Roosevelt's election in 1932, work on national parks was largely concentrated west of the Mississippi River. New parks were established in the West and the South; and throughout the East a host of federally owned historic sites, battlefields, and monuments were consolidated under NPS administration. The inclusion of federal parks and monuments in and around Washington, DC, gave the NPS its first significant urban footprint. A foundation for the nation's future network of urban, recreational national parks was also being built. The NPS was directed to complete the first of a number of national recreation studies and plans, taking into account the needs of American urbanites who lacked access to existing national parks.

In the post–World War II years additional recreation studies assessed the potential for adding new national parks near the nation's growing population centers. By the beginning of the 1960s, Congress was ready to expand the system with a generation of new seashores and lakeshores, including Cape Cod, Fire Island, Indiana Dunes, and Point Reyes, each with beaches within driving distance of major cities like Boston, New York, Chicago, and San Francisco. These coastal landscapes were still largely undeveloped, though they were on the edges of rapidly expanding metropolitan areas. Adding them to the national park system represented an evolutionary stage in national park–making and the realization of a broader suite of values: not only the preservation of the nation's significant scenery and natural and cultural heritage, but also the preservation of traditional landscape and community character, as well as the potential for large-scale public use and regional recreation.

Three years after reading the Hartzog profile, while in graduate school in 1974, I landed a job as a planner and landscape architect with the NPS. As luck would have it, my first assignment was the start-up of one of the urban parks that Hartzog championed: Golden Gate National Recreation Area. The politics behind the establishment of Golden Gate in the San Francisco Bay Area and its companion site, Gateway National Recreation Area in New York City, were complex, to say the least. In fact, I had written my master's thesis on the subject. I thought this was the most exciting work I could ever find.

I was surprised to find in those early days at Golden Gate that there appeared to exist among park staff a subtle geographic pecking order. Park employees who were working up in the Olema Valley, adjacent to Point Reyes National Seashore, seemed to feel they were in a more traditional national park environment than their colleagues working further to the south, closer to San Francisco. The people assigned to the former military lands of the Marin Headlands believed they were still in the "backcountry" compared to their colleagues across the Golden Gate Bridge in San Francisco. Those working at Fort Mason, at park headquarters, or at one of San Francisco's other park offices, such as the Maritime Museum or Ocean Beach, may have felt at times as if they were working in a different park, if not for a different service altogether, myself included.

In 1978 I was pleased to accept a detail to New York to help with the completion of a general management plan for Gateway. Before departing for the East Coast for my new assignment, I traveled to Glacier Bay National Park and Preserve, in Alaska, to attend the wedding of an old college friend who was working as a seasonal ranger, and also to do a little kayaking. One evening, while I was sitting around a stove on a floating tent platform with half a dozen of my friend's ranger colleagues, someone asked about my immediate plans. When I mentioned I was soon headed for Gateway, they all stared at me in disbelief, as if I had told them I had volunteered for an assignment on Mars. I was asked, "How can you be working for the NPS and end up in New York City?" I reminded them that there have been national park sites in New York City since the 1930s, including the Statue of Liberty. "But why," as someone pointed to the wide bay just outside the tent, "Why would you ever go there, when you could work in places like this?"

The conversation in that tent at Glacier Bay demonstrated the service's culture and self-perception, one that has not always mimicked the evolution of its geography and mission. Most organizations develop what historian Ed Linenthal refers to as a "first narrative," one that continues to dominate even in the face of changing circumstances and revised context and interpretation.[4] In the case of the NPS, the first narrative is rooted in the agency's earliest years as a largely homogeneous, Western-based, natural-resource-oriented organization. Though the system has greatly diversified over time, many traditions and stories associated with that early narrative are still honored today, as they should be. But as a recent task force on NPS core values has explained, the agency should respect tradition but not be bound or limited by it.[5]

Today the National Park Service comprises more than 390 national parks in a system with remarkable breadth and diversity—from the mountain peaks of Gates of the Arctic National Park and Preserve in Alaska to the evocative story of the struggle for the right to vote told along the Selma to Montgomery National Historic Trail in Alabama. But the NPS is about more than the sum of its park units. It provides support for fifty national heritage areas, hundreds of natural and national historic landmarks, and a broad portfolio of technical and community-assistance programs. NPS parks and programs are active in every corner of the United States and its outlying territories. Between 2008 and 2009, the National Parks Conservation Association (NPCA) convened the National Parks Second Century Commission, made up of twenty-six national leaders, experts, and thinkers drawn from a broad range of backgrounds, to produce a comprehensive report on the park system as it nears its hundredth anniversary in 2016 and embarks on a second century.[6] The commission chose five key parks to visit during their meetings on the future direction of the National Park System. Two of them, Santa Monica Mountains National Recreation Area and Lowell National Historic Park in Massachusetts, were urban national parks, exemplars for innovation that the commissioners hope to see adopted throughout the national park system. At Santa Monica, commissioners heard from a panel of representatives from Los Angeles youth service organizations that testified to the great usefulness of the Santa Monica Mountains in connecting the parklands to urban neighborhoods, as well as underserved and at-risk youth. The panel also discussed how much their organizations benefit from association with a highly regarded, high-profile national institution like the NPS. In response, Milton Chen, a commissioner, succinctly summed up the message of the presentation, and perhaps one of the dominant themes of the commission, by observing that the NPS was in the business of "building human capital," perhaps where it was needed the most: in urban America.[7] At Lowell, this message was further reinforced by a national park-community partnership that, over time, has made it increasingly challenging to recognize where the national park ends and the city begins, and vice versa.

These examples are representative of decades of hard work and substantial investment of both people and resources. They are indicative of a more inclusive narrative beginning to emerge within the NPS. Speaking to the Second Century Commission at Lowell, Jon Jarvis, then the NPS's Pacific West regional director (now NPS director) spoke metaphorically of changing the agency's image from that of twentieth-century park ranger on horseback, crossing America's continental divide, to the twenty-first-century park ranger crossing America's social divide in the nation's urban communities.[7] Ironically, as the agency matures and accepts a much more nuanced, contemporary image of itself and its increasingly complex purpose, the first narrative is still stubbornly embedded in public consciousness—the common if not stereotypical image of the national park system as exclusively some combination of Yellowstone, Grand Canyon, and Yosemite.

Recently I re-read McPhee's 1971 profile of Hartzog, who, sadly, passed away in 2008. I also revisited some of the original planning documents for Gateway and Golden Gate, as well as a provocative article written some time ago by historian Ronald Foresta, a thoughtful chronicler of the NPS. Foresta, like me, was particularly curious about how expectations for these urban parks have been met or not met in the years since their establishment.[8] It has now in fact been more than thirty-five years since Gateway and Golden Gate were established, approximately the span of my career with the NPS. So here are a few reflections on how the federal agency has changed our urban landscape, and how parks such as Gateway have forever changed the NPS.

One of the greatest assets of the NPS is the professionalism of its employees and the breadth and depth of its national system. The "brand" is broadly recognizable and is generally associated with integrity, competency, and durability. It has a deep bench with many resources: historians, biologists, water-quality specialists, lifeguards, architects, museum curators, geographic information specialists, educators, and other well-trained professionals. This is not to say that parks such as Gateway have not presented the NPS with huge new problems and issues—at a scale not encountered before. But the agency has demonstrated throughout its history the capacity to adapt itself to a remarkably diverse variety of environments and circumstances. However, the staggering number of resource management issues at these parks, particularly the decayed infrastructure, can consume most of the park's funding, to the detriment of other programmatic needs such as visitor services, recreation, and education. At Gateway and Golden Gate, with many hundreds of needy historic structures inherited from the military, priorities have been difficult to set and the challenge has been to avoid an outcome where resources are spread too thin.

At Golden Gate, the establishment of the Presidio Trust, with its broad leasing authority, and the creation of the classic Cavallo Point Lodge at Fort Baker suggest some different paths to achieving both the sustainable preservation of historic resources and expanded public use. In both situations, all other issues aside, public access to valuable waterfront and related recreational activity has been dramatically expanded as a key component of the final equation. The Presidio Trust example, in particular, bears close watching, as it represents an unprecedented broad and complex experiment in urban park design and management, on a scale not seen before in this country.

As time goes on, there is no doubt that lessons learned from urban national parks can be applied broadly to the national park system as a whole. Perhaps most importantly, urban national parks have already demonstrated a remarkable potential for building and sustaining citizen stewardship. Organizations like Golden Gate National Parks Conservancy,

Cuyahoga Valley National Park Association, and the National Parks of New York Harbor Conservancy provide the national park system with valuable new models for mutually beneficial and durable partnerships, significantly expanded educational collaborations, and youth service programs that engage young people, first with programs and then with jobs.

In 2006 the National Park System Advisory Board convened a group of distinguished scholars to reflect on the decline of historical literacy and civic participation in public life. William Kornblum, chairperson of the Center for Urban Research at the City University of New York and chief of the Center's Cooperative Park Studies Unit, told an instructive story about students in his environmental history field course:

> You can't help but feeling this melancholy for the loss of these species and the terrible mayhem that took place. And so what we do after we own this melancholy, we take a trip to the Jamaica Bay Wildlife Refuge. The Jamaica Bay Wildlife Refuge for me is one of those very, very moving places in American environmental history and contemporary environmental history, because what the students see there, is that first of all, they have within their own city a genuine bona fide wildlife refuge that you can get to by the subway or by bus. So it's the story of the resiliency of nature that we can restore, that can start coming back again, we can co-exist with it in the flight pattern of the biggest airplanes we can figure out how to get up into the air. And it instructs us about how to preserve that Jamaica Bay ecosystem and also shows the students that, you know, "I can make a difference. I might have some job some day and I might really be able to make a difference even in my own backyard."[9]

Kornblum's story provides reason for optimism and hints at a direction for the further evolution of Gateway. Daniel Botkin argues that city environments should not be dismissed as bad places that we can only attempt to make less bad. Rather, he states, "Urban life will succeed when we recognize the positive potential of urban settings."[10] Ecologists like to talk about edge or ecotone—the place where the transitions between habitat communities occurs—as being the most productive. This is analogous to the situation of urban national parks where the sharp environmental contrasts of their urban/wild interfaces, however challenging, create extraordinary opportunities and laboratories for learning. These are laboratories where people can learn about adaptation to change, environmental recovery, and public health and well-being, and, perhaps most importantly, hone problem-solving skills.

Author Wendell Berry has written, "There is no significant urban constituency, no formidable consumer lobby, no noticeable political leadership, for good land use practice, for good farming and forestry, for the restoration of abused land."[11] If national parks such as Gateway can be designed and organized in ways that intentionally advance citizen engagement, with emphasis on inclusion, youth participation, and stewardship—and if they create meaningful opportunities to demonstrate resilience, recovery, and sustainable practices—these public venues may yet build the kind of land ethic renewal Berry is searching for.

In their report, Advancing the National Park Idea, the National Parks Second Century Commission envisioned an NPS "animated by the conviction that their work is of the highest public importance. They are community-builders, creating an enlightened society committed to a sustainable world."[12] I think George Hartzog was at heart a community builder—a nation builder. His vision for Gateway reflected a commitment to parks, empathy for America's cities, and a well-developed nose for re-positioning the NPS in ways that enhanced its usefulness and relevance. A good friend and writer in my home state of Vermont, John Elder, could have been speaking of George Hartzog's legacy when he wrote, "We must pursue stewardship not simply as the maintenance of valuable resources, but also as a way of fostering a broader experience of democracy and community."[13] He could have also been speaking of Gateway's future, and perhaps the future of all national parks.

This essay was adapted from the lecture, "The Urban Park as Cultural Catalyst," presented at the Nature Now conference on October 14, 2006, at Columbia University's Graduate School of Architecture, Planning and Preservation.

ENDNOTES

1 John McPhee, "Ranger," *The New Yorker* (September 11,1971).

2 Oral History Interview with George B. Hartzog Jr., National Park Service (2007): 59.

3 Harlan D. Unrau and G. Frank Williss, "Administrative History: Expansion of the National Park Service in the 1930s," http://www.nps.gov/history/history/online_books/unrau-williss /adhi4i.htm.

4 Edward T. Linenthal, "Healing and History: The Dilemmas of Interpretation," Rally on the High Ground: The National Park Service Symposium on the Civil War, http://www.nps.gov /history/history/online_books/rthg/chap3b.htm.

5 http://www.nps.gov/training/uc/npsdcv.htm.

6 Advancing the National Park Idea, National Parks Second Century Commission Report, National Parks Conservation Association, 2009.

7 Notes from the Meeting of the National Parks Second Century Commission, Lowell National Historical Park, Lowell, Massachusetts, October 2008.

8 Ronald Foresta, "America's Urban National Parks," *Urbanism Past & Present* (Summer/ Fall 1984).

9 Scholars Forum: The National Park Service and Civic Reflection, Summary Report, NPS Conservation Study Institute, Conservation And Stewardship Publication No. 13, 2006, 28.

10 Daniel B. Botkin, *No Man's Garden, Thoreau and a New Vision for Civilization and Nature* (Washington, DC: Island Press, 2001), 250.

11 Wendell Berry, "Distrust of Movements," *Orion Magazine*, Summer 1999.

12 Advancing the National Park Idea, National Parks Second Century Commission Report, National Parks Conservation Association, 2009, 16.

13 John Elder, "Inheriting Mt. Tom," *Orion Magazine*, Spring 1997, 29.

COPING WITH COMPLEXITY
CHRISTOPHER HAWTHORNE

Of all of the major divisions separating architects from landscape architects—education and training, job description, temperament, and philosophical outlook—none has loomed quite so large in recent years as the gap between how the two fields deal with complexity. Many of the world's best-known contemporary architects, in particular those with roots in or a fidelity to the movement known as deconstructivism, use new buildings to extend, elaborate upon, or tease out complexities latent in the culture at large. In significant contrast to the modernist architects who preceded them by two or three generations, the goal is not to reconcile the challenges posed by site, budget, or program—or the larger issues of working as an architect in an inequitable, violent, or consumerist society—but rather to make those obstacles and tensions legible by giving them dramatic formal expression.

There are exceptions to this emerging rule, of course. Many architects have held fast to the modernist notion that the architect's chief responsibility is to use design to iron out nettlesome challenges, not advertise their intractability. But quite a few and perhaps even a majority of the architects now sitting at the top of the profession's heap see a pure, smooth facade as something to be crinkled, torn, stretched, punctured, folded, or ruptured before it is fit to be called a meaningful piece of contemporary design. For them, any tidy resolution of an architectural or sociopolitical challenge is immediately suspect, on philosophical as well as aesthetic grounds. When they encounter complexity, their first inclination is to redouble it. The result is often what one architect described to me recently as a "sculpture of complexity" rather than the thing itself.

For many of today's contemporary landscape architects, on the other hand, particularly those working on large-scale multipurpose sites, treating complexity in that manner must seem like a fetish—or, more to the point, like the sort of luxury they barely have time to consider, let alone pursue. In their work, complexity is often a given, a starting point, a factor that exists not outside the sites they work on, but stitched right into their fabric. They therefore deal with it more urgently and more productively than many architects do.

That fact adds a degree of engagement and brisk forthrightness to their designs. After all, these days landscape architects often face the nearly impossible task of trying, in a single design concept, to pursue environmental remediation, establish robust wildlife corridors, and provide new cultural or recreational facilities while bringing together warring political factions, reluctant or cash-strapped funders, and a range of public and private entities. Often, they are also expected to stamp a site with a signature, even "iconic" design solution while working to attract tourists and please critics, scholars, and bloggers alike. And at the same time, many are trying to coax the flickering flame of public awareness in American design tenderly back to life.

Under those conditions, the notion of adding a new layer of essentially symbolic complexity would be absurd. I suppose some enterprising landscape architect could turn this rising tide of complexity into the metaphorical organizing principle for an entire design concept. Short of that kind of creative obfuscation, though, the chief challenge for landscape architects working in such conditions is not to create or symbolize complexity, but simply to corral it.

There is a second area where the gap between contemporary architects and landscape architects seems to be widening. It has to do with vulnerability. There is no question that contemporary global culture, and American culture in particular, has come face to face with its own fragility in recent years. The chief reason has been a growing sense of alarm about global warming, rising sea levels, and other environmental threats. In addition, the recent economic meltdown and subsequent global recession have thoroughly discredited those economists who argued, through the boom years of the previous decade, that the world had entered a smooth, postcyclical age where deep economic troughs, not to mention panics, were relics of the past. In this country, the attacks of September 11, 2001, and the destruction wrought in 2005 by hurricanes Rita and Katrina—and the troubled efforts to recover and rebuild after those disasters—have opened new sources of doubt about America's ability to protect its built and natural landscapes, its skyscrapers as well as its wetlands. The Iraq War has done the same for notions of American power and influence around the world.

Nonetheless, architecture seems increasingly enamored these days with an unshakable heroism. The surprise for me has been the extent to which this heroism has been, like the complexity I described earlier, driven as much by the ambitions of architects as by those of the clients. Large-scale architecture has always been about aggrandizing someone or something.

Even rising worries about further terror attacks have ultimately helped promote the hulking architecture of aggressive defense, with buildings like Skidmore, Owings & Merrill's

One World Trade Center, formerly known as the Freedom Tower, wrapping themselves in bunkerlike layers of blast-proof concrete. Instead of grappling honestly or openly with the realities of a new, more dangerous society, most new public projects in this country are so armored against potential threats that they show the world a helmeted face. Landscape architecture, by contrast, is in the midst of a great and productive exploration of vulnerability as a design concept as well as a political, social, and ecological reality. One reason is that ambitious landscape architecture projects—those that aim not just to reorder discrete gardens, but also to grapple practically and symbolically with larger issues, from ecology to contemporary urbanism—simply can't escape a larger admission of vincibility, and regret for past decisions and environmental misdeeds.

Even as architects complain that they are losing their traditional role as leaders of the construction process for new buildings, landscape architects continue to take on a new professional and cultural prominence. Particularly when civic or other clients choose to organize a competition to produce new design solutions for a large or complicated site, they increasingly turn to landscape architects to oversee teams of experts. Landscape architecture, too, has a long history of competitions for large-scale projects in this country —a complicated and multichaptered one that extends back to Eero Saarinen's design for the Gateway Arch in St. Louis (1947) and Frederick Law Olmsted and Calvert Vaux's for Central Park (1873). But the latest batch has taken on increasingly sprawling, complex, and environmentally troubled or threatened sites, ones where remediation or at least restoration is the first requirement of any design intervention.

This new competition process for sizeable landscape projects, often for sites along the periphery of major metropolitan areas, therefore raises a long list of ancillary questions that, generally speaking, elude easy answers: How do landscape architects bring a consistent design sensibility to sites too large to be understood as a whole by the naked eye, and where the client is often a multiheaded one with a varied set of expectations and interests? How can they treat those sections of new parks that are not actually for people but rather for wildlife corridors, wetlands, and the like—and how should they demarcate the divisions between the two realms? How can they communicate the essence of a concept to a media and a public who, quite often, think design means a single author producing an iconic or monumental gesture? How should they tackle issues like vulnerability, vincibility, and regret?

These questions make up the context in which the Envisioning Gateway competition, and the recent history of the more than 26,000-acre Gateway National Recreation Area site, needs to be considered. As established elsewhere in this volume, the site seems in nearly every way to demand the opposite of a top-down, one-note design solution. Established as a National Recreation Area in 1972, Gateway is multifunctional and sprawling, its land-scape and history little understood by the public at large or even by those who use it on a regular basis.

As Kate Orff notes in her essay, Gateway's Jamaica Bay Unit is not just at the terminus of an urban watershed, it's "a site of muddy ecologies and complex politics." For her, that muddiness seems to imply not only a lack of political and aesthetic clarity, but also in many respects a degree of opportunity. The fact is that the process, which is the subject of this book, is itself quite muddy: When the National Parks Conservation Association, Columbia University GSAPP, and Van Alen Institute set out to organize a design competition for the site, they were in essence creating a new possible reality for the park, alongside the existing and functioning (however imperfect) one that exists there today. Even as the winners of the Envisioning Gateway competition bring needed clarity to our understanding of the site and its potential, the notion of who the client is, or to what degree the NPS will take up the ideas generated by the competition, remains unclear.

What we have is a large, complex site mixing urban recreation, infrastructure, and troubled wetlands and wildlife areas, and stretching across land and sea and across a number of jurisdictional and cartographic boundaries. We have a collection of public and private interests who have come together to revitalize the recreation area, or at least expand and clarify the ways in which the public considers the site and its future. And we have, finally, a design competition conceived as a means not of redesigning the area, but of extending or bringing attention to that process of clarification and education. To be sure, in its mixture of opportunity and indeterminacy, the Envisioning Gateway process is emblematic of the current state of landscape architecture and landscape urbanism—full of rich potential and minefields, conceptual and practical, at virtually every turn.

The finalists in the design competition emerge from that mud—from the morass of one hundred separate entries, from nearly two dozen countries. The majority of finalists respond with refreshing frankness to the complexity of the site, the threats posed to it by environmental problems, and the challenges of roping its various sections and constituencies into a single park. One of the honorable-mention winners, Frank Gesualdi and Hayley Eber's H2grOw, embraces the "precarious environment" of the park not by trying to barricade the site against the onslaught of rising sea levels, but by flooding much of it on purpose, accelerating the transition from land to water, and making that transition a mechanism for education. The second-place winner, North Design Office's Reassembling Ecologies, is up-front about the range of programmatic and environmental demands the site places on any landscape architect. Its proposal is anchored in an attempt to concentrate uses and users at the park along a strongly etched central spine that would operate variously as "gateway, sound barrier, viewing platform, seating, and protection from future sea-level rise."

But it is the elegant first-place project, Mapping the Ecotone—created by the team of Ashley Kelly and Rikako Wakabayashi, now students at Harvard's Graduate School of Design—that brings these varied demands into sharpest and most compelling focus. It would allow Gateway visitors to move along new, sparely designed jetties and piers directly out into Jamaica Bay. At the same time, the design is centered on an acknowledgment that shifting tides and even rising water levels will play a dramatic role in how the park looks and is used in the future. The proposal imagines a park where designers leave their mark on the landscape but where the reverse is also true. In purely formal terms the design takes cues from modernism and minimalism. But in the way it considers the effects of time and future environmental changes, it is flexible and open-ended, and admits a sense of fragility and flux, in ways no doctrinaire modernist could ever abide.

Indeed, the designers themselves describe the project very much along the lines of inquiry and sensibility I described at the start of this essay. Defined by its honesty about the fragility of the landscape, it seeks to engage and ultimately redefine; the design is immersed—in ways both refreshing and productive—with anxiety. In the words of Kelly and Wakabayashi, the winning proposal seeks "to help register and reframe our environmental doubts and insecurities." It seeks to find resilience in exposure to and the understanding of "disturbances" and the prospect that the site's relationship with the waterfront, thanks to rising sea levels, may "violently shift" over time. Finally, the design does not dominate or loom over the site or its public through intimidating scale or posture. It doesn't seek to vanquish complexity, nor to advertise it. Instead, to borrow Kelly and Wakabayashi's telling verb, it "copes."

To a degree, the dilemmas that mark projects like Envisioning Gateway are examples of a careful-what-you-wish-for problem. Now that landscape architects are being asked to lead large teams of experts in creating new plans for sprawling sites, they are settling into the role they have long considered themselves uniquely qualified for. This new prominence of landscape architecture, of course, also leaves them facing the nerve-wracking question of whether they can pull off the sort of design magic required to bring such sites to life—or back to life, as the case may be. In certain cases, the expectations we now routinely pile on the shoulders of landscape architects may prove overwhelming. It may be that in some cases engineers or ecologists are better qualified to oversee teams of experts seeking to salvage and reorder compromised landscapes. It may be that the real healer will be time.

Nonetheless, reviewing the Gateway finalists has provided another reminder of why I so often find writing about landscape architecture these days measurably more rewarding than writing about architecture. Compared to that highly ritualized process, the task of turning an abused brownfield site or a stretch of forsaken waterfront into a striking piece of landscape architecture seems endlessly trickier, richer, and more revealing.

CIVIC LIFE IN THE MAKING
ADI SHAMIR

As with most matters concerning government, architecture told most.
—Daniel Patrick Moynihan, *A Dangerous Place*

For Senator Moynihan, public architecture, a term he used to reference landscape, building, planning, and infrastructural works, served as the critical underpinning of economic and cultural productivity. At its best it possessed an intimacy that brought people together in an experience of confidence and trust. It had the power to reveal and represent, to express and inculcate civic values.

Moynihan, who grew up in the New York City of Central Park, City College, the New York Public Library, and the old Pennsylvania Station, declared in a lecture to members of the American Institute of Architects in 1969:

> The American polity—the experience as well as the sense of community
> and shared convictions has…atrophied in our time because of the retreat
> from architecture and public buildings as a consensus element of public policy
> and a purposeful instrument for the expression of public purposes.…If we
> are to save our cities and restore to American public life the sense of shared
> experience, trust and common purpose that seems to be draining out of it,
> the quality of public design has got to be made a public issue because it is
> a political fact.[1]

And while he championed the material and physical impact of public architecture, for him the rebuilding of cities demanded the enactment of programs and policies that enabled institution building and the strengthening of a civil society's foundations. When, for example, in 1993 he insisted on maintaining the deductibility of gifts of appreciated property to nonprofit institutions such as universities and museums, he demonstrated the necessity of these gifts as vital elements of the "unplanned flowering" of learning and culture in a huge and diverse society.[2] But he struggled to reconcile the oppositional forces of individual interest and common good weighing down either side of the civil ballast.

His nuanced assessment of American national character, impassioned public advocacy, and the many trajectories of his career echoed that of another New Yorker a century before. In his essay "Democratic Vistas," Walt Whitman mounted a sustained criticism of Reconstruction Era failures—the "depravity of our business classes" while unequivocally affirming "democracy's convictions [and] aspirations."[3] In a great, rambling depiction of civic life, more exuberant and moving than any other, he wrote:

> After an absence, I am now again…in New York…. The splendor, picturesqueness, [its] oceanic amplitude and rush, the unsurpass'd situation, rivers and bay, sparkling sea-tides, costly and lofty new buildings, facades of marble and iron, of original grandeur and elegance of design, with the masses of gay color, the preponderance of white and blue, the flags flying, the endless ships, the tumultuous streets, Broadway, the heavy, low, musical roar, hardly ever intermitted, even at night; the jobbers' houses, the rich shops, the wharves, the great Central Park, and the Brooklyn Park of hills, (as I wander among them this beautiful fall weather, musing, watching, absorbing)—the assemblages of the citizens in their groups, conversations, trades, evening amusements, or along the by-quarters—these…completely satisfy my senses of power, fulness, motion, &c., and give me…a continued exaltation and absolute fulfilment. Always and more and more, as I cross the East and North rivers, the ferries, or with the pilots in their pilot-houses, or pass an hour in Wall street, or the gold exchange, I realize…that not Nature alone is great in her fields of freedom and the open air, in her storms, the shows of night and day, the mountains, forests, seas—but in the artificial, the work of man too is equally great—in this profusion of teeming humanity—in these ingenuities, streets, goods, houses, ships—these hurrying, feverish, electric crowds of men, their complicated business genius…and all this mighty, many-threaded wealth and industry concentrated here.[4]

Whitman's observations speak in ways that we today cannot muster the energy or the confidence to utter. The century since, with the abominable march of 1914, 1929, 1945, 1968, and 2001, has deafened and deadened our senses to such universally heroic truths. But as the cartoonist Art Spiegelman has illustrated in his book *In the Shadow of No Towers*, civic life endures, though its forms and reforms may be wholly unfamiliar and new.[5]

It was in fact a new form that Whitman witnessed and conceived, one that emerged from within a generation Lewis Mumford called "the brown decades."[6] The term was coined to identify "our buried renaissance," a sober though charged period of American history from 1865 to 1895 that began with the Civil War and which propelled democratic realization in the artistic practices of Winslow Homer and Thomas Eakins, in the landscapes of Olmsted and Charles Eliot Norton, in the engineering of John A. Roebling, the architecture of Henry Hobson Richardson, and in the industry and philanthropy of Andrew Carnegie and John D. Rockefeller.

It was the transformation of civic life that Norton, also a social reformer and liberal activist, alluded to when he said of Olmsted toward the close of his career that of all American artists, he stood "first in the production of great works which answer the needs and give expression to the life of our immense and miscellaneous democracy."[7]

As much a testament to Olmsted's genius as a confirmation of the correspondence that exists between great works and social imperatives, and the necessity to imbue productive expression with political ideals, Norton's elegy admits to the inherent messiness of civic enterprise and its open-ended conclusions.

Olmsted had in fact observed, "It is a common error to regard a park as something to be produced complete in itself, as a picture to be painted on a canvas. It should rather be planned as one to be done in fresco, with constant consideration of exterior objects."[8] And the exterior objects, boulders and bedrock, political and physical, resisted. To fulfill Olmsted's living vision, a fundamental and total reshaping of the site's topography was required. Workers moved nearly 3 million cubic yards of soil and planted more than 270,000 trees and shrubs, and transverse roads were blasted through rocky ridges 8 feet below the surface to carry crosstown traffic while maintaining a continuous, expansive parkscape. When Central Park first opened to the public in the winter of 1859, thousands of New Yorkers skated on lakes constructed on what had been swamps.

Mumford contends that Olmsted and Eliot "humanized and subdued the feral landscape."[9] But it might be more useful to consider the work as the invention of a language of inchoate public values, a crucible which, rather than tame, caused the reconstitution of the very marrow of life in the city. Whitman understood modern material accomplishments, like the Suez Canal and the Atlantic Cable, as answers to the most important "aged fierce enigmas" at the heart of spiritual questions:

> For, I say, the true nationality of the States, the genuine union, when we come
> to a mortal crisis, is, and is to be, after all, neither the written law, nor, (as
> is generally supposed,) either self-interest, or common pecuniary or material
> objects—but the fervid and tremendous idea, melting everything else with
> resistless heat, and solving all lesser and definite distinctions in vast, indefinite,
> spiritual, emotional power.[10]

A year after "Democratic Vistas" was first published in 1871, Yellowstone became the first national park in the United States and the world—a radically new public program born of those "brown decades" and met with a veritable legion of what Olmsted had termed "exterior objects."

One hundred years forward, the first of two urban national recreation areas was designated at Gateway, perched at the very edge of the continent at the mouth of New York's outer harbor. But in the interval since 1972, endangered birds at Gateway have grown more so, and drowning marshes continue to do just that, as sewer outfalls fill and abandoned buildings remain empty. And it would seem that the public is, as political journalist Walter Lippmann once asserted, "phantom."[11]

Lament for the loss of an idealized critical publicity is not unwarranted. It may well be that the public sphere as it once was, is no longer. And yet, with no reliable end in sight nor the clarity of a perfect resolution, the efforts of philanthropic entities, citizen groups, and individual volunteers—on behalf of the tremendous challenges that are Gateway—persist. These champions of a not yet fully formed great public work, lead as they follow. Mumford insisted of Olmsted, that he had done "something more than design a park, battle insolent and rascally city appointees, and protect his plantations against vandals: he had introduced an idea—the idea of using the landscape creatively. By making nature urbane he naturalized the city."[12]

To give expression as Olmsted did to the vitality "of our immense and miscellaneous democracy" is to produce anew its promise, and in the making to enact civic life.[13]

ENDNOTES
Epigraph: Daniel Patrick Moynihan, *A Dangerous Place* (Boston: Little Brown, 1978), 65.
1 Robert A Katzmann, ed., *Daniel Patrick Moynihan: The Intellectual in Public Life* (Baltimore, MD: Johns Hopkins University, 1998), 91.
2 Robert Peck, "Remembering Daniel Patrick Moynihan," in *Daniel Patrick Moynihan: The Intellectual in Public Life*, ed. Robert A Katzmann (Baltimore, MD: Johns Hopkins University, 1998), 143.
3 Walt Whitman, *Democratic Vistas* (London: Walter Scott, 1888), 13.
4 Whitman, 13.
5 Art Spiegelman, *In the Shadow of No Towers* (New York: Pantheon Books, 2004).
6 Lewis Mumford, *The Brown Decades: A Study of the Arts in America, 1865–1895*, rev. ed. (New York: Harcourt, Brace, and Co., 1931; New York: Dover Publications, 1971). Citations are to the Dover edition.

7 Charles Eliot Norton, quoted in Mumford, 30.
8 Frederick Law Olmsted, "Public Parks and the Enlargement of Towns," lecture, the American Social Science Association at the Lowell Institute, Boston, MA, Feb. 25, 1870 (Cambridge, MA: The Riverside Press, 1870), 26.
9 Mumford, 40.
10 Whitman, 10.
11 Walter Lippmann, *The Phantom Public* (New York: Macmillan Co., 1927).
12 Mumford, 40.
13 Ibid., 37.

215

A Vision for Park Planning and Design Stephanie Toothman

America's public parks face unprecedented challenges in the twenty-first century. Shifting demographics, climate change, rapidly evolving communications technologies, new transportation prototypes, and economic constraints are but a few of the urgent issues confronting park designers, planners, and managers. Aging infrastructure and changing use-patterns demand new approaches to park design, creating opportunities for park planners and designers to focus on energy conservation, sustainability, and engagement with local communities. How we plan and design our parks in response to these changing imperatives will have an enormous impact on our success in creating welcoming, meaningful, healthy, and enduring public places that will last well into the future.

Gateway National Recreation Area embodies both the challenges and the potential of America's parklands. All national park unit managers must find a way to reconcile the NPS's dual mandates of resource stewardship and visitor experience. Gateway's diverse natural resources, the stories represented by its historic military and aviation sites, and the recreational opportunities it represents for the 22 million residents in the tri-state region, coupled with deteriorating infrastructure, degraded habitat, and 8 million visitors a year, present some of the most complex planning, design, and management challenges in the National Park System.

In 2008, in recognition of the issues facing Gateway and parks throughout the nation, the National Park Service, the National Parks Conservation Association, and Van Alen Institute joined other partners in cosponsoring "Designing the Parks"—a two-part bicoastal conference that brought together more than five hundred practitioners, academics, park policy-makers, nonprofit groups, and federal, state, and local park managers, who together considered and debated the past, present, and future of designing public parks. Out of these sessions emerged six proposed principles to guide future park planning and design:

1. Reverence for place—understand and preserve the essential character of a place
2. Engagement of all people—connect people of diverse cultures, ages and interests to community, nature, and mankind
3. Expansion beyond traditional boundaries— build, design, and promote dynamic linkages and networks among parks, communities, and natural systems
4. Advancement of sustainability—inspire stewardship through, and exercise leadership through, demonstration of sustainable practices
5. Informed decision-making—ensure that planning and design is based on a comprehensive knowledge of resources and attributes
6. Integrated research, planning, design, and review process—reconcile a clear understanding of conflicting mandates through a clear determination of resource values, park management goals, and informed discussions.

Participants agreed that a transparent, inclusive design and planning process open to innovative thinking was essential to implementing these principles. A key recommendation was to test and refine these principles through design studios or competitions that would address a variety of park issues.

The collaboration that produced Envisioning Gateway reflects these principles and anticipated the recommendation for using a design competition to test them. Extensive research and outreach to stakeholders, an ongoing dialogue incorporating the perspectives of environmentalists and preservationists, planners, designers, and managers, and a commitment to the unique role of national parks in the country's increasingly urbanized landscape all informed the visions for Gateway's future presented here. The international design competition provides a model for further testing these principles in national park settings, and for promoting innovative new ways of understanding our parks. For those who participated in "Designing the Parks," and for all of those committed to the renewal of our parks to meet present and future challenges, the Envisioning Gateway project provides an exciting illustration of the future of park planning and design.

PARTNERS & PARTICIPANTS

NATIONAL PARKS CONSERVATION ASSOCIATION

Since 1919, the nonpartisan National Parks Conservation Association (NPCA) has been the leading voice of the American people in protecting and enhancing our National Park System. NPCA, its members, and partners work together to protect the park system and preserve our nation's natural, historical, and cultural heritage for generations to come. For more information, visit www.npca.org.

COLUMBIA UNIVERSITY GRADUATE SCHOOL OF ARCHITECTURE, PLANNING AND PRESERVATION

The Columbia University Graduate School of Architecture, Planning and Preservation (GSAPP) is an independent academic institution dedicated to fostering a leadership role in acting as a laboratory for testing new ideas about the possible roles of designers in a global society. GSAPP's goal is not a certain kind of architecture but a certain evolution in architectural intelligence, and is united in its commitment to the global evolution of the twenty-first-century city. The school uses explorative studio projects, working in different directions and "reporting back" through juries, exhibitions, and publications. With continually evolving research trajectories, the school operates as a multi-disciplinary think tank, an intelligent organism thinking its way through the uncertain future of the discipline and the global society it serves. For more information, visit www.arch.columbia.edu.

VAN ALEN INSTITUTE

Van Alen Institute promotes innovative thinking about the role of architecture and design in civic life. Among our activities are design competitions, lectures and symposia, exhibitions, publications, research, and advocacy. Our programs engage a broad constituency of people in New York City, the nation, and around the world who participate in shaping the designed environment, from architecture students to emerging and established professionals to the interested public. For more information, visit www.vanalen.org.

Competition Jury, May 12, 2007:
Ethan Carr, University of Massachusetts, Amherst
Andrew Darrell, Environmental Defense Fund
Patricia Harris, New York City Office of the Mayor
Marian Heiskell, *The New York Times*
Walter Hood, Hood Design
Peter Latz, Latz + Partner Landscape Architects
John Loring, Tiffany & Co.
Randall Luthi, U.S. Fish and Wildlife Service
Anuradha Mathur, Mathur/da Cunha and University of Pennsylvania
Wendy Paulson, The Nature Conservancy and Rare Conservation
Steward Pickett, Cary Institute of Ecosystem Studies
Lindy Roy, ROY Co.
Adi Shamir, Van Alen Institute (co-chair)
Mark Wigley, Columbia University Graduate School of Architecture, Planning and Preservation (co-chair)

Nature Now Conference Speakers, October 14, 2006:
Glenn Allen, Hargreaves Associates
Daniel Botkin, University of California, Santa Barbara
Ethan Carr, University of Massachusetts, Amherst
Rolf Diamant, Marsh-Billings-Rockefeller National Historical Park (NPS)
Matthew Gandy, Geographer and Writer
Billy Garrett, Gateway National Recreation Area (NPS)
Anuradha Mathur, Mathur/da Cunha
Robert W. McIntosh, National Park Service

Columbia University Graduate School of Architecture, Planning and Preservation:
Mark Wigley, Kate Orff, Sarah Williams, Tse-Hui Teh and Li-Chi Wang

National Parks Conservation Association:
Alexander Brash, Tom Kiernan, Darcy Shiber-Knowles, Linda Rancourt, and Shannon Andrea

Van Alen Institute:
Adi Shamir, Jamie Hand, Andra Eglitis, Chris Dierks, Ari Duraku, Caroline Snyder, Ori Topaz, Claudia Kotowicz, and Omar Toro

Special thanks to:
Bryan Cave LLP, Maria Burks, Craig Cook, John Daskalakis, Lisa Eckert, John Hnedak, Pete McCarthy, NYC Visual Group, Rob Pirani and Elizabeth Case / Regional Plan Association, Linda Pollak, Eric Ratkowski, Don Riepe, Travis Roozée, Marie Salerno, Nanette Smith, Barry Sullivan, Dave Taft, Kim Tripp, and Webokraft

Sponsor:
Underwritten by The Tiffany & Co. Foundation

Sponsored by The Tiffany & Co. Foundation

BOOK CONTRIBUTORS

Alexander Brash is the senior director of National Parks Conservation Association's Northeast Regional office.

Ethan Carr is an associate professor of landscape architecture at the University of Virginia School of Architecture.

Rolf Diamant is superintendent of Marsh-Billings-Rockefeller National Historical Park.

Jamie Hand is the former program director at Van Alen Institute.

Christopher Hawthorne is the *Los Angeles Times* architecture critic.

Olympia Kazi is the executive director of Van Alen Institute.

Fernanda Kellogg is president of The Tiffany & Co. Foundation.

Thomas Kiernan is president of the National Parks Conservation Association.

Laura McPhee is a landscape photographer and a professor at the Massachusetts College of Art in Boston.

Kate Orff is an assistant professor and director of the Urban Landscape Lab at the Columbia University Graduate School of Architecture, Planning and Preservation.

Adi Shamir is the former executive director of Van Alen Institute.

Stephanie Toothman is the chief of Cultural Resource Programs for the Pacific West Region of the U.S. National Park Service.

Mark Wigley is the dean of the Columbia University Graduate School of Architecture, Planning and Preservation.

Sarah Williams is director of the Spatial Information Design Lab at the Columbia University Graduate School of Architecture, Planning and Preservation.

COMPETITION WINNERS

Ashley Scott Kelly and Rikako Wakabayashi
Ashley Scott Kelly and Rikako Wakabayashi established Urban Found Architecture in 2007, a research-based practice pursuing the increasingly cogent overlaps of design, global ecology, microniches, and social geographies of our urban landscapes. They both currently attend the architecture program at Harvard University's Graduate School of Design.

North Design Office
North Design Office is a landscape architecture, urbanism, and design firm, founded by partners Pete North and Alissa North in 2005. North Design Office has developed a praxis where research and theory inform their process-based approach to solving complex design issues, with the idea that well-designed urban environments and open spaces create vibrant communities and ecologies.

Virginia Polytechnic: Laurel McSherry, Terry Surjan, Rob Holmes
Laurel McSherry, a native of Highlands, New Jersey, is an associate professor and director of the Graduate Program in Landscape Architecture at the Washington-Alexandria Architecture Center of Virginia Tech. Terry Surjan, a native of Joliet, Illinois, is an associate professor of architecture at Virginia Tech, Blacksburg. Rob Holmes is a graduate student in the landscape architecture program at the Washington-Alexandria Architecture Center of Virginia Tech.

W Architecture and Landscape Architecture
Founded in 1999 by Barbara Wilks, W Architecture and Landscape Architecture builds on the links between architecture and landscape to create spaces and buildings that engage both nature and urbanism. Working at various scales from the regional to the interior, the practice seeks to foster a greater awareness of the special qualities of each place by reimagining the boundaries between nature and city, new and old, land and water.

Frank Gesualdi and Hayley Eber
EFGH is a multidisciplinary architectural partnership founded in 2007 by principals Hayley Eber and Frank Gesualdi, located in New York City. EFGH practices a research-driven architecture focusing on responsive design concepts and building techniques that redefine conventional notions of program, material, and context.

Christopher Marcinkoski and Andrew Moddrell
Based in New York and Chicago, PORT Architecture + Urbanism is an innovative design and research collaborative founded by Christopher Marcinkoski and Andrew Moddrell. The practice combines expertise in architecture, urbanism, landscape, and planning to provide exceptional solutions to unique design challenges at every scale of the urban landscape—from the domestic to the civic—with projects ranging from architectural design to institutional and urban strategy.

COMPETITORS

82.m
Ayvind Karlsen, Jonathan Lundstrom,
Mounir Tawadrous
Philadelphia, Pennsylvania, USA

A Studio
Jeanine Brandi, Con Murphy, Charles Ramsay
Santa Barbara, California, USA

Abruzzo Bodziak Solomon
Emily Abruzzo, Gerald Bodziak, Jonathan Solomon
Brooklyn, New York, USA

Lorjan Agalliu, Pin Wei (Dylan) Kuo, Steven Hong,
Shih-Feng Huang
New York, New York, USA

Claire Agre, Liat Margolis, Darlene Montgomery
Somerville, Massachusetts, USA

Mohammad Hassan Almamun, Julian Williams
Stamford, Connecticut, USA

Anas Alomaim, Deniz Guneri, Bernard Malafaia
New York, New York, USA

Joshua Anderson, Sohith Perera, Joann Green
Indianapolis, Indiana, USA

Archipelago Architecture and
Landscape Architecture
New York, New York, USA

Bad Architects Group
Innsbruck, Austria

Bagrose
Femke Bakker, Ruben Groot, Jeroen Semeijn
Utrecht, the Netherlands

Scott A. Battaglia
Broad Channel, New York, USA

Brady Shipman Martin Landscape Architects
Limerick, Ireland

Case Brown
Clyde, North Carolina, USA

En-Ming Chang, Gregory Mell, Nick Potts
Minneapolis, Minnesota, USA

Civitas Inc.
Denver, Colorado, USA

Siqing Chen
Auburn, Alabama, USA

Melissa Dittmer, Tadd Heidgerken,
Noah Resnick, Kleber Salas
Detroit, Michigan, USA

Susannah Drake, Rebecca Leising,
Anne Clark, Chad Smith, Mike Jacobs
Brooklyn, New York, USA

Olga Drobinina, Ximena Valle
Berwyn, Pennsylvania, USA

E+I Architecture
New York, New York, USA

Hayley Eber, Frank Gesualdi
New York, New York, USA

EDAW Limited
Hong Kong, China

Mark Ericson, Katherine Harvey
Philadelphia, Pennsylvania, USA

Suzanne Ernst-Zathureczky
Montreal, Quebec, Canada

Abby Feldman, Daniela Jimenez,
Frank Ruchala Jr., Elizabeth Stoel
Brooklyn, New York, USA

Beth Fenstermacher
Amherst, Massachusetts, USA

F. F. Rudsy
Susan Day, Robin Washco
Blacksburg, Virginia, USA

Foisgaetanistudio
Carolina Fois, Lorenzo Gaetani
Paris, France

Ford/Agnoli
Matthew Ford, Vasco Agnoli
Pittsboro, North Carolina, USA

Forrest Fulton
Cambridge, Massachusetts, USA

Gateway Design Team JV
Michael Cetera, Eiki Danzuka, Johanes Knesl,
Rod Knox, Toshio Sasaki, Sakae Sugiura
New York, New York, USA

Farzana Gandhi, Jonathan Lee
Jersey City, New Jersey, USA

General Design Office
Jhaelen Eli, Juliet Hernandez
New York, New York, USA

Shaney Gomez, David Hays, Martin Holland,
Patrick Petersen, Julie Sajtar
Urbana-Champaign, Illinois, USA

Thanassis Gounaris, Eleni Livanis, Mairi
Mantouvalou, Chrysostomos Theodoropoulos
Athens, Greece

GRO Architects, PLLC
New York, New York, USA

Emilie Hagen, Annie Suratt, Michael Szivos
New York, New York, USA

HWH
Andrew Cocke, Sonya Hals, Ted Whitten
Richmond, Virginia, USA

Jack L. Gordon Architects
New York, New York, USA

Rachel Johnston, Elizabeth Campbell Kelly,
Meaghan Pierce-Delaney, AJ Pires, Steven Tupu
New York, New York, USA

K+L
Melanie Kramer, Svetlana Lavrentieva
Toronto, Ontario, Canada

Kiduck Kim
Cambridge, Massachusetts, USA

Jason Kentner
Columbus, Ohio, USA

Ashley Kelly, Rikako Wakabayashi
Brooklyn, New York, USA

Kim+Claudio+Gregory
Pedro Claudio, Erick Gregory, Soo Jin Kim
New York, New York, USA

Caroline Kim, Yu-ju Lin, Zhaojie Wu
Hoboken, New Jersey, USA

Leander Grayson Krueger
Stamford, Connecticut, USA

Michelle Lazar, Matthew Sweig
Toronto, Ontario, Canada

Stephen Lee, Mike McAtee
Hoboken, New Jersey, USA

Huei-Lyn Liu, Mel Yip
Singapore

LSU-1
Frank Chaffin (Faculty Advisor),
Daniel Raggio, Beth Sansovich
Baton Rouge, Louisiana, USA

LSU-2
Frank Chaffin (Faculty Advisor), Brad Bennett, Bo
Danos, Austin Evans, Chad Prejean
Baton Rouge, Louisiana, USA

LSU To4
Henry Dalton, Blake Guidry,
David Newman, Dudley Thiel
La Place, Louisiana, USA

M+
Kenneth Yeung, Urtzi Grau
Princeton, New Jersey, USA

Daniel Markiewicz
Brooklyn, New York, USA

Marniquet Associes
Paris, France

Albert Miller
San Diego, California, USA

Marc Miller
St. Paul, Minnesota, USA

Meredith Miller
Cambridge, Massachusetts, USA

Ryan Moody
Charlottesville, Virginia, USA

Mundus Bishop Design, Inc.
Denver, Colorado, USA

…Ninja
Chris Wilson, James McReynolds
Blacksburg, Virginia, USA

Ninja Bella
Natalie Deck, Pamela Jean Reitter, Ana Sosa
Blacksburg, Virginia, USA

Ninja, Eh?
Laura Bowe, Ryan Cole
Powell, Ohio, USA

North Design Office
Toronto, Ontario, Canada

Office42
Los Angeles, California, USA

Out-fo Design
Brooklyn, New York, USA

PORT Architecture + Urbanism
Christopher Marcinkoski, Andrew Moddrell
Chicago, Illinois, USA

Pratt Alums
Michael R. Tom
New York, New York, USA

PrattGrads
Christina Ficicchia, Christine Fitzgerald,
Eleni Glekas, Justin Kray, Vlada Smorgunov
Astoria, Queens, New York, USA

Jeffrey Pronovost
Granby, Massachusetts, USA

Pryo
Ola Nielsen, Markus Magnusson
Malmo, Skåne, Sweden

Adam Rothwell, Stephen Suen,
Taku Suzuki, Erika Uribe
London, England, United Kingdom

Richard Rudnicki
Central, South Carolina, USA

Sdrawkcab Ajnin
Thomas Keller, Josh Smith, Sean Witty
Blacksburg, Virginia, USA

Chihiro Shinohara
Charlottesville, Virginia, USA

Tshen Shue, Dimitris Vlachopoulos
New York, New York, USA

Skye Design Studio, Ltd.
Washington, DC, USA

Studio Sassy Ninja
Rebekah Martin, Michelle Meyer
Manassas, Virginia, USA

Rachel Smith
Blacksburg, Virginia, USA

SWA Group–LA
Los Angeles, California, USA

Ritsumeikan University Landscape Design
Lab + WinLandscape Architect Partners:
Eri Imose, Junnichi Inada, Ryohei Inoue,
Saki Kojima, Shiro Takeda, Yusuke Yoshida
Kusatsu-shi, Shiga-ken, Japan

Tango With Danger
Mercedes Kiss, David Yount
Blacksburg, Virginia, USA

Paula Tomisaki
New York, New York, USA

TypicalState
Jason Addington, Anthony Corso,
Matt Fordham, Ryan Wilson
Chicago, Illinois, USA

Urban Progress Studio
Amsterdam, Noord-Holland, the Netherlands

VertNY
Martha Desbiens, Nicholas Desbiens,
Tricia Rubenstein, Kristi Stromberg Wright
Brooklyn, New York, USA

Virginia Polytechnic
Rob Holmes, Laurel McSherry, Terry Surjan
Alexandria, Virginia, USA

Vogt Landscape Architects |
Lars Müller Publishers
Guenther Vogt, Lars Müller
Zurich, Switzerland

www.noise-ae.org
Sean Gallagher, Michael Stewart
Brooklyn, New York, USA

Joel Wenzel
Charleston, South Carolina, USA

Jessica Young, Philip Lee, Jane Kim
Houston, Texas, USA

Nanguo Yuan
Urbana-Champaign, Illinois, USA

Zurita Architects
New York, New York, USA

IMAGE CREDITS

Endpapers New York City Parks Photo Archive
4 Don Riepe / American Littoral Society
7 Harpers Ferry Center, National Park Service, Historic Photograph Collection
12–17 Graphics by Spatial Information Design Lab (SIDL)
21–47 Laura McPhee
52, top Regional Plan Association (RPA)
52, bottom Library of Congress
56, top Taken from Henry Collins Brown, *Valentine's Manual of the City of New York* (New York, NY: 1862).
56, bottom Brooklyn Public Library—Brooklyn Collection
58 *Report of the Jamaica Bay Improvement Commission*, May 31, 1907
61 "Jamaica Bay to Be a Great World Harbor," *New York Times*, March 13, 1910
64, top left, right Brooklyn Public Library—Brooklyn Collection
64, bottom Photograph by Kate Orff
68, top The New York Public Library
68, bottom U.S. Navy National Museum of Naval Aviation
69 Brooklyn Public Library—Brooklyn Collection
72, top Adapted from New York City Department of Environmental Protection
72, bottom Image courtesy of NOAA/NY/NJ Baykeeper
78 Niagara Falls (Ontario) Public Library
79, top left Photograph by Alexander Brash
79, bottom left Photograph by Alexander Brash
79, top right Women's Rights National Historical Park
79, bottom right Photograph by Alexander Brash
82 Photograph by Alexander Brash
84 Reproduced under GNU Free Documentation License, http://en.wikipedia.org/wiki/File:Gettysburg_National_Military_Park_33.jpg
93, top Photograph by Katrina Thomas, Courtesy of National Park Service
93, bottom Image courtesy of Avery Library, Columbia University
96 New York City Parks Photo Archive
99 Photographs by Eric Ratkowski
101 Graphic by Spatial Information Design Lab (SIDL)
103 Graphics by Spatial Information Design Lab (SIDL)
105 Image files sourced online by GSAPP Research Report team.
106–09 Christopher Marcinkoski and Andrew Moddrell
110, middle right Melissa Dittmer, Tadd Heidgerken, Noah Resnick, Kleber Salas
110, bottom right VertNY: Martha Desbiens, Nicholas Desbiens, Tricia Rubenstein, Kristi Stromberg Wright
110, middle left Emilie Hagen, Annie Suratt, Michael Szivos
110, bottom left Abby Feldman, Daniela Jimenez, Frank Ruchala, Jr., Elizabeth Stoel
110, top Michelle Lazar, Matthew Sweig
111 Michelle Lazar, Matthew Sweig
112 Emilie Hagen, Annie Suratt, Michael Szivos
113 Melissa Dittmer, Tadd Heidgerken, Noah Resnick, Kleber Salas
114 Abby Feldman, Daniela Jimenez, Frank Ruchala, Jr., Elizabeth Stoel
115 VertNY: Martha Desbiens, Nicholas Desbiens, Tricia Rubenstein, Kristi Stromberg Wright
117 Graphics by Spatial Information Design Lab (SIDL)
119 Graphics by Spatial Information Design Lab (SIDL)
121–23 W Architecture
124, middle right skye design studio, ltd.
124, bottom left PrattGrads, Christina Ficicchia, Christine Fitzgerald, Eleni Glekas, Justin Kray, and Vlada Smorgunov

124, top right Brady Shipman Martin Landscape Architects
124, middle left K+L, Melanie Kramer and Svetlana Lavrentieva
124, bottom right Joshua Anderson, Sohith Perera, and Joann Green
125 Brady Shipman Martin Landscape Architects
126 K+L, Melanie Kramer and Svetlana Lavrentieva
127 skye design studio, ltd.
128 PrattGrads, Christina Ficicchia, Christine Fitzgerald, Eleni Glekas, Justin Kray, Vlada Smorgunov
129 Joshua Anderson, Sohith Perera, Joann Green
131 Graphics by Spatial Information Design Lab (SIDL)
133 Graphics by Spatial Information Design Lab (SIDL)
134–37 New York State Department of Environmental Conservation
139–40 Ashley Kelly and Rikako Wakabayashi
142, bottom left Olga Drobinina and Ximena Valle
142, middle left SWA Group–LA
142, top right Mundus Bishop Design, Inc.
142, middle right Adam Rothwell, Stephen Suen, Taku Suzuki, and Erika Uribe
142, bottom right Chihiro Shinohara
143 Mundus Bishop Design, Inc.
144 SWA Group–LA
145 Adam Rothwell, Stephen Suen, Taku Suzuki, and Erika Uribe
146 Olga Drobinina and Ximena Valle
147 Chihiro Shinohara
149 Graphics by Spatial Information Design Lab (SIDL)
150–55 Image files sourced online by GSAPP Research Report team
156–59 North Design Office
160, bottom left EDAW Limited
160, middle left TypicalState, Jason Addington, Anthony Corso, Matt Fordham, and Ryan Wilson
160, bottom right Jason Kentner
160, middle right M+, Kenneth Yeung and Urtzi Grau
160, top right Huei-Lyn Liu, Mel Yip
161 Huei-Lyn Liu, Mel Yip
162 TypicalState, Jason Addington, Anthony Corso, Matt Fordham, and Ryan Wilson
163 M+: Kenneth Yeung, Urtzi Grau
164 EDAW Limited
165 Jason Kentner
167 Graphics by Spatial Information Design Lab (SIDL)
168–69 Courtesy of Brookhaven National Laboratory
171–73 Frank Gesualdi and Hayley Eber
174, top right Richard Rudnicki
174, middle left 82.m, Ayvind Karlsen, Jonathan Lundstrom, and Mounir Tawadrous
174, bottom right Paula Tomisaki
174, bottom left SWA Group–LA
174, middle right office42
175 Richard Rudnicki
176 82.m, Ayvind Karlsen, Jonathan Lundstrom, and Mounir Tawadrous
177 office42
178 SWA Group–LA
179 Paula Tomisaki
181 Graphics by Spatial Information Design Lab (SIDL)
182 Work Projects Administration Poster Collection (Library of Congress)
183, top right Photograph by Nathaniel R. Ewan, Historic American Buildings Survey (Library of Congress)
183, bottom George Grantham Bain Collection (Library of Congress)

183, top left Courtesy of the National Archives
185–87 Laurel McSherry, Terry Surjan, and Rob Holmes
188, middle right Case Brown
188, top right Claire Agre, Liat Margolis, and Darlene Montgomery
188, bottom right Civitas Inc.
188, middle left Leander Grayson Krueger
188, bottom left skye design studio, ltd.
189 Claire Agre, Liat Margolis, and Darlene Montgomery
190 Leander Grayson Krueger
191 Case Brown
192 skye design studio, ltd.
193 Civitas Inc.
196, top left Courtesy of the National Park Service, Jefferson National
Expansion Memorial
196, top right Photograph by Rolf Diamant
196, bottom left Photograph by Rolf Diamant
196, bottom right Courtesy of Department of Interior, National Park Service
Historic Photograph Collection, Harpers Ferry Center